# Where Are They Now?

Liverpool

Liam Moore

www.where-are-they-now.co.uk/club/liverpool

First published in 2020 by
Media House Books

© Media House Books 2020

ISBN 978-1-912027-57-6

Original cover design by Marten Sealby

# Dedication

This book is dedicated to every player who has
contributed to the success of Liverpool Football Club.

## A'COURT, Alan

*Winger*
**Born:** *1934 Rainhill*
**Died:** 2009
**Playing career:** *Liverpool, Tranmere R (1952-1966)*

Alan A'Court was in demand as a youngster but chose to join Liverpool rather than Bolton or Everton. Went on to make over 350 appearances in red which saw him at Anfield for 11 years. A'Court was just as influential off the pitch as he was seen as a dressing room leader during Bill Shankly's early reign. He also won 5 England caps. Later coached both at home and in Zambia and New Zealand. After retirement from the game as a whole, he ran a tobacconist's shop in Birkenhead. Died on 14th December 2009, he had been suffering from cancer.

## ABLETT, Gary

*Defender*
**Born:** *1965 Liverpool*
**Died:** 2012
**Playing career:** *Liverpool, Derby County, Hull City, Everton, Sheffield United, Birmingham City, Wycombe Wanderers, Blackpool, Long Island Rough Riders (1983-2001)*

One of the rare breeds of players who played for both Merseyside clubs. He also repeated the feat as a coach, by first joining Everton as Under 17 coach in 2002 and then switching to become Liverpool's reserve team manager in 2007. In 2009 he was appointed manager of Stockport County but left the club when new owners took over the following year. Ablett died in Liverpool on 1st January 2012. He had been battling against non-Hodgkins lymphoma for some time.

Ablett House

Derek Acorah

## ACORAH, Derek

**Born:** *1950 Bootle, Merseyside*
**Died:** *2020*
**Playing career:** *Wrexham, Liverpool, Glentoran, Stockport County*

Derek Acorah is probably not a name that you expected to see here. The now famous TV medium was quite a nifty footballer in his youth and had a spell on the books at Liverpool. Ironically, Acorah came from a family of Everton supporters, who were horrified by his decision to represent the red side of the Mersey. His father rang Bill Shankly in an attempt to sabotage the potential signing. Although never quite making the first team at Anfield, he did play in Northern Ireland and Australia before injuries ended his career. It was then that he decided to use his psychic powers on a full time and lucrative basis. Now a permanent fixture on our screens and probably best known for the series, 'Most Haunted'. Acorah went on tour in the UK and Norway to present his show *Whispers From Heaven* and most recently he had appeared on the twentieth instalment of Celebrity Big Brother. He passed away on 3 January 2020 after a brief illness. His wife confirmed that he had been hospitalised with pneumonia and later contracted sepsis.

## AGGER, Daniel

*Defender*
**Born:** *1984 Hvidovre, Denmark*
**Playing career:** *Liverpool, Brondby (2004-2014)*
Daniel Agger signed for Liverpool during the January transfer window in 2006. He was bought for £8.5 million from Brondby. The Dane spent eight years with Liverpool, featuring 175 times and scoring on nine occasions. A real fans' favourite declared his loyalty to the club in 2012. There was interest in Agger's services throughout Europe, but the defender decided to get 'YNWA' tattooed across his knuckles to reaffirm his love for Liverpool. He won the 2012 League Cup with Liverpool before moving back to boyhood club Brondby in 2014. He was capped 75 times by Denmark before he finished his playing career in 2016. He left Denmark upon retiring and moved to Marbella in Spain. There, he co-owns a sewerage business with his brother, uncle and childhood friend. Additionally, he invested in Tattoodo, which is a website that shares tattoos so others can find inspiration. In 2017 he also set up a charity project for Save the Children and frequently runs golfing competitions for the cause.

## AJDAREVIC, Astrit

*Attacking midfielder*
**Born:** *1990 Pristina, Yugoslavia*
**Playing career:** *Falenbergs FF, Liverpool, Leicester City , Hereford United, Djurgardens IF*
His father had been a professional footballer in the Yugoslavian First Division before moving his family to Sweden. Liverpool gave him the chance to play in England after a successful trial but he returned home after stops at Leicester City and Hereford United but having played only half a dozen league games in total. He has represented Sweden at the 2016 Rio Olympics but in 2017 he was capped by Albania in international football. He is currently playing for Djurgardens IF Fotboll in Sweden.

## ALDRIDGE, John

*Striker*
**Born:** *1958 Liverpool*
**Playing career:** *Newport County, Oxford United, Liverpool, Real Sociedad, Tranmere R (1979-1998)*
John Aldridge had to earn his spurs at Newport County and Oxford United before a £750,000 move took him back to his hometown, Liverpool, in 1987. A prolific scorer for all of his clubs, Aldridge amassed a tally of over 300 goals in his 20+ year career and still regularly finds the back of the net while playing for Liverpool Masters side. The former Republic of Ireland international – who made 69 caps and grabbed 19 goals for his country - managed Tranmere from 1996 until 2001 but is now a partner in Aldo's on Victoria Street in Liverpool and pundit on local sports programmes. He also writes an opiniated weekly column on Liverpool Football Club for the Liverpool Echo.

John Aldridge

## ALLAN, George
*Striker*
**Born:** *1875 Linlithgow, Scotland*
**Died:** 1899
**Playing career:** *Broxburn Shamrock,Bo'ness, Leith Athletic, Celtic, Liverpool (1891-1899)*

When George Allan arrived in Liverpool in 1895, he was a mere 20-year-old boy who made quite the impact at his new club. Known for his fine physique and bravery, he amassed an incredible goalscoring record for the club. In the 96 games that he played, he netted 56 times – a goal ratio of just 1.71. His important goals in his debut season helped Liverpool gain First Division status. He moved to Celtic in 1897 where he helped the club to their fourth championship by scoring 15 goals in only 17 league games. He returned back to Liverpool and 11 more goals for the striker helped his team finish second in the First Division. Prior to the 1899/00 season, Allan was too ill to train and remained in Scotland as he suffered with lung problems. These issues forced his retirement from football and he died from tuberculosis on 16 October 1899 at his mother's home in Fife. His unexpected death was described as a 'thunderclap' for Liverpool fans.

## ALLMAN, Dick
*Forward*
**Born:** *1883 Burslem*
**Died:** 1943
**Playing career:** *Burslem Port Vale, Reading, Portsmouth, Plymouth Argyle, Stoke City, Liverpool, Wrexham, Grantham, Ton Petre, Leicester Fosse, Croydon Common.. (1903-1916)*

Dick Allman started his career with Burslem Port Vale before being picked up by Reading in 1907. He eventually earned a transfer to Liverpool in 1908 but only featured for the side once – where Bristol City ran out as 2-1 winners at Anfield. His subsequent move away kept to a similar theme in his career, as he was constantly on the move to another club. He finally found a home with Croydon Common, where he made 113 appearances and scored 34 goals. He enlisted in the army in 1915 and served in France, but he still made appearances during the wartime. He remained settled in Croydon and later worked as a tramway conductor before he died in 1943.

Xabi Alonso

## ALONSO, Xabi
*Midfielder*
**Born:** *1981 Tolosa, Spain*
**Playing career:** *Antiguoko, Real Sociedad B, Real Sociedad, Eibar (loan), Liverpool, Real Madrid, Bayern Munich (1999-2014)*

Xabi Alonso completed his transfer from Real Sociedad in 2004 for a fee of £14.4 million. It would be during his debut season that Alonso established himself as a true fan favourite. With Liverpool being 3-2 down in the 2005 UEFA Champions League final, Alonso took responsibility to take the penalty awarded to Liverpool. The initial penalty was saved, but Alonso managed to scramble the ball into the net to draw Liverpool level. He moved to Real Madrid in 2009 before finishing his career in Germany, playing for Bayern Munich. He was capped 114 times for Spain. Alonso retired from playing in 2017 and in 2018 he completed his UEFA coaching course and took charge of Real Madrid U14s in the same year. He was then appointed manager of Real Sociedad B on the 1st June 2019 and has remained in the role since.

Nicolas Anelka

## ANELKA, Nicolas

*Forward*
**Born:** *1979 Le Chesnay, France*
**Playing career:** *Mumbai City, Trappes Saint-Quentin, Clairefontaine, Paris Saint-Germain, Arsenal, Real Madrid, Liverpool (loan), Manchester City, Fenerbahce, Bolton Wanderers, Chelsea, Shanghai Shenhua, Juventus (loan), West Bromwich Albion (1983-2014)*

Nicolas Anelka was brought to Anfield in 2001 when he was loaned from Paris Saint-Germain. He featured for Liverpool 20 times, scoring four goals. The following season he moved to Manchester City, where he spent four years with the club. When he retired from as a player, Anelka joined the technical staff at Dutch Eredivisie side Roda JC in February 2017, claiming he wanted to help his friend and shareholder Aleksey Korotaev. However, the following year he moved to Lille as a youth offensive coach and remains with the club.

Alberto Aquilani

## AQUILANI, Alberto

*Midfielder*
**Born:** *1984 Rome, Italy*
**Playing career:** *Roma, Triestina (loan), Liverpool, Juventus (loan), Milan (loan), Fiorentina, Sporting CP, Pescara, Sassuolo (loan), Las Palmas (1999-2018)*

Alberto Aquilani moved to Liverpool in 2009 after seven years with Roma - he was viewed as a potential replacement for the recently departed Xavi Alonso. Limited first team opportunities saw him loaned to Juventus and AC Milan in two successive years. He made 18 appearances for Liverpool, scoring once before moving to Fiorentina in 2012. He was capped 38 times by Italy during his career. He signed a two-year deal with Las Palmas in 2018 but it was terminated after a year. He hung up his boots after the termination as he could not find another club whilst listed as a free agent.

## ARBELOA, Alvaro

*Full-back*
**Born:** *1983 Salamanca, Spain*
**Playing career:** *Real Madrid, Deportivo La Coruna, Liverpool, Real Madrid, West Ham. (2003-2017)*

Spanish international who played in their World Cup winning side of 2010. He became a regular for Liverpool following his move from Deportivo La Coruna and stayed for three seasons. Real Madrid lured him back home in 2009 and paid the Reds £5,000,000 for his signature. He remained at Los Blancos for seven years, before briefly featuring for West Ham prior to retiring as a player. Since then, he has returned to Real Madrid to work as an ambassador for the club.

## ARNELL, Alan
*Striker*
**Born:** *1933 Chichester*
**Died:** 2013
**Playing career:** *Worthing, Liverpool, Tranmere Rovers, Halifax Town, Runcorn (1953-1964)*
Alan Arnell started his professional football career with Liverpool in 1953 and he remained with the club until 1961. He was primarily used as a squad player during his eight years at Anfield but he did net 33 times in only 56 appearances! He moved to local club Tranmere where he scored a further 34 goals for the side. Finished his career playing non-league football. When he retired from the game he returned to Chichester where he went into licensed trade but also worked as a declaration officer at racecourses before his death in May 2013.

## ARPHEXAD, Pegguy
*Goalkeeper*
**Born:** *1973 Abymes, Guadeloupe*
**Playing career:** *Lille, Lens, Leicester City, Liverpool, Stockport County (loan), Coventry City, Notts County (loan), Olympique Marseille. (1990-2005)*
Arrived in the Premier League and Leicester City via France where he had made a handful of appearances for Lens and Lille. He was used mainly as back up to Kasey Keller and Tim Flowers but did save two penalties for the Foxes in an FA Cup penalty shootout against Arsenal in 2000. Joined Liverpool on a free transfer in 2000 but was only called upon twice and eventually moved on to Coventry and finally back to France. Despite only making very few appearances, he did return home at the end of his career with a remarkable number of trophies on the basis of being an unused substitute. In March 2016 he visited Leicester and he was forced to deny rumours that he had become a porn star! He told reporters that he was now working in sports insurance.

## ARROWSMITH, Alf
*Striker*
**Born:** *1942 Ashton-under-Lyne* **Died:** 2005
**Playing career:** *Liverpool, Bury, Rochdale, Macclesfield Town (1960-1973)*
Alf Arrowsmith was described by Bill Shankly as 'a born goal scorer', but injuries seriously hindered his true potential in front of goal. He arrived at Anfield at the age of 17 and he had set a club record for Derbyshire Club Tintwistle after he scored 96 goals during the 1959/60 season – a record that remains intact today. During his debut season he scored 19 goals in 24 games which helped Liverpool win their first league title for 17 years. Sadly, he injured his left knee badly whilst playing against West Ham in the 1964 Charity Shield. He died in May 2005 and his daughter paid tribute to his love from Liverpool by stating that away from his family, Liverpool Football Club was always in his heart.

## ASHCROFT, Charlie
*Goalkeeper*
**Born:** *1926 Chorley* **Died:** 2010
**Playing career:** *Liverpool, Ipswich Town, Coventry City, Chorley (1946-1962)*
Charlie Ashcroft spent nine years at Anfield after the conclusion of the Second World War and was instantly hailed a hero after saving a penalty from Preston legend Tom Finney on the opening day of the 1952/53 season. In December he lost his starting place and the arrival of Dave Underwood the following year further restricted his playing opportunities. He eventually moved to Ipswich – to play under World Cup-winning coach Sir Alf Ramsay - in the Third Division South. After only seven games for the club, he broke his arm and moved to Coventry but failed to make an impact as his injury never fully recovered. He later moved into the non-league with Chorley and spent 30 years working for the Royal Ordnance factory at Euxton. He died at the age of 83 in March 2010.

# Pegguy Arphexad: Former Liverpool and Leicester keeper denies he became a porn star

## ASHURST, Len

*Defender*
**Born:** *1939 Liverpool*
**Playing career:** *Liverpool, Prescot Cables, Sunderland, Hartlepool United (1957-1973)*

Len Ashurst joined Liverpool's academy as a youngster but was released in 1957. He was signed by Sunderland in the same year and stayed with the club for 13 years, recording 409 league appearances. He moved into management after playing and spent 19 years with ten clubs - including a short stint back with Sunderland. In the mid-1990s he moved into an administrator's role with the Football Association and in 2002 he became a Premier League match delegate, assessing the performances of match officials.

## AURELIO, Fabio

*Left-back/left winger*
**Born:** *1979 Sao Carlos, Brazil*
**Playing career:** *Sao Paulo, Valencia, Liverpool, Gremio (1997-2013)*

Fabio Aurelio was the first Brazilian to feature for the Club. After his six-year contract expired at Valencia, the Brazilian arrived at Anfield on a free transfer. Aurelio was a consistent player for the first team during his debut season before suffering an injury in the Champions League first leg tie against PSV in 2007. After returning from injury, the Brazilian established himself as  first choice left-back but continued to suffer with injuries. In total, he made 134 appearances, scoring four goals. Little is known about Aurelio's life after retiring as a footballer but he will return to Anfield in 2020 to take part in a legends charity game where Liverpool will play Barcelona's legends.

## AYALA, Daniel

*Centre-back*
**Born:** *1990 El Saucejo, Spain*
**Playing career:** *Liverpool, Hull City (loan), Derby County (loan), Norwich City, Nottingham Forest (loan), Middlesborough (2009-)*

Daniel Ayala signed for Liverpool before he could sign a professional contract with Sevilla, who he had spent the majority of his youth career with. Despite the excitement around the signing, the Spaniard failed to make a huge impression and was restricted to just five appearances in his three years with the club.

He stayed in England for the remainder of his playing career and is still currently contracted to Middleborough, where he has been since 2014 after making his loan move permanent.

## BABB, Phil

*Centre-back*
**Born:** *1970 Lambeth*
**Playing career:** *Millwall, Bradford City, Coventry City, Liverpool, Tranmere Rovers, Sporting Lisbon, Sunderland (1988-2004)*

Phil Babb was born in Lambeth in 1970 but qualified to play international football for the Republic of Ireland. Made his name at Bradford City and Coventry City before a £3.5m move took him to Liverpool in 1994. Ended his career at Sunderland and moved into management where he managed Hayes & Yeading United for two years before leaving by mutual consent. He also invested in a magazine called 'Golf Punk' along with some of his former teammates. Babb is now a Players' agent and UK-Football Academy Consultant. You can also hire out the former Irish international to play football with. He is signed with playwithalegend.com and he will play in matches, make public appearances and work in co-operation with commercial partnerships.

Markus Babbel

## BABBEL, Markus

*Centre-back/right-back*
**Born:** *1972 Munich, West Germany*
**Playing career:** *FC Luzern, TSV Gilching-Argelsried, Bayern Munich, Hamburger SV, Bayern Munich, Liverpool, Blackburn Rovers (loan), VfB Stuttgart (1979-2007)*

Having shone for Bayern in the Bundesliga, a £5 million move to Manchester United was lined up but never concluded. This allowed Gerard Houllier and Liverpool to secure his signature in 2000. Was a member of the 2001 treble winning squad but a nervous system disorder meant that he could not play for over a year after that.

Ben-Howard Baker

Upon recovery, he had a spell with Blackburn Rovers, but then went back home to play for VfB Stuttgart (where he became assistant manager), and Hertha Berlin. The former West German international was sacked from his post as coach in December 2011 when he announced that he did not intend to stay with the club beyond the end of the season. He is now the manager of A-League side Western Sydney Wanderers.

## BARON, Kevin

*Striker*
**Born:** *1926, Preston* **Died:** 1971
**Playing career:** *Liverpool, Southend United, Northampton Town, Aldershot (1947-1960)*

Kevin Baron came through the youth academy at Liverpool and was offered a professional contract in 1945. Due to his youthful looks, he was once denied entry to an away ground, with the doorman claiming: "Don't tell me you're a player. You are a boy"! Despite being only a 'boy' he certainly knew how to perform in a red shirt. He made his breakthrough during the 1949/50 season where he only missed four league matches and played in Liverpool's FA Cup final team against Arsenal. He settled in Suffolk after retiring as a player and worked as an insurance agent whilst managing Maldon Town. He died in June 1971 after a long illness, only 45 years old. His brother Gerard Baron, was the oldest victim of the Hillsborough tragedy in 1989.

## BAKER, Benjamin Howard

*Goalkeeper*
**Born:** *1892 Aigburth, Liverpool* **Died:** 1987
**Playing career:** *Blackburn Rovers, Preston North End, Liverpool, Corinthian, Everton, Chelsea, Everton, Oldham Athletic (1913-1929)*

Ben-Howard Baker was an amateur football player throughout his career but he also excelled within the athletic arena too. He played as a goalkeeper after his ankle was damaged by a naval mine during World War I. At one stage, he held the British record for high Jump and competed in the 1912 and 1920 Olympic Games, finishing in 6th and 11th. When he retired as a sportsman he joined the family-run business producing soap and chemicals and became a renowned businessman in the Liverpool area. He died in Warminster at the age of 95.

Jack Balmer

## BALMER, Jack

*Striker*
**Born:** *1916 West Derby*
**Died:** 1984
**Playing career:** *Liverpool (1935-1952)*

When Everton decided not to renew Jack Balmer's amateur contract, it did not take long for their dearest rivals to snap up the striker. In August 1935, he signed professional forms with Liverpool and remained at the club until 1952. He came back to haunt Everton in 1938, when he scored inside the first 30 seconds to help his side to a 3-1 victory at Goodison Park. World War II potentially stole the greatest years of his career away from him, but once the normal footballing calendar resumed, he was Liverpool's joint top scorer that helped the club win the 1946/47 League Championship. It was during this season that he scored a hat-trick in three consecutive league games with Portsmouth, Derby and Arsenal bowing down to the brilliance. Balmer was a brilliant asset to Liverpool and is one of only a few to have scored 100 goals for the club, but his refusal to tackle did frustrate the locals. He was given the captaincy during the 1947/48 season and became a coach with the club. When he left Liverpool as a coach he solely focused on his building business in West Derby Village before his death on Christmas Day 1984.

## BAMBER, Jack

*Half-back*
**Born:** *1895 St Helens* **Died:** 1973
**Playing career:** *Liverpool, Leicester City, Tranmere Rovers, Prescot Cables (1915-1932)*

Jack Bamber started his career playing as a right-winger but was later developed into a right-half, where he gained a lot of praise. He joined Liverpool during World War I and did not cost the club a single penny. After a four-year absence of the Football League, Bamber made 23 appearances in his debut season. 30 more matches the following campaign saw Bamber called up for his sole England cap against Wales – England ran out 1-0 victors. Unfortunately, the half-back was struck with appendicitis and his illness made room for Jock McNab to impress. Bamber never regained his starting position and due to a lack of appearances, he missed out on medals as Liverpool won the Championship twice in successive seasons, 1922 and 1923. He moved to Leicester for two seasons before returning to Merseyside to finish his career with Tranmere Rovers. He died 26 May 2013 in St Helens, the same place as his birth.

## BANKS, Alan

*Striker*
**Born:** *1938 Liverpool*
**Playing career:** *Liverpool, Cambridge City, Exeter City, Plymouth Argyle, Exeter City (1958-1974)*

Local lad Alan Banks impressed in Liverpool's reserves and was rewarded with a professional contract. He made his debut for the senior side a few days short of his twentieth birthday. He could not have dreamt of it being better, as he slotted in Liverpool's third goal in a convincing 5-0 victory. He played eight times for Liverpool and scored six goals before moving to Exeter. He never got to experience top-tier football whilst at his former club but was a talisman for Exeter. He scored 109 goals in 285 games during two spells with the club and was voted Exeter's all-time greatest player in a PFA survey as he was said to have been quite the entertainer on the pitch. Banks continued to play football for Exeter's Legends football team well into his sixties after retiring professionally. He was also awarded a silver salver by the Mayor of Exeter in 1971 after he broke the individual record of goals for the club.

## BARMBY, Nick
*Midfielder*
**Born:** *1974 Hull*
**Playing career:** *Tottenham Hotspur, Middlesbrough, Everton, Liverpool, Leeds United, Nottingham Forest (loan), Hull City (1991-2012)*

Prolific goal scorer who is one of very few players who have scored for six different Premier League sides. Featured in a number of £5 million+ moves during his career and was a runner-up in the PFA Young Player of the Year awards in 1993. Ended up at Hull and was confirmed as their Manager on a full-time basis in January 2011 but only lasted a sole season. In March 2019, Scunthorpe United announced that Nick Barmby would join the club as a coach but left the club only two months later when Paul Hurst was hired.

John Barnes

## BARNES, John
*Left winger*
**Born:** *1963 Kingston, Jamaica*
**Playing career:** *Watford, Liverpool, Newcastle United, Charlton Athletic, Celtic (1981-2000)*

John Barnes was a fantastic servant for Liverpool and represented the club more than 400 times. He arrived in England after his father was hired as Jamaica's military attaché in London. He started his youth career as a centre-back after turning out for local side Stowe Boys Club. However, he was quickly transitioned into a winger, where he would be so effective for Liverpool in future years. Kenny Dalglish brought the English international from Watford for £900,000 and completed the clinical trio of John Aldridge and Peter Beardsley. He finished his career with Charlton Athletic and was capped 79 times by England. After his appointment of head coach at Celtic, he momentarily removed his status of retired but never featured for the club on the pitch. He also managed Jamaica and Tranmere Rovers throughout his managerial career. He frequently writes for FourFourTwo magazine's Perfect XI, where former players compile their best XI that they have either played with or against. His opinion is also published across an array of newspapers and in October 2019, he was linked with the vacant Bangor City manager's job.

Nick Barmby

## BARNETT, Charlie

*Midfielder*

**Born:** *1988 Liverpool*
**Playing career:** *Liverpool (youth), Tranmere Rovers, Accrington Stanley, AFC Telford United (2005-2015)*

Charlie Barnett was destined for the big time when he was awarded a professional contract with Liverpool in 2006. He was part of their youth team that won the FA Youth Cup in 2006 and 2007. However, two years after his signing he was released by the club without making a sole senior appearance. He moved to Tranmere in 2008 and stayed with the club for two years, before signing for Accrington Stanley. He was released in 2013 and signed for AFC Telford United. He then fell out with the manager and after only 17 appearances, was released. He currently plays for fellow non-league side Marine.

## BAROS, Milan

*Striker*

**Born:** *1981 Czechoslovakia*
**Playing career:** *Banik Ostrava, Liverpool, Aston Villa, Lyon, Portsmouth (loan), Galatasaray, Antalyaspor, Mlada Boleslav, Slovan Liberec (1998-date)*

Milan Baros joined Liverpool in 2002 and stuck around long enough to help his team record history on the most memorable evening of the club's history in the 2005 Champions League Final. The striker was a goal-hungry machine but suffered a major injury during his second season with the club. He finished as the top scorer in the 2004 EUFA European Championships with

Milan Baros

five goals but left Liverpool in August 2005 to join Aston Villa. In 2009, he was banned indefinitely from playing for his national side after several breaches of discipline. He was, however, recalled back into the team after the appointment of Ivan Hasek. He finished his career with 93 caps for Czech Republic and scored 41 goals. He was once arrested in France for driving at 168 mph in his black Ferrari F430, which was more than double the speed limit – it was the fastest speed ever recorded in the region! He is currently contracted with Banik Ostrava, where he has been since 2017.

2005 Victory Parade

## BARTON, Harold

*Forward*
**Born:** *1910 Leigh* **Died:** 1969
**Playing career:** *Whitegate Juniors, Liverpool, Sheffield United (1927-1946)*

Harold Barton made 12 appearances during his debut season with Liverpool, but was a regular from November 1930 onwards. His most successful year in a Liverpool shirt came during the 1932/33 season, where he netted 13 goals from 36 matches - which included a hat-trick when his side crushed league champions Everton 7-4 in an entertaining derby. It still remains the highest scoring Merseyside derby to this day. He moved to Sheffield United in 1934 and was a member of the side that lost 1-0 to Arsenal in the 1936 FA Cup final. He did not return to playing professional football after World War II. Instead, he became a publican in Sheffield, where he passed away in the summer of 1969.

## BARTON, Joey

*Midfielder*
**Born:** *1982 Huyton*
**Playing career:** *Everton, Liverpool, Manchester City, Newcastle United, QPR, Marseille (loan), Burnley, Rangers (1996-2017)*

Came through the ranks at Manchester City making 130 league appearances and collected his one England cap before transferring to Newcastle. Always a controversial figure, he has been involved in numerous disputes both on and off the field. In December 2004 he was fined six weeks' wages after he stubbed a cigar into the eye of a younger teammate at the club's Christmas party. He served 77 days of a six-month sentence for common assault. He is currently managing Fleetwood Town.

## BARTROP, Wilf

*Outside-forward*
**Born:** *1887 Worksop* **Died:** 1918
**Playing career:** *Barnsley, Liverpool (1908-1915)*

Wilf Bartrop started his career in the Midland League, where he was playing for Worksop Town before earning a move to Barnsley in 1909. He had an interesting spell with the club as they reached the FA Cup final in his first season, losing 2-0 to Newcastle. The following season Barnsley were almost relegated but during the 1911/1912 campaign, they went one better and won the FA Cup. Prior to moving to Liverpool, he had played in 187 matches for the Tykes. He arrived alongside teammate Phil Bratley in May 1914 but only played three games for the club due to the outbreak of the war. Bartrop joined the Royal Field Artillery as a gunner and was killed in action in Belgium on 7 November 1918.

## BATTLES Sr., Barney

*Full-back/half-back*
**Born:** *1875 Springburn, Glasgow*
**Died:** 1905
**Playing career:** *Heart of Midlothian, Celtic, Liverpool (1896-1902)*

Barney Battles was a Scottish International defender who won trophies with Celtic and three Scottish caps before his death from pneumonia in 1905. He was only 30 years old and it is claimed that 40,000 people turned out to pay their respects on the day of his funeral. Unlike today's top players, Barney would not have earned much money during his career and, in a commendable tribute to their former player, Celtic donated the proceeds from an international match held at Celtic Park to support his family.

## BEADLES, Harry

*Forward*
**Born:** *1897 Llanllwchaiarn, Wales*
**Died:** 1958
**Playing career:** *Liverpool, Cardiff City, Sheffield Wednesday, Southport, Dundalk. (1921-1930)*

Harry Beadles' story is interesting. Due to economic reasons, he was forced to leave school at the age of 12 and work at the Pryce Jones Welsh Warehouse as a furrier and hosier. When the First World War broke out he enlisted and within a year he was serving as a rifleman in Gallipoli – he was awarded the Serbian Gold Medal for 'Gallantry'. After the war concluded he returned to play for his local side before he moved to Liverpool to play for amateur side Grayson's of Garston. In May 1921 he signed for Liverpool Football Club and started well, scoring six goals in his first 11 appearances as Liverpool won the league for the first time in 16 years. However, he never fully established himself in the first team and moved to Cardiff City. He was part of the team who lost 1-0 to Sheffield United in the 1925 FA Cup final. A knee injury brought an end to his playing career in the English league and he moved to Ireland to play and coach Dundalk, which ultimately became his last club. After retiring he returned to Merseyside and spent a short amount of time working as a prison officer at Walton Jail, whilst juggling another job at a local sports equipment retailer.

# BEARDSLEY

••••••••••••••••••••••••••••••

Peter Beardsley
@Realbeardsley

He later managed a hotel that was popular with American soldiers that were stationed in Liverpool because of World War II. Due to ill health he was forced to retire in the 1950s and on 29 August 1958 he passed away in the village of Sychdyn after a long illness.

## BEARDSLEY, Peter

*Forward/midfielder*
**Born:** *1961 Hexham, Northumberland*
**Playing career:** *Carlisle United, Vancouver Whitecaps, Manchester United, Newcastle United, Liverpool, Everton, Bolton Wanderers, Manchester City, Fulham, Hartlepool United, (1979-1999)*

When Peter Beardsley arrived at Anfield, he had already compiled quite the resume. His performances for Newcastle did not go unnoticed and he arrived around the same time as John Barnes and John Aldridge. His goals contributed to Liverpool's two league titles in 1987/88 and 1989/90 and he also won the 1989 FA Cup. He finished his playing career in Australia playing for Melbourne Knights and was capped 59 times by England. When he retired as a player he moved into management and his first role was assistant to Kevin Keegan. He then spent the majority of his career in management with Newcastle but only managed the senior team on a temporary basis. He is currently Newcastle's Football Development Manager but was issued a 32-week ban from football by the Football Association in 2019 after it was alleged he was racially abusive towards a youth coach with the club.

## BECTON, Frank

*Inside-forward*
**Born:** *1873 Preston*
**Died:** 1909
**Playing career:** *Preston North End, Liverpool, Sheffield United, Bedminster, Preston North End, Swindon Town (1889-1904)*

Frank Becton joined the famous Preston team that had won the first titles of the Football League, where they earned the nickname of 'The Invincibles', in 1891. Upon his arrival, Preston finished runners-up in three consecutive seasons! His best season was the 1892/93 campaign where he was the side's top scorer with 25 goals in both the league and the cup. He demanded a substantial pay rise as he claimed that Aston Villa, Manchester City and Bolton

Wanderers were after his signature. He was eventually sold to Liverpool for a hefty fee of £100. His four goals from the final five games would not save the club though, as they were relegated to the second tier. They went straight back up the following year as Becton, George Allan and Jimmy Ross scored a combined 66 goals. Unfortunately, Becton's attitude saw him dropped to the reserves and a last-minute move to Aston Villa fell through before the player and the club settled their differences. He later moved to Sheffield United before heading back to Preston but could not save his local club from relegation. He worked in a mill after retiring but died of tuberculosis on 6th November 1909, aged just 36. His brothers, Martin and Tom, were both professional footballers who also played for Preston.

## BEGLIN, Jim

*Left-back*
**Born:** *1963 Waterford, Republic of Ireland*
**Playing career:** *Waterford Bohs, Shamrock Rovers, Liverpool, Leeds United, Plymouth Argyle (loan), Blackburn Rovers (loan) (1980-1991)*
Prior to being Forced to quit after a short comeback following a serious leg break, Jim Beglin was a member of the famous Liverpool side that won the 1986 double. He was also capped 15 times for Republic of Ireland. Since retiring as a player he has carved himself a career in the media working for Radio Five, Granada and Sky amongst others – which also included commentating in the 2014 and 2018 FIFA World Cup for RTÉ. He has also done voice over work and can be heard as co-commentator on the Pro Evolution Soccer 2011 game. He is currently working for Premier League Productions and BT Sport in similar media roles.

## BELLAMY, Craig

*Forward*
**Born:** *1979 Cardiff, Wales*
**Playing career:** *Bristol Rovers, Norwich City, Coventry City, Newcastle United, Celtic (loan), Blackburn Rovers, Liverpool, West Ham United, Manchester City, Liverpool, Cardiff City. (1990-2014)*
Craig Bellamy began his nomadic career with Bristol Rovers youth team before moving onto a relatively successful career with a variety of Premier League clubs - including two spells with Liverpool.

Craig Bellamy

Also collecting over 60 Welsh caps along the way. No stranger to controversy, Bellamy is alleged to have been involved in several violent incidents, although he has never been convicted. The unreported side of Bellamy is his charitable work in Sierra Leone, where he has personally spent over a million pounds in setting up the Craig Bellamy Foundation for disadvantaged children, a non-profit football academy in the Kono region. In January 2019, Bellamy stepped down from his youth coaching role with Cardiff City after it was alleged he was bullying a youth player. The following June he signed a three-year contract to become the U-21 team coach at Anderlecht, where he was reunited with former Manchester City player Vincent Kompany.

## BENAYOUN, Yossie

*Midfielder*
**Born:** *1980 Dimona, Israel*
**Playing career:** *Maccabi Haifa, Hapoel Dimona, Hapoel Be'er Sheva, Ajax, Racing Santander, West Ham United (loan), Liverpool, Chelsea, Arsenal (loan), QPR, Maccabi Haifa, Maccani Tel Aviv, Beitar Jerusalem, Maccabi Petah Tikva, Beitar Jerusalem (1989-Date)*
Yossie Benayoun was a starlet in the making when he established himself at both club and international level. He was voted Player of the Year as Maccabi won their first title in seven years during the 2000/01 campaign. They retained their champions status the following year before he moved to northern Spain to represent Racing Santander. He shone in a side that was rather lacklustre which caught the eye of West Ham, who signed the Israelian for £2.5 million in the summer of 2005.

His performances against Liverpool during the subsequent season certainly influenced Rafael Benitez into signing the attacking-midfielder. He was a member of the West Ham team that lost the FA Cup final to Liverpool on penalties after a pulsating 3-3 draw in 2006. When he signed for Liverpool, it was under controversial circumstances as he had verbally agreed to sign an extension with his current club. Nevertheless, West Ham accepted the £5 million bid and he was on his way to Merseyside. His first season with the club was relatively successful, he featured in 47 of Liverpool 59 competitive matches – although he was used as a substitute on 21 occasions. He grabbed two hat-tricks in his inaugural season with the club, one in the FA Cup against Havant & Waterlooville and one in the Champions League when playing Besiktas. His second season brought more success and he was widely hailed as a match winner, but he was still primarily used as an impact sub. Ironically, Benayoun's best season at the club was awarded with a move to Chelsea in the summer of 2010! He claimed the reason he left was because of Benitez himself, and his lack respect shown to the Israeli international. He had a loan spell with Arsenal before moving permanently to Queens Park Rangers in 2013. He momentarily moved home to play for Maccabi and brought an end to a glittering career in April 2019 when he announced that he was going to retire at the end of the season. He is the most capped Israelian player with 102 appearances and is arguably the greatest footballer to ever be produced by the country.

## BERGER, Patrik
*Left winger/attacking midfielder*
**Born:** *1973 Prague, Czechoslovakia*
**Playing career:** *Slavia Prague, Borussia Dortmund, Liverpool, Portsmouth, Aston Villa, Stoke City, Sparta Prague (1991-2010)*

Patrik Berger knew what it took to win at a young age, having been a part of the Czech Republic U-16 squad that became European champions in 1990. He started on the books at Sparta Prague but it was their rivals who snapped him up when he was 18 and eligible to sign a professional contract. He moved to Borussia Dortmund and spent a sole season with the German side. They won the league but he spent a large proportion of the campaign sat on the bench. Roy Evans brought the winger to Liverpool for a fee of £3.25m in 1996 and he started his time with the club in blistering fashion. In only his second appearance, he came off the bench and scored twice as Liverpool beat Leicester. Kasey Keller, then Leicester keeper, stated: "I've never seen a ball move so fast in my life. It's a good job I didn't get in the way of either shot or I'd have been back in the net with them". His first appearance in the starting line up resulted in two more goals against Chelsea and he was voted Liverpool's player of the month in his first with the club! However, controversy soon surrounded the Czech international as he reportedly refused to sit on the bench in a Premier League game against Bolton - this seriously damaged the relationship he had with the man who signed him. Berger was actively looking for a move away before Evans left Liverpool and Gerard Houllier was his replacement. Four goals in five games proved to the new manager that his trust was safely placed in him. During Liverpool's successful season of 2000/01, Berger was injured for five months due to a knee ligament injury and continued to play less frequently before moving to Portsmouth in 2003. Injuries continued to plague the twilight years of his career and after a brief spell back home with Sparta Prague, he hung up his boots in January 2010 due to his consistent knee issues. Instead of going into management he continued his ties with Liverpool by working for the club as an ambassador and continues to play for the Liverpool Masters team in addition to featuring in legends games.

Patrik Berger

## BERRY, Arthur
**Born:** *1888*
**Died:** 1953
**Playing career:** *Liverpool, Fulham, Everton, Wrexham, (1900's)*

Arthur Berry won two gold medals with England in the 1908 and 1912 Olympics, having been a member of their football team. He was only one of two men who were victorious at both of the Games. He studied at Denstone College and Wadham College in Oxford and was awarded two Blues in 1907 and 1908 - which recognise sporting excellence from students at the highest level. He studied law at his colleges and was even the cricket captain for the institutions, being known for his resilience with the bat. Coincidentally, his father Edwin Berry, was Liverpool's chairman from 1904-1909, which resulted in Berry's first spell with the club. He made his first team debut in April 1908 where the Reds lost 3-1 to Newcastle. He left for Fulham but as he remained stationed up north, he found the commute difficult which led to his signing for Everton. He re-joined Liverpool in June 1912 but only played one more game for the club, bringing his overall tally to four. He remained an amateur throughout his career and his only silverware was winning the FA Amateur Cup with Oxford City in 1913. He retired from football in 1914 and severed as Adjutant of the Lancashire Fusiliers during World War I. After the conclusion of the war, he joined the family law firm, where his father was the head of the company. He also later served as chairman and director of Liverpool Football Club. He died in Liverpool on March 15, 1953.

## BEST, John
*Defender*
**Born:** *1940 Liverpool*
**Died:** 2014
**Playing career:** *Liverpool, Tranmere Rovers, Stockport County, Philadelphia Ukrainians, Philadelphia Spartans, Cleveland Stokers, California Jaguars, Dallas Tornado, Seattle Sounders (1958-1974)*

John Best started his footballing career with Liverpool. Having spent two years in the reserves, he failed to force his way into the senior side and moved to Tranmere Rovers, where he spent one season. In 1962, he moved to America to feature for Philadelphia Ukrainians.

Indoor Soccer League

He spent the remainder of his career in the States and eventually retired with Seattle Sounders, where he then moved into a management role with the club. He played once at international level, for the United States as they lost 4-0 to Bermuda. He moved to Vancouver Whitecaps and became the general manager of the side, winning the 1979 NASL Championship. When he retired from coaching he remained in the Seattle area, founding Tacoma Indoor Soccer Inc. and was inducted into the Tacoma-Pierce County Sports Hall of Fame. In 1990, he was diagnosed with kidney disease and in 2002 he received a kidney transplant from his wife. He died on 5 October 2014 from a lung infection while visiting family in Ireland.

## BIRCH, Trevor
*Midfielder*
**Born:** *1958 Liverpool*
**Playing career:** *Liverpool, Shrewsbury Town, Chester City, Marine, Runcorn, Northwich Victoria (1974-1988)*

Was the last player to be signed for Liverpool by Bill Shankly. Became a Chartered Accountant and has since worked as Chief Executive for Chelsea and Derby. When employed at the former, he oversaw the sale to current owner Roman Abramovich for £180 million. He has also been Chairman at Leeds United and has been CEO at Sheffield United since 2009. Birch became the chairman of Swansea City on 18 March 2019.

### "DID YOU KNOW?"

*"In 1892, to get the club started, the club president John Houlding went to Scotland and signed 13 players."*

## BISCAN, Igor

*Midfielder/defender*

**Born:** *1978 Zagreb,* Croatia
**Playing career:** *Samobor (loan), Liverpool, Panathinaikos, Dinamo Zagreb (1995-2012)*

Igor Biscan was brought to Liverpool to rival Didi Hamann for the defensive-midfielder position. He was signed for £5.5m by Gerard Houllier but he failed to make an instant impact and struggled during his first year with the club. He was used primarily as a sub for the following two seasons before becoming a regular in the team during the 2003/04 campaign. He was occasionally used in defence by the Frenchman but when Rafael Benitez arrived, the Croatian was under strict instructions to solely focus on being a midfielder – which relieved the player as he hated playing at the back! He was informed that he was no longer part of the plan in December 2004 and would be sold in the subsequent summer. However, this only fuelled him as he played a big part in Liverpool's 2005 Champions League success. Injuries forced him to retire in 2012 but he did return to the game in 2016 to manage Croatian second tier team Rudes. He won promotion with the club which led to him becoming the manager of Olimpia Ljubljana. He won the league and cup double in 2017/18 but was sacked by the owner and he returned to Croatia to manage Rijeka before coaching the Croatia U-21 national team, a role he still fulfils today.

Igor Biscan

Stig Inge Bjornebye

## BJORNEBYE, Stig Inge

*Left-back*

**Born:** *1969 Elverum, Norway*
**Playing career:** *Strommen, Kongsvinger, Rosenborg, Liverpool, Brondby, Blackburn Rovers (1987-2003)*

Stig Inge Bjornebye's move to Liverpool was nothing short of a dream. He scored the winning goal for Rosenborg in the Norwegian Cup final which resulted in then Liverpool boss Graeme Souness to ring the full-back and offer him a contract with one of the biggest clubs in the world! His debut, however, was the polar opposite of that cup final. Liverpool lost 5-1 to Coventry – which was their biggest defeat in 16 years. He struggled in his first two seasons with the club but his breakthrough came in the 1994/95 campaign. Unfortunately, he broke his leg as his studs remained grounded into the floor in April 1995 and he only played two games in the following season. He did revive his Liverpool career when his side were on the charge for their first Premiership title, but they fell short. He provided brilliant assistance for Robbie Fowler and Stan Collymore and his performances did not go unnoticed, as he made the Premier League Team of the Year. Sadly, when Gerard Houllier took over, Bjornebye was one of the first to leave Anfield, as the Frenchman looked to assemble his own squad. He linked back up with Souness at Blackburn and helped the club gain Premier League status before a freak training ground incident saw him fracture his eye-socket.

He injured his foot whilst playing Wigan in 2002 and was forced to have a surgery that by-passed two arteries in a five-hour operation to save his foot from being amputated. The surgery was a success, but it forced the Norwegian to retire from football in March 2003. He returned in the following December when he was named as Norway's assistant manager and he remained there until 2006, where he was appointed manager of IK Start. He was dismissed in his second season with the club as the threat of relegation loomed greater. In 2015 he became the sports director at Rosenborg and remains there today.

## BLENKINSOP, Ernie

*Left-back*
**Born:** *1902 Cudworth, Barnsley* **Died:** 1969
**Playing career:** *Hull City, Sheffield Wednesday, Liverpool, Cardiff City (1921-1938)*
Ernie Blenkinsop may be one of the only players in the history of football to have a barrel of beer as part of the transfer! Hull City captured the full-back's services after paying his local club £100 and 80 pints of beer. He worked in the Grimethorpe and Brierley pits from the age of 13 until he was 18 and he once cheated death when the roof collapsed in the gallery in which he was working in – he was certain if he had not reacted quickly and fell to the floor he would have died. He was very skilful on the ball, had brilliant positional awareness and held pinpoint accuracy. Sheffield Wednesday bought the left-back and he went on to play 424 games for the club in an 11-year spell. He eventually moved to Liverpool for £6,500 in March 1934 which caused great unrest by Wednesday fans. By then, he had played and captained England and helped his former side win the League Championship in two successive years in 1929 and 1930. Whilst at Liverpool he shared the captaincy with Tom Cooper. but moved on to Cardiff after 71 appearances. During his career, he kept a detailed autograph book that he would leave outside of the dressing room for players to print their autograph in – he amassed quite the collection from his playing days at Sheffield Wednesday, England and Liverpool. When he retired from the game he went into the pub trade and died whilst serving a customer on his premises on 24 April 1969.

Bob Bolder

## BOLDER, Bob

*Goalkeeper*
**Born:** *1958 Dover*
**Playing career:** *Dover F.C, Sheffield Wednesday, Liverpool, Sunderland, Charlton Athletic, Margate, Dagenham & Redbridge (1977-1995)*
Was predominantly back up to Bruce Grobbelaar while at Liverpool but did become first choice for Charlton Athletic. He played for seven seasons at the Valley before injury forced him to retire from the game but he still works for the club's community scheme. He also represents Liverpool's Masters team and plays in goal for the side. Bolder now works as a public speaker/dinner host and he can be hired to speak at any formal event.

## BOWEN, George

*Winger*
**Born:** *1875 Walsall*
**Died:** 1945
**Playing career:** *Bridgetown Amateurs, Liverpool, Wolves, Burslem Port Vale (1899-1905)*
George Bowen impressed Liverpool when he scored both of Wolves' goals in a 2-1 win at Molineux six months prior to him joining the club. He had enjoyed success at Wolves having scored 13 goals in 48 games before moving to Merseyside. However, he would not emulate that success purely because of bad luck. His second game against Sunderland saw him suffer a leg break that kept him out of football for over a year. He did eventually return to the reserves but decided to move back to Wolves, still slightly injured. He only made three appearances on his return before he was shipped off to Burslem Port Vale during the 1904/05 season. He continued to play non-league football after retiring professionally whilst working in a factory in Bilston until his death in 1945.

## BRADLEY, James

*Wing-half*

**Born:** *1881 Stoke-upon-Trent* **Died:** 1954
**Playing career:** *Stoke City, Liverpool, Reading, Stoke City (1898-1915)*

James Bradley started his career with local side Goldenhill Wanderers, in the coalmining village of Goldenhill, where he was born and raised. After a sole season with the club he was snapped up by Stoke and made 199 league appearances in a 7-year spell. He was supposed to move to Plymouth in 1905 but the Football Association could not sanction the deal, which allowed Liverpool to sweep in for the wing-half. Prior to signing, whilst Bradley was at Stoke, himself and Liverpool's Fred Buck had a fight on the pitch with both men being dismissed! However, he clearly put the issue past him and signed for the club in September 1905. In his inaugural season with the club Liverpool won the League Championship and he played in 32 matches that season. He became an integral player for Liverpool and would only miss 18 league matches over the next four seasons. On Christmas day 1909, he was required to go in goal and managed to keep a clean sheet in a 3-0 win over Bolton Wanderers! He rejoined Stoke in 1913 after the club had resigned from the Football League and helped them back up to the Second Division.

James Bradley

After he retired from football he worked in the Stoke-on-Trent highways department whilst becoming a part-time coach for Stoke's reserves. When he retired he moved to Blackpool to live out the remainder of his life until his death on 12 March 1954.

## BRADSHAW, Harry

*Forward*

**Born:** *1873 Liverpool* **Died:** 1899
**Playing career:** *Liverpool Nomads, Liverpool, Northwich Victoria, Tottenham Hotspur, Thames Ironworks (1889-1899)*

Harry Bradshaw was the first Liverpool player to be called up to play international football when he played outside-left as England beat Ireland 6-0 on 20 February 1897. At the time, Bradshaw was Liverpool's centre-forward and without a doubt the biggest star that had ever represented the club. He scored seven goals from 14 games to help Liverpool win the 1893/94 Second Division Championship in his debut season. Despite his efforts in the top tier scoring 17 goals, his side were immediately relegated again. Nevertheless, they went back up the following season and he contributed with 11 more goals. He had switched to play on the wing during this season, which would explain his lack of goals in contrast to the previous two. His performances caught the eye of Tottenham and he moved to London before the start of the 1898/99 season – he played in 52 matches during his debut season with the club. He moved to Thames Ironworks (now West Ham) in the summer of 1899 and was made club captain. On Christmas day 1899 Bradshaw watched Spurs play Portsmouth and once he arrived back home he was vomiting excessively and complained of head and chest pains. Before a doctor could be present he suffered a fit and passed away at the age of 26. His widow Elizabeth later stated that four years prior, he was kicked on the head in a football game and the same thing happened the following week. It was from then on that he suffered from pain in the head and discharges from his ear. When he headed the ball, he had to put his hands on his ears to ease the pain. The post-mortem showed that he had died due to a ruptured blood vessel in the brain. On April 2 1900, Tottenham and Thames Ironworks played a charity match to raise money for his young family.

## BRADSHAW, Tom

*Wing-half*
**Born:** *1904 Bishopton, Scotland*
**Died:** 1986
**Playing career:** *Woodside Juniors, Bury, Liverpool, Third Lanark, South Liverpool (1920-1939)*

Tom Bradshaw – nicknamed tiny – was an absolute giant of a player for Liverpool Football Club. Prior to his arrival, he had played in 208 league games for Bury. His one and only cap for Scotland turned out to be one of the greatest victories they had over England, thumping the hosts 5-1 in front of 80,000 people at Wembley! The Scottish team were dubbed 'The Wembley Wizards' after the feat. Bradshaw primarily started out as wing-half during his debut season with Liverpool but he was moved to centre-half for the remainder of his time – a position he completely dominated. He was one of the brightest stars in a rather average Liverpool side at the time. He returned to Scotland to play for Third Lanark for a sole season before retiring professionally in 1939. After he retired as a player he worked as a scout for Norwich City before moving back to Scotland, where he remained until his death on 22 February 1986.

## BREDBURY, Tim

*Striker*
**Born:** *1963 Hong Kong*
**Playing career:** *Liverpool Reserves, Ryoden, Seiko, Rangers (HKG), South China, Lai Sun, Sydney Olympic, Selangor, Sabah, South China, Voicelink, Sing Tao, Frankwell, Instant-Dict (1979-1999)*

Tim Bredbury was born in Hong Kong to English parents and was on Liverpool's books for three years after he signed as an apprentice professional in 1979. He was restricted to the reserve side whilst at Liverpool and never made a senior appearance.

After the expiration of his contract he was approached by Hong Kong side Ryoden. He decided to take up the offer and he returned home. He was the top scorer in Hong Kong on two separate occasions before he moved to Australia. He moved back home again finishing his career with Instant-Dict and he represented his country 34 times, scoring 14 goals before hanging up his boots in 1999. When he retired as a player he worked as a marketing manager, professional coach, sports journalist and a television presenter on ATV's World channel. In 2005 he returned to football and was appointed the head coach at La Salle College. He has managed a whole host of clubs including: Rangers (HKG), Biu Chun Rangers, Sun Hei SC and Tai Chung. He is currently employed coaching the U14's at Kitchee Football Club.

## BROMILOW, Tom

*Left-half*
**Born:** *1894 Liverpool*
**Died:** 1959
**Playing career:** *Liverpool (1919-1930)*

Having been demobilised by the army in 1919, Tom Bromilow rather confidently approached Liverpool asking for a trial. Then secretary of Liverpool, George Patterson claimed: "I should think that is one of the luckiest signings I have made". He certainly wasn't wrong. The local lad would stay with the club for ten years and make 375 appearances. He played 28 times during his debut season but he would incredibly go on to miss only five matches for the next three campaigns – assisting Liverpool with their third and fourth League Championship in 1922 and 1923. His final game came against Blackburn that brought an end to a marvellous career in red. A poll was conducted for Liverpool fans to vote for their greatest ever player in 1939 and Bromilow came fifth. He was capped five times by England before bringing an end to his career in 1930. He swiftly moved into management and rather strangely, started his managerial career with AFC Amsterdam. He moved to Burnley in 1932 and became the first manager of the club who was a former player. His last involvement in football was working as a scout for Leicester City, it was during his employment there that he died suddenly on a train on 4 March 1959.

## BROWN, Owen

*Forward*
**Born:** *1960 Liverpool*
**Playing career:** *Liverpool, Carlisle United, Crewe Alexandra, Tranmere Rovers, Chester-City, Hyde United (1978-1985)*

Owen Brown was part of the youth academy at Liverpool but the club felt he had not progressed enough to offer him a professional contract. Carlisle picked him up after his release, but he only lasted a sole season before fellow Merseyside club Tranmere signed him. When his career finished he moved into coaching with Prescot Cables. From 1996 to 1999 he was the manager of Barrow, winning the UniBond Premier title in 1998. However, with the club struggling in the Conference, he was relieved of his duties. He then became a coach for Liverpool's U-19s before moving back into management with Dyoylsden – a tenure that lasted only a matter of weeks. Whilst managing Vauxhall Motors FC, he dropped home a player and received a phone call only minutes later that he had been shot after getting out of the car! He returned to Liverpool to work in various positions, including a scout, player liaison officer and advisor to then-manager Rafael Benitez.

## BROWNBILL, Derek

*Forward*
**Born:** *1954 Liverpool*
**Playing career:** *Liverpool, Port Vale, Cleveland Cobras, Wigan Athletic, Stafford Rangers, Oswestry Town, Morecambe, Witton Albion, Warrington Town (1972-1982)*

Derek Brownbill impressed Liverpool's youth coaches which resulted in a professional contract. However, the local lad quickly learned that it was very difficult to break into the senior side and was restricted to just one appearance for them in a league match away to Birmingham in 1973.

He left Anfield in 1975 and played 140 games for lower-league outfits Wigan and Port Vale. He emigrated to America to play for Cleveland Cobras before returning back to England to play as a semi-professional. He became player-manager at Warrington Town in 1989 and remained in that role for six seasons, before briefly joining Curzon Ashton for a year. He managed Runcorn for four years before returning to Warrington. He stepped down as the club's director of football after 20 years of service in 2009. However, he has kept his ties with the club intact and still assists the board of directors today.

## BUCK, Fred

*Inside-forward/Centre-half*
**Born:** *1879 Audley* **Died:** *1952*
**Playing career:** *Stafford Wesleyans, Stafford Rangers, Liverpool, Plymouth Argyle, West Bromwich Albion, Swansea Town (1895-1917)*

Fred Buck arrived from West Brom in 1903 and his most memorable moment in a Liverpool shirt was being sent off – and subsequently banned for six weeks – for kicking and punching Preston's James Bradley. He only made a handful of appearances for the club after that incident and his only goal came in the Boxing day defeat by Blackburn Rovers in 1903. He returned back to his former club and racked up over 300 league appearances whilst scoring more than 70 goals. He moved to Swansea for three seasons but injuries resulted in him only being used in eight league fixtures during his time in Wales and decided to retire in May 1917. During 1915 to 1918 he served in the Army Service Corps where he gained the British War Medal. After retiring he became a publican in Rugby, Warwickshire and worked as a clerk in the Grinding Wheel Works in Stafford. He died on 5 June 1952 and was buried in the Eccleshall Road Cemetery.

## BURKE, Tom

*Wing-half*

**Born:** *1863 Wrexham, Denbighshire, Wales*
**Died:** 1914
**Playing career:** *Wrexham Grosvenor, Wrexham February, Wrexham Olympic, Liverpool Cambrian, Newton Heath LYR, Wrexham Victoria (1882-1891)*

Tom Burke started his career playing for Wrexham and was awarded eight Welsh international caps throughout his career. He moved from Wales to Liverpool to feature for Liverpool Cambrians before he transferred to Newton Heath in 1886. The club's parent company, the Lancashire and Yorkshire Railway, was able to employ Burke as a painter, which was his trade. He mainly played as a left-half but could play anywhere along the back. He finished his career where it started before going back to painting. He died in February 1914 at the age of 50 as a result of lead poisoning.

## BURKINSHAW, Keith

*Defender*

**Born:** *1935 Higham, Barnsley*
**Playing career:** *Wolves, Denaby United, Liverpool, Workington, Scunthorpe United (1953-1968)*

Keith Burkinshaw made just one appearance for Liverpool, which came in a home fixture against Port Vale on 11 April 1955. He had to stay with the reserves for two years before being granted a move away to Workington in December 1957. He racked up over 300 appearances for the club and is one of their fondly remembered players. He also made over 100 appearances for Scunthorpe. However, he is largely remembered by the football community for his services as a manager. He spent eight years managing Tottenham between 1976 and 1984, where he won the FA Cup two years in succession in 1981 and 1982 and the UEFA Cup in his last season with the club. His last involvement in football was assistant manager at Watford, a role he held for two years between 2005 and 2007 before he was forced to leave due to a serious family illness and he retired at the age of 71.

## BURROWS, David

*Left-back*

**Born:** *1968 Dudley*
**Playing career:** *West Bromwich Albion, Liverpool, West Ham United, Everton, Coventry City, Birmingham City, Sheffield Wednesday (1985-2003)*

Just a few days before David Burrows twentieth birthday, Kenny Dalglish signed the youngster from West Brom. He was thrown straight into the team for a home match against Coventry only two days later and would go on to make a further 20 league appearances during his debut season. He was a member of the 1989/90 League Championship side and also played his part in the 1992 FA Cup run that saw Graeme Souness win his only silverware whilst manager of the club. He moved on to West Ham in 1993 and later revealed that he had a sour relationship with Souness, claiming it was obvious that he did not fancy him in the team. He moved back to Merseyside to join rivals Everton but failed to make an impact before heading to Coventry for four years. He joined Birmingham and had bust ups with both Trevor Francis and Steve Bruce – where he was thrown out of the club! He was forced to retire at 34 whilst at Sheffield Wednesday as injuries were a frequent occurrence. He has since moved to France with his wife and three children where he has been investing in holiday homes and coaching part-time sides.

## BUSBY, Sir Matt

*Right-half/Inside-forward*
**Born:** *1909 Orbiston, Bellshill, Scotland*
**Died:** *1994*
**Playing career:** *Denny Hibs, Manchester City, Liverpool, Hibernian (guest) (1928-1943)*

Sir Matt Busby is a prominent figure in English football. As a player, he spent eight years at Manchester City and five years at Liverpool. His greatest achievements, however, come from his managerial career. It was his stint as Manchester United where tragedy struck. His current team were nicknamed the 'Busby Babes' after the youthful looks of many of his players. After an away trip to Red Star Belgrade, the plane carrying the Manchester United staff crashed and ten died at the scene - which included seven players. Busby rebuilt his team and enjoyed great success at Old Trafford. In total, he won one European Cup, five Division One Championships and two FA Cups whilst Manchester United manager.

## BUSH, Tom

*Defender*
**Born:** *1914 Hodnet, Shropshire*
**Died:** *1969*
**Playing career:** *Shrewsbury Amateurs, Liverpool (1930-1947)*

Tom Bush was one of many English footballers that had their careers disrupted by World War II. He first featured for Liverpool at the end of December 1933 in a 1-1 draw against Wolves. Bush started his career as a centre-forward and his second and last time playing in that role for Liverpool came in the St James' massacre on New Year's Day 1934 that saw Liverpool absolutely thrashed 9-2. A hiatus of almost three years until he appeared again for the senior side, but by this time the war had broken out. He returned to Anfield after the war was over but had to fly back from Liverpool's American pre-season tour before the 1946/47 season to be by his daughter's side. Tragically, she lost her life on 29 May 1938, just nine months old. His final appearance came against Preston on 7 April 1947, over 13 years since he had made his debut. After he retired as a player, he had the responsibility of bringing players through the youth system at Liverpool and preparing them for the reserves and potentially the senior side. A lot of his work was done away from Anfield, interviewing parents of youngsters who the club had an interest in. Arguably, the greatest feat in his career was when Liverpool won the FA Cup in 1965 and five academy players were on the pitch. In total, he spent 37 years at Anfield and can go down as a brilliant servant to Liverpool Football Club.

## BYRNE, Gerry

*Left-back*
**Born:** *1938 Liverpool*
**Died:** *2015*
**Playing career:** *Liverpool (1957-1969)*

Having spent four years in the academy at Liverpool, he was awarded a professional contract at the age of 17. He made his league debut against Charlton on 28 September 1957, but that would be his only game of the season. Unfortunately, Liverpool lost the game 5-1 and he did score an own goal. However, it was the arrival of Bill Shankly that truly gave Gerry Byrne his first chance of senior football.

Gerry Byrne

He broke into the team in the autumn of 1960 after Ronnie Moran sustained an injury and he kept his spot for many years. During the 1965 FA Cup final, Byrne suffered an injury early into the match but continued to play for the entirety of the game – it was revealed after that he had broken his collarbone. Shankly was impressed by his left-back's commitment, stating: "it was a performance of raw courage from the boy". He was also in England's World Cup-winning squad in 1966 but failed to make an appearance during the finals. In 2009 he wasfinally presented with a winner's medal at a ceremony in London. He was awarded with a testimonial match at the end of his career, where more than 40,000 fans were present. He suffered from Alzheimer's disease in later life and died in a Wrexham nursing home in 2015 at the age of 77.

## CALLAGHAN MBE, Ian

*Midfielder*
**Born:** *1942 Toxteth, Liverpool*
**Playing career:** *Liverpool, Ft Lauderdale Strikers (loan), Swansea City, Canberra City (loan), Cork United, Sandefjord, Crewe Alexandra (1960-1982)*
When Billy Liddell was retiring, he was questioned if there was anyone who would be able to replace the gaping hole that he would leave. He responded with one name: Ian Callaghan.

The local lad played his first game only six days into his eighteenth birthday replacing his boyhood hero Liddell. Liverpool beat Bristol Rovers 4-0 and the youngster was awarded with a standing ovation from not only the home fans, but everyone in the stadium – including the referee! However, Bill Shankly was cautious on relying on someone so younger and brought Kevin Lewis to Anfield in 1960, which forced Callaghan to settle for limited opportunities. When Liverpool were promoted in the 1961/62 season, he became a regular for the club and stayed for the next 15 years! He won the League Championship four times and set the winning goal up for the 1965 FA Cup final victory. During the 1970/71 season, Callaghan had a knee operation and Shankly decided to play him in central midfield, a decision that prolonged his Liverpool career by seven years. His ability to read the game, mobility and quick speed suited his new role. He won two EUFA Cups before adding two European Cups to his already sensational trophy cabinet. In September 1978, he brought an end to his Liverpool career and moved to Swansea before finishing his career with Crewe, retiring just two months short of his fortieth birthday. In total, Callaghan played 857 times for Liverpool – which is a club record – and he was the first Liverpool player to be voted Footballer of the Year in 1974.

Ian Callaghan

Titi Camara

## CAMARA, Titi

*Striker*
**Born:** *1972 Conakry, Guinea*
**Playing career:** *Saint Etienne, Lens, Marseilles, Liverpool, West Ham, Al-littihad (loan), Al-Siliya, Amiens (1990-2006)*

When Titi Camara arrived at Liverpool in 1999, he quickly established himself as a fan favourite. Despite only being at Anfield for 18 months, he occasionally showcased his remarkable footballing ability. From his 37 appearances for Liverpool, 13 were from the bench. His most emotional moment in a red shirt came when he scored the winning goal against West Ham in October 1999, only hours after he was told that his dad had passed away. His sour relationship with Gerard Houllier spelt the end for him at Liverpool, and he moved to West Ham. However, his time at the Hammers was largely unsuccessful, playing in only 14 games and failing to find the net on every occasion. He was loaned out to Saudi side Al-lttihad and scored a hat-trick in his second game, where he was awarded with three luxury cars. He was living in a five-star hotel and even had servants! He returned to France to finish his career and had a season with Amiens, scoring nine goals in 26 games. He scored 23 times in 38 caps for Guinea and was appointed their manager in 2009, which ended after only three months before being replaced. Then in 2010, he was declared Sports Minister of Guinea before being replaced again two years later. In 2015, he established his own football academy in his country which remains in business today.

## CAMPBELL, Bobby

*Wing-half*
**Born:** *1937 Liverpool*
**Died:** 2015
**Playing career:** *Liverpool, Portsmouth, Aldershot (1958-1967)*

Bobby Campbell started his football journey with Liverpool after signing professional forms in 1958. He was used sparingly in Bill Shankly's inaugural season as manager in the 1959/60. However, it was clear that he was not in the manager's plans and he moved to Portsmouth before finishing his career with Aldershot. Although he was not too prominent as a player, he moved into management where he truly made his name. He started his career managing George Best's Fulham side for four years before being sacked. He moved to Portsmouth and made them Third Division champions in 1983 but was sacked the following season. In 1988 he was appointed assistant manager at Stamford Bridge and took over as caretaker manager later into the season but could not keep the Blues up. He was hired on a full-time basis the following season and took them back up before finishing fifth in the First Division. Once again, he was sacked the follow season. He moved to Kuwait and stayed for one year before retiring as a manager in 1994. Before retiring officially, Bobby collected old AHU filters from maintenance companies in London. He lived close to Stamford Bridge and Roman Abramovich would often invite him to Chelsea games. He died on 6 November 2015 and Chelsea players wore black armbands in the following game against Stoke City as a sign of respect to the man who promoted them back to the top tier of English football the first time of asking, a reign that remains today.

## CAMPBELL, Don

*Full-back*
**Born:** *1932 Bootle*
**Died:** 2016
**Playing career:** *Liverpool, Crewe Alexandra, Gillingham, Folkestone Town, Margate, Canterbury City (1950-1967)*

Don Campbell was a local lad who signed as a professional for Liverpool in November 1950, when he was just 18 years old. He was forced to wait three years for first team opportunities - when he was one of 31 players who featured for Liverpool during the 1953/54 season where the club were relegated. It was clear that Don Walsh did not fancy the full-back and he had to wait for a change of manager before being given more time in the senior side. He appeared 28 times under Phil Taylor but was transferred to Crewe in the summer of 1958 – who were in the fourth division. He made 169 appearances there before moving to Gillingham in 1962. He subsequently moved into the non-leagues and eventually finished his career at Margate, whilst working as a painter and decorator. He passed away in September 2016, at the age of 83.

## CAMPBELL, Ken

*Goalkeeper*
**Born:** *1892 Cambuslang, Scotland* **Died:** 1971
**Playing career:** *Liverpool, Partick Thistle, New Brighton, Stoke City, Leicester City (1911-1931)*

Ken Campbell was given his first Liverpool opportunity when he became their number one for the last seven league games of the 1911/12 season. The club were in deep relegation trouble and Tom Watson showed a lot of faith in an unexperienced 20-year-old. That faith was restored when Liverpool won three of their last four games and survived the drop by the skin of their teeth. Campbell quickly established himself as Liverpool's 'keeper after Sam Hardy moved to Villa Park in the summer. He eventually lost his place before the advent of World War I, but after the conclusion of the war he returned between the sticks for the club. However, Elisha Scott took over from Campbell, which saw him move back home to play for Partick Thistle. He moved to Wallasey and played for New Brighton, as he wanted to set up a sports retailer – which became the base for the remainder of his career after he finished with football. He died on 28 April 1971.

## CAREY, Johnny
*Right-back*
**Born:** *1919 Dublin, Ireland* **Died:** 1995
**Playing career:** *Manchester United, Manchester United (wartime), Cardiff City (guest), Manchester City (guest), Shamrock Rovers (guest), Middlesbrough (guest), Everton (guest), Liverpool (guest), Played in Italy (guest) (1936-1943)*

Johnny Carey spent 17 years with Manchester United when he was signed as a 17-year-old for £250. During his first season with the club, he helped United gain First Division status. The outbreak of World War II disrupted the usual footballing calendar, but Carey stayed with the club and recorded 112 wartime appearances. He also served in the British Army during the war and was sent to both Italy and the Middle East. Whilst in Italy he played part-time football and after the conclusion of the war he had several offers to stay in the country, but he opted to return back to England. When he returned he became the first Irish player to win a major trophy with United after winning the 1948 FA Cup Final. When he retired as a player he moved into management and managed his country for two years between 1955 and 1957. He left football for good in 1971 after he was sacked from Blackburn and went on to work at a textiles company before working in the treasurer's office of Trafford Borough Council before retiring in 1984. Carrey died in Macclesfield on 22 August 1995.

## CARLIN, John
*Striker*
**Born:** *1878 Leith, Edinburgh, Scotland* **Died:** 1935
**Playing career:** *Tranmere Rovers, Barnsley, Liverpool F.C, Preston North End F.C (1902-1903)*

John Carlin only spent two years at Anfield and his stay was relatively unsuccessful. He first appeared in Liverpool's forward-line at Stoke in 1903 but this was his only game of the season as he was used as cover for Sam Raybould – who scored 32 times in 34 games. The following season he failed to settle into the team but he did score six goals that helped Liverpool win their second league title in 1906. When he retired from football he worked as a brick setter in the Mersey Docks. He also ran with the Liverpool Harriers and was a member of Eton Bowling Club for over thirty years. He died on 29 June 1935.

## CARLIN, Willie
*Central midfielder*
**Born:** *1940 Liverpool*
**Playing career:** *Liverpool, Halifax Town, Carlisle United, Sheffield United, Derby County, Leicester City, Notts County, Cardiff City (1959-1973)*

Inside-forward Willie Carlin came through the youth ranks at Liverpool but only made one senior side appearance for the club, featuring in a 2-2 draw against Brighton on 10 October 1959. Despite his lack of success at Liverpool, he did go on to play in 445 league matches, throughout the top four divisions of English football. His career took off when he signed for Brian Clough's Derby in August 1968 and helped the club win the Second Division. He featured rarely in the following season and was transferred to Leicester, where he once again won the Second Division. After retiring from football, he ran a bar in Majorca before returning home to retire indefinitely. Unfortunately, in April 2011 his house was targeted by burglars and his winners medal from Derby's successful season was stolen, in addition to the gold commemorative bracelet that was awarded to the players.

## CARR, Lance
*Outside-left*
**Born:** *1910 Johannesburg, South Africa* **Died:** 1983
**Playing career:** *Johannesburg Calies, Boksburg, Liverpool, Newport County, South Liverpool, Newport County, Bristol Rovers, Merthyr Tydfil, Gloucester City (1933-1946)*

Lance Carr was the ultimate sportsman. He was an accomplished cricketer and boxer and he was the son of a professional runner. So, it would come as little surprise to learn how impactful he was from the left-wing. However, despite all of his attributes, he played occasionally for the Reds and only had one decent run in team where he played in 23 of a possible 28 matches. The highlight of his Liverpool career was when they beat their bitter rivals by a record 6-goal margin and he setup the first two goals – a record that still stands today. Lance eventually moved on after three years with the club and he won the Third Division South with Newport County in 1939. After World War II he played for Bristol Rovers. He became a businessman in London after his footballing days and he died in Greenwich on 28 April 1983, aged 73.

## CARRAGHER, Jamie

*Defender*
**Born:** *1978 Bootle, Merseyside*
**Playing career:** *Liverpool (1988-2013)*
Jamie Carragher is Liverpool through and through, which is quite ironic as he grew up as an Everton fan! Nevertheless, the commitment and loyalty that he showed his club is second to none. He once stated: "there may be more skilful players in the squad, but no one can ever say I don't give 100%", and it's hard to argue against. Roy Evans handed the youngster his first opportunity in a red shirt in January 1997 when he came on as a substitute in a League Cup tie at Middlesbrough. Throughout his Liverpool career he scored 5 goals in 737 appearances and he netted on his first start for the club when a fine header from a left-wing corner found the back of the net – he almost scored on his final game for Liverpool too, as his thunderbolt strike from 25-yards cannoned off the post and back into play! Carragher won two FA Cups with Liverpool (2001, 2006), three League cups (2001, 2003, 2012), and a UEFA Cup in 2001 to complete a historic treble. The most famous of them all, was the 2005 Champions League. He is the second highest capped player by Liverpool behind only Ian Callaghan. He retired in 2013 to bring the curtain down on 17 wonderful years at Liverpool Football Club. The same year, he signed a contract with Sky Sports and became a pundit with the broadcaster, a role he still fulfils.

## CARTER, Jimmy

*Winger*
**Born:** *1965 Hammersmith, London*
**Playing career:** *Millwall, Liverpool, Arsenal, Oxford United, Portsmouth, Milwall (1983-1999)*
A tricky winger who made his name at Millwall before his £800,000 move to Liverpool in 1991. Despite the price tag, he couldn't quite make the grade at his new club and only featured eight times. Graeme Souness' arrival spelt the end for Jimmy Carter, as it was clear the Scotsman was not a fan of the player. He later moved to Arsenal for £500,000 and Liverpool lost £300,000 for only eight games. He had to retire at the age of 33 due to a consistent back problem and he is now back at Millwall working as a matchday host for the club.

## CASE, Jimmy

*Midfielder*
**Born:** *1954 Liverpool*
**Playing career:** *Liverpool, Brighton, Southampton, Bournemouth, Halifax Town, Wrexham, Wanneroo British, Darlington, Brighton. (1973-1996)*
Jimmy Case signed for Liverpool on 1st May 1973 but had to wait two years before making his debut, in a 3-1 home win against QPR. By 1976, he was an integral player for Liverpool and one of the rare midfielders who would constantly pop up with important goals in crucial matches. Whilst at Liverpool he won the First Division title four times, the UEFA Cup once, FA Charity Shield four times, European Cup three times, European Super Cup once, Football League Cup once and the FA Cup once. Quite frankly, Case won everything that could be won in domestic and European football! He was also issued the Bravo Award by Italian magazine *Guerin Sportivo*, which awards the best young player in Europe. Case didn't retire until the age of 41 despite his claims of eating – and definitely drinking – whatever he liked! Since retiring Case has worked as the manager of Brighton and Barnsley. He then played in veteran teams for many years whilst working in the media as a match summariser before returning home to Anfield to work as a pre-match host and feature on LFC TV.

## CAVALIERI, Diego

*Goalkeeper*
**Born:** *1982 Sao Paulo, Brazil*
**Playing career:** *Palmeiras B, Palmeiras, Liverpool, Cesena, Fluminense, Crystal Palace, Botafogo (2001-)*
6ft 3in Brazilian keeper Diego Cavalieri, signed for Liverpool for £3 million and was given the difficult task of uprooting Pepe Reina as Liverpool's number one. He was the third Brazilian to play for the club and that task proved too difficult, as he was restricted to just ten appearances . After two years at Anfield he returned back to brazil to sign for Fluminense, where he helped the club to the Brazilian Championship in 2012. He did return to England with Crystal Palace when he was signed on a short-term deal that lasted three months but he was released at the end of his contract without playing a league game. He is currently back in Brazil playing for Botafogo at the age of 37.

Jamie Carragher

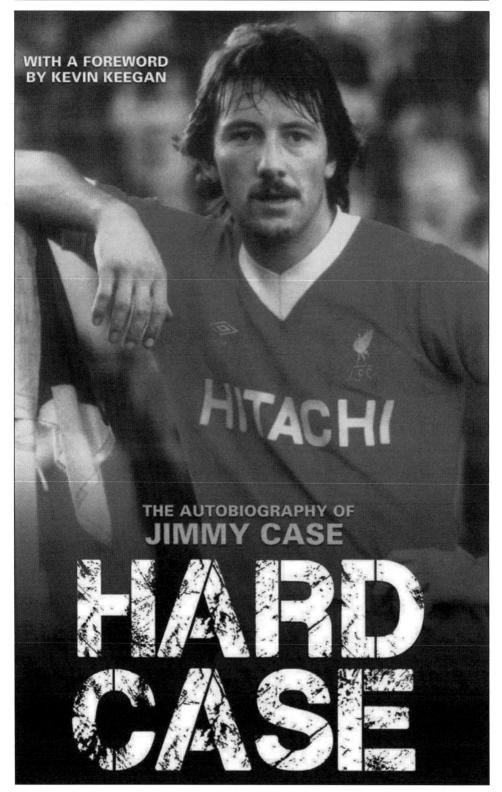

WITH A FOREWORD
BY KEVIN KEEGAN

HITACHI

THE AUTOBIOGRAPHY OF
JIMMY CASE

HARD
CASE

## CAVANAGH, Peter
*Right-back*
**Born:** *1981 Bootle, Merseyside*
**Playing career:** *Liverpool, Accrington Stanley, Fleetwood Town, Rochdale, Altrincham (1991-2015)*

Peter Cavanagh was a product of Liverpool's youth system but failed to make the breakthrough into the first team. He joined Accrington Stanley in 2001 where he became their youngest ever captain. Was selected for the England C team but later banned from the game having been found guilty of betting against his own team. Joined Fleetwood when the ban came to an end in June 2010. He is currently a manager for Everton's youth teams.

## CHADWICK, Edgar
*Inside-left*
**Born:** *1869 Blackburn* **Died:** 1942
**Playing career:** *Blackburn Rovers, Everton, Burnley, Southampton, Liverpool, Blackpool (1884-1908)*

'Hooky' was an England international who excelled as a player with both Everton and Liverpool but it was as a coach that he may well be remembered. After a spell in Germany, he moved to Holland and ultimately became the Dutch national coach.

It was during this stint, that he guided their team to a Bronze medal in both the 1908 and 1912 Olympic Games. After the First World War he returned to Blackburn and to his original trade, which was as a baker.

## CHAMBERLAIN, Alec
*Goalkeeper*
**Born:** *1964, Ramsey, Cambridgeshire*
**Playing career:** *Ipswich Town, Colchester United, Everton, Tranmere Rovers, LutonTown, Chelsea (loan), Sunderland, Liverpool (loan), Watford (1980-2007)*

Well-travelled 'keeper who had loan spells at both Chelsea and Liverpool. Notched up 678 League appearances before retiring in 2007. He spent a year with Liverpool in 1995 after he was loaned from Sunderland. He failed to make a single league appearance during his time there. He is now goalkeeping coach at Watford after retiring with the club.

## CHAMBERS, Harry
*Striker*
**Born:** *1896 Willington Quay* **Died:** 1949
**Playing career:** *Liverpool, West Bromwich Albion, Hereford United (1915-1934)*

Harry Chambers had confidence from a young age. In 1915, he knocked on Tom Watson's door and enquired about a potential trial. Ultimately, he would be the final player that Watson signed before his passing on 6 May 1915. Prior to World War I, Chambers only played a few reserve games before the breakout of the conflict. He became a soldier during the war but was invalided by the army and recovered in Ireland, where he guested for Belfast distillery and Glentoran. After the war had finished, he returned to Liverpool and soon became a fan favourite after his lethal left-foot would find the net frequently.

He won two League Championships whilst at Liverpool in two consecutive seasons, 1922 and 1923. During his final season he was knocked over by a car whilst riding a bicycle. He took the driver to court but failed to win any compensation, despite claiming the incident lost him his place in the side. He moved to West Brom in 1928 before dropping down to non-league level. He ran a pub called The Stafford Arms whilst player-manager at Oakengates Town before moving into a factory job. He was still playing for Oakengates up until his death in 1949, aged 52.

## CHARNOCK, Phil
*Midfielder*
**Born:** 1975 Southport
**Playing career:** Liverpool, Blackpool (loan), Crewe Alexandra, Port Vale, Bury, Linfield, Ballymena United, Fleetwood Town, Leigh RMI (1992-2008)

When Phil Charnock became the youngest Liverpool player to play in a European contest, big things were expected from the midfielder. Unfortunately, he would only go on to record one more appearance for the club before a blight of injuries ruined his opportunities at Liverpool – a similar theme that would plague his career. He moved to Crewe in 1996 and would play in over 150 league matches, but injuries kept him out for extended periods of time. He transferred to Bury before heading out to Northern Ireland. Injuries finally brought his career to an end in 2007 and he established his own driving school of which he is the managing director and since 2012, he juggles his position there with a part-time coaching role at Liverpool Football Club.

## CHEYROU, Bruno
*Midfielder*
**Born:** 1978 Suresnes, France
**Playing career:** Lille, Liverpool, Marseille, Bordeaux, Rennes, Anorthosis, FC Nantes. (1998-2012)

When Bruno Cheyrou arrived at Anfield for a £3.7 million fee, big things were expected from the 25-year-old. Fans were quickly disappointed as the Frenchman looked out of his depth in the Premier League. However, he did have some highlights with the club. His brilliant goal against Chelsea in 2004 secured Liverpool's first win at Stamford Bridge during the Premier League era. He also netted twice against Newcastle in the FA Cup fourth round that saw him voted as the best player of the round. His stint in the first team was only temporary, and he soon found himself on loan to to teams in France, firstly Marseille took him before he had a spell with Bordeaux. He eventually found a move away from England with Cypriot team Anorthosis Famagusta but after six months he returned to France to play for Nantes. He was released in 2012 and never played professionally again. He has since worked as a consultant for BeIN Sports and in 2017 he was appointed as sporting director for Paris Saint Germain's women's teams.

## CHILTON, Allenby
*Centre-half*
**Born:** 1918 South Hylton
**Died:** 1996
**Playing career:** Liverpool, Manchester United, Grimsby Town (1938-1956)

A dominating central defender who was tough enough to give up te game for a while to try his hand at boxing. Allenby Chilton played his first League match just before the War, then had a frustrating wait during which time he sustained a wartime injury. However, by the time hostilities had finished, he had established himself as a first team regular, a position he managed to maintain, well into the 1950s. In 1955, with two England caps and over 350 United appearances under his belt, the Geordie man moved a little closer to home when he took over as player manager at Grimsby Town. Chilton later went on to manage Wigan Athletic and Hartlepool United. He left the game to run a shop for five years and then worked in a steelwork for 14 years. He died in June 1996, aged 77, after retiring to Sunderland in 1981.

## CHISNALL, Phil
*Forward*
**Born:** 1942 Manchester
**Playing career:** Manchester United, Liverpool, Southend United, Stockport County (1959-1972).

Having started his career with Manchester United, Phil Chisnall was a talented youngster who spent five years on the books at Old Trafford. He fell down the pecking order at the club and eventually moved to Liverpool but a lack of opportunities with the club only saw him feature in six league matches before moving to Southend and finishing his career with Stockport County. He was the last player to transfer from Manchester United to Liverpool. Injuries took their toll on the winger and he was forced to retire from the game at the age of 29. His grandson joined Manchester United's academy, playing in a similar position. After retiring from the game, he ran several betting shops and worked in a pre-retirement job as a factory processor in Trafford Park before retiring. In 2014 he suffered from a stroke that left him in a wheelchair and left him with severe speech problems.

Djibril Cisse

## CISSE, Djibril

*Striker*

**Born:** *1981 Arles, France*
**Playing career:** *Arles-Avignon, Nimes, Auxerre, Liverpool, Marseille (loan), Sunderland (loan), Panathinaikos, Lazio, QPR, Al-Gharafa (loan), Kuban Krasnodar, Bastia, Saint-Pierroise, Yverdon, A.C. Vicenza 1902 (1989-2019)*

After joining Auxerre and winning the golden boot for the French league, Gerard Houllier brought the French international to Anfield. However, two weeks before Djibril Cisse arrived at Liverpool, Houlier left the club by mutual consent. Rafael Benitez was appointed the new manager, and it was now him who Cisse must impress. He scored 24 goals from 79 games but failed to cement a regular spot in the team until his final season with the club. He suffered a nasty leg break in Liverpool's league game against Blackburn Rovers in 2004. His most memorable moment in a Liverpool shirt would have been his penalty to complete the ultimate comeback and win the 2005 Champions League. He had a brief spell with QPR before moving back to France and is currently playing for A.C. Vicenza 1902.

## CLARK, Robert

*Forward*

**Born:** *1903 Newburn* **Died:** 1970
**Playing career:** *Spencer's Welfare, Hawthorn Leslie, Newburn Grange, Prudhoe Castle, Newcastle United, Liverpool, Nottingham Forest (1919-1932)*

Primarily known for his weight, Robert Clark was 'built like an elephant'. He signed for Liverpool in 2008 for a fee of £3,000 from Newcastle United. He featured for Liverpool on 42 occasions, netting 11 goals. This included 32 consecutive league matches during the 1928/29 season. Despite being remembered as a strong forward, his ability to waltz around the opposition brought plenty of praise from national media. Clark died in 1970 at the age of 67.

## CLEMENCE, Ray

*Goalkeeper*

**Born:** *1948 Skegness, Lincolnshire*
**Playing career:** *Notts County, Scunthorpe United, Liverpool, Tottenham Hotspur (1965-1988)*

Bill Shankly promised Ray Clemence that he would be in the side within six months if he signed for Liverpool in June 1967. The 18-year-old accepted but had to serve two and a half years as an apprentice in the reserves with the exclusion of one League Cup tie against Swansea in 1968. It wasn't until the next decade where he was given his first real opportunity in the team as Shankly started to dismantle the side that was so successful only a few years prior. Incredibly, he would only go on to miss 6 league games throughout the next 11 years! He is another player on this list that had won everything on offer in both English and European football. Five League Championships, one FA Cup, one League Cup, two UEFA Cups and three European Cups. He spent 13 years at Liverpool and featured in 665 matches for the club. He later moved to Tottenham, where he recorded his 1000th career appearance, an incredible feat. He retired in 1988, well into his forties and initially joined his last club, Spurs, as goalkeeping coach before taking on the role of Manager at Barnet in 1994. Has been involved with the England set-up since 1996. Was awarded the MBE for his service to the sport. His son Stephen played for Birmingham City and Leicester City while daughter Sarah is married to former Crystal Palace manager Dougie Freedman.

Ray Clemence

## CLOUGH, Nigel

*Striker/Midfielder*

**Born:** *1966 Sunderland*

**Playing career:** *Nottingham Forest, Liverpool, Heanor Town (loan), Manchester City, Nottingham Forest (loan), Sheffield Wednesday (loan), Burton Albion (1982-2008)*

Having truly shone and spending nine years at his first club Nottingham Forest, Clough moved to Liverpool for £2.28m in 1993 after his former club were relegated and his father resigned from his managerial position.

Nigel Clough

His debut for the club is one of the best, scoring twice as Liverpool beat Sheffield Wednesday on the opening day of the season. However, after this game several subdued performances were scattered across the remainder of his time with Liverpool, with exception to his two crucial goals that turned a 3-0 loss into a 3-3 draw against Manchester United. It was clear that Roy Evans had a lack of trust in the player and he was offloaded to Manchester City midway through the 1995/96 season. In October 1998 Clough accepted the role of player-manager at Burton Albion and helped them gain two promotions. By the time the club were in the football league though, Clough had moved on to Derby where he remained until he was dismissed on 28 September 2013 and took over at Sheffield United. He remained in Yorkshire for two years before leaving on mutual consent after failing to get the Blades promoted, despite a League Cup run that took the side to the semi-finals. He is currently into his second spell with Burton, after taking over from Jimmy Floyd Hasselbaink, who moved to Queens Park Rangers in 2015.

### "DID YOU KNOW?"

*"The red shirts that we are used to today were previously blue and white quarters!"*

## COHEN, Avi
*Defender*
**Born:** *1956 Cairo, Egypt* **Died:** 2010
**Playing career:** *Maccabi Tel Aviv, Liverpool, Rangers, Maccabi Tel aviv, Maccabi Netanya (1974-1990)*

Israeli defender who joined Liverpool in 1979 from Maccabi Tel Aviv for £200,000. Once risked the wrath of fellow Jewish members by playing a game in Yom Kippur. However, this did not stop him being picked to appear for his country 51 times and ultimately ending his playing career back in Israel. Sadly, Avi died in a motorbike accident in December 2010 but not before he had appeared in the Israeli version of Dancing with the Stars and becoming the Chairman of the Israel Professional Footballers Association.

## COLE, Joe
*Attacking midfielder/Winger*
**Born:** *1981 Paddington, London*
**Playing career:** *West Ham United, Chelsea, Liverpool, Lille (loan), Aston Villa, Coventry City (loan), Coventry City, Tampa Bay Rowdies (1994-2016)*

Prior to Joe Cole's move to Anfield in 2010, he had spent his career in London playing firstly for West Ham and Chelsea. Whilst at the latter, he became a valuable asset for the club and was used frequently by Jose Mourinho. He won three Premier Leagues, two FA Cups, one League Cup and finished runner-up when his team lost to Manchester United on penalties during the 2008 Champions League final. He had been capped 56 times by England too, so Liverpool managed to land a man with vast experience in the footballing world. Annoyingly for fans of the club, Cole's debut season was rather disappointing – in fact, it was nothing short of disastrous. He was sent off on his Premier League debut after just 45 minutes against Arsenal and his next game he missed a penalty against Trabzonspor in the Europa League.

Joe Cole

He was restricted to limited opportunities but he was handed a rare start on the final day of the 2010/11 season against Aston Villa, he once again failed to show his capabilities. He was loaned out to Lille the following season and was relatively successful with the French club before leaving Liverpool on a free to return to West Ham. He gradually dropped down the divisions before finishing his career in America with Tampa Bay Rowdies on 13th November 2018 before returning to Chelsea the following month as an academy coach. He also appears as a pundit occasionally with BT Sport. He remains at his post with Chelsea.

### "DID YOU KNOW?"

*"Rafa Benitez loved Bruce Lee and reached brown belt at Judo himself before the age of thirteen."*

# Tributes for 'diamond of a guy' Avi Cohen, killed at 54 after motorbike crash

Stan Collymore

## COLLYMORE, Stan

*Striker*

**Born:** *1971 Stone, Staffordshire*
**Playing career:** *Walsall, Wolverhampton Wanderers, Stafford Rangers, Crystal Palace, Southend United, Nottingham Forest, Liverpool, Aston Villa, Fulham (loan), Leicester City, Bradford City, Real Oviedo (1988-2001)*

To say that Stan Collymore is a controversial character would be a fundamental understatement. He was rejected at both Walsall and Wolves because of his antics but his undeniable ability saw him scouted by John Griffin whilst playing for Conference side Stafford Rangers. Initially, Griffin had gone to scout their goalkeeper, but it was Collymore who truly stole the show. When he returned to Crystal Palace he told Steve Coppell that he had: "just seen the best non-league player ever". Collymore signed for Palace for £100,000 in January 1991 but as his new team were promoted to the Premiership, he failed to get a look in. This prompted a move to Southend who were in Division One and he truly shone with the club, scoring 18 goals in only 33 games. He moved to Nottingham Forest and continued his fine form, helping the club win promotion back to the top tier of English football. A huge price tag was placed on him, which discouraged top teams to sign the striker – this influenced Andy Cole's move to Manchester United. In the summer of 1995 he made his England debut, which was swiftly followed by a move to Anfield a month later where he broke the British transfer record for a fee of £8.5 million.

He introduced himself to Liverpool by rifling a rocket into the top corner on his debut against Sheffield Wednesday from 25 yards out! He failed to further impress after his first appearance and Ian Rush returned to the side to partner Robbie Fowler. He was selected to play against former club Forest at Anfield and when the visiting team went 2-0 up there were cries of 'Judas' and 'what a waste of money' by the fans, as their former idol had become the enemy. However, he responded by assisting three goals that saw Liverpool overcome a 2-goal deficit to a 4-2 victory. Collymore's second season with the club saw himself and strike partner Fowler score a combine 47 goals, but his attitude and stuttering form saw Roy Evans lose patience with the striker, who was subsequently sold to Aston Villa for £7 million. Throughout his Liverpool career, he scored 35 goals in 81 games, but it was his lack of application that cost him his time at Anfield. He retired with Spanish side Real Oviedo in 2001 before consistent injuries brought an end to his career in football at the age of 30. When he retired from football he had a stint as an actor when he starred in the film Basic Instinct 2. He also stated in his autobiography that he had been diagnosed with borderline personality disorder, which could explain his eccentric personality. He also works frequently as a football pundit, where he has gained relative success.

## COOPER, Tom

*Right-back*
**Born:** *1904 Stoke-on-Trent* **Died:** 1940
**Playing career:** *Port Vale, Derby County, Liverpool (1924-1940)*

When Tom Cooper arrived at Anfield in 1934, he had spent 10 years playing football and he had compiled 280 league appearances for both Port Vale and Derby County. He is considered one of England's greatest full-backs and even captained the national side. He was a strong tackler and had great vision to pick out accurate passes. Undoubtedly, he would have won more caps for his country if he had not been injured so frequently. He signed for Liverpool for £7,500, which was an extraordinary fee at the time. He shared the skipper's duties with Ernie Blenkinsop for a couple of seasons before being named the club captain for the following two.

He made his debut for the club when he came on as a substitute at Chelsea on 8 December 1934 and impressed so much that he would only miss two more league matches for the remainder of the season. During his four seasons with the club, he played in 127 of the 168 games, which is substantial proof of how much Liverpool valued his services. However, it was the advent of World War II that subsequently finished his career in professional football. He made nine wartime appearances for the club during the 1939/40 season but failed to play competitively again. He was also a keen golfer and won the Merseyside Professional Association Footballer's Golf Championship for three consecutive years. He enlisted for the Second World War, joining the Royal Military Police. On 25 June 1940 he was sent out on his despatch motorcycle when he collided with a lorry and died in the incident. An enquiry followed which resulted in an order that stated despatch riders were no long allowed to ride their motorcycles without wearing a crash helmet.

## CORMACK, Peter

*Midfielder*
**Born:** *1946 Edinburgh, Scotland*
**Playing career:** *Tynecastle Boys Club, Heart of Midlothian, Hibernian, Toronto City (guest), Nottingham Forest, Liverpool, Bristol City, Hibernian, Partick Thistle (1961-1980)*

The arrival of Peter Cormack added the creativity that was missing from the squad. His tricks on the ball, slick movement and pinpoint accuracy gave Liverpool their final piece of the puzzle.

PETER CORMACK

He joined in the summer of 1972 and would help his team go on to win the League Championship after they narrowly missed out the previous season. He also aided the club win the UEFA Cup in the same season. The following year, he added further silverware with the FA Cup and he featured in all of Liverpool's 42 league games that season. He had one more full campaign with the club before a knee injury spelt the end of his time at Liverpool. He moved to Bristol City before returning home to Scotland to play for Partick Thistle before retiring in 1980. He was appointed manager of the club in December 1980 and spent three and a half years there before moving to manage Cypriot team Anorthosis Famagusta. He finished his managerial career with Greenock Morton in 2002 before retiring from the sport. He then moved into the karaoke business and worked as an after-dinner speaker for many years before retiring indefinitely. He now spends his time playing in celebrity golf events, working in his garden and helping with his six grandchildren. It was publicly announced in October 2019 that Peter is suffering from dementia and his wife Marion is convinced that it was football that contributed to his illness.

## COTTON, Charles

*Goalkeeper*
**Born:** *1880 Plymouth* **Died:** *1910*
**Playing career:** *Sheppey United, Reading, West Ham United, Southend United (1897-1910)*

Charles Cotton started as West ham's number one during the 1903/04 season before his differences with the club's directors had led to his move to Liverpool. Unfortunately, his one and only season with the club ended in relegation to the Second Division as he featured 13 times for the side. He had won his place after a fine performance against Wolves on 28 December 1903 before losing his starting position after Liverpool were thrashed 5-2 in the Merseyside derby on April's Fools' day. He would fail to represent the club again and returned to West Ham before moving to Southend two years later. During his four years with the club, he only missed one match before he contracted Bright's disease. After a five-week illness, he lost his life on 3 January 1910, aged only 29.

## COUSINS, Tony
*Forward*
**Born:** *1969 Dublin, Ireland*
**Playing career:** *Longford Town, Belvedere, Chelsea, Middlesbrough, Dundalk, Liverpool, Hereford United, Bohemians, Shamrock Rovers, Bray Wanderers (1985-2003)*

Tony Cousins had seriously impressed in his native land and was awarded the Professionals Footballers' Association of Ireland Players' Young player of the Year in 1990. His incredible form in Ireland influenced a move to Liverpool in the same year for a fee of £70,000. Annoyingly, injuries seriously hindered his time with the club and after no appearances in three years, he moved to Middlesbrough. He suffered identically with his new club and around the time of his 27th birthday he moved back to his home city to play for Shamrock Rovers, where he was successful and stayed with the club for six years. He had a sole season with Bray Wanderers before retiring in 2003. He swiftly moved into coaching and was appointed the U-21 coach at Shamrock Rovers before becoming the assistant manager at the club. In 2006 he had his first taste of management when Galway United appointed him manager. He moved to Longford Town in 2009 and spent seven years with the club, before departing in 2016 as his team's form was poor. After a three year hiatus, he returned to coaching in 2019 and is currently working with Shamrock Rovers' U-17's.

## COX, Jack
*Winger*
**Born:** *1877 Liverpool* **Died:** 1955
**Playing career:** *South Shore, Blackpool, Liverpool, Blackpool (1897-1912)*

Jack Cox started his professional career with Blackpool before being purchased by Liverpool for £150. It would become one of the greatest signings during that time period. Cox played for Liverpool 361 times, scoring 80 goals. He was part of the 1900/1901 Liverpool team that were only top of the league at two occasions that season – after the first and the last game! After Liverpool's relegation in 1904, he pushed for a move away. However, as Liverpool paid the player the maximum wage, the Football Association blocked any potential move. He stayed and was a significant factor in

JACK COX

Liverpool's promotion to the First Division and then champions of the First Division in back-to-back years. He returned to Blackpool to finish his playing career as player-manager before retiring in 1912. His brother Bill was also a footballer but died of his wounds he suffered as a result of serving during World War I. Cox passed away on 11 November 1955.

## CRAWFORD, Robert
*Defender*
**Born:** *1856 Blythswood, Renfrewshire, Scotland*
**Died:** 1950
**Playing career:** *Barhead BC, Arthurlie, Liverpool (1909-1915)*

Tom Watson brought Robert Crawford to Liverpool in 1909 and he stayed with the club for six years. He made his debut in a 4-1 home win against Leicester City on 13 February 1909, but his second game could not have been any worse as Liverpool were thrashed 5-0 by Arsenal. He was left out of the side for six weeks before returning to play against Everton. He again lost 5-0! This certainly failed to instil confidence in the Scotsman and his new team. The majority of the backline were replaced, but Crawford kept his place in the squad and made four more appearances that season as Liverpool narrowly survived the drop.

The highest tally of games he played in one year was 33 during the 1910/11 season. Tom Chorlton lost his place in the team following Liverpool's poor start to the season and Crawford was moved from right-back to left-back, where he was relatively successful. The advent of World War I brought an end to his footballing career and he enlisted into the army. He was discharged in 1919 from the Royal Engineers with war and victory medals before becoming a plumber up until his retirement.

## CRIBLEY, Alex
*Defender*
**Born:** *1957 Liverpool*
**Playing career:** *Liverpool, Wigan A (1978-1987).*
Alex Cribley spent the first two years of his professional career contracted to Liverpool. He failed to make a single appearance for the club before moving to Wigan in 1980. He would become a legend with the Latics in a stay that kept him there for eight years, recording 272 league appearances in the process. He was part of the Wigan team that won the 1985 English Football League trophy. He managed Wigan for a year in 1985 before moving into a role as a physiotherapist, where he remains today.

## CROWTHER, Ryan
*Winger*
**Born:** *1988 Stockport*
**Playing career:** *Stockport County, Liverpool, Stalybridge Celtic, Ashton United, Hyde, Fleetwood Town, Halifax Town, Altrincham. Ashton United, Hyde (2006-)*
Stockport-born winger Ryan Crowther spent nine years in his local club's academy before signing professional forms with them in 2006. He was made captain during a 2-2 draw against Cheltenham when he was aged just 17, making him the youngest captain in the club's history. Liverpool came knocking in the same year asking to give him a trial for the upcoming pre-season tour of Milan. He went to the tour and he had agreed terms with Liverpool on 9 July 2007. He featured for the successful reserve team during the 2007/08 season but in 2009 he was released by Liverpool without making a single appearance for the senior team. After several trials, he joined non-league team Stalybridge Celtic and has stayed in the non-leagues of English football since.

Is currently contracted to Hyde. In 2010 he was jailed for four months after drunkenly assaulting a taxi driver on a night out.

## CUNNINGHAM, William
*Defender*
**Born:** *1899, Radcliffe, Lancashire* **Died:** 1934
**Playing career:** *Blyth Spartans, Liverpool, Barrow, Mid-Rhondda United (1920-1922)*
William Cunningham made his debut for Liverpool on the left-wing against Middlesbrough in a First Division fixture played at Anfield on 12 March 1920 before playing his second game for the club in the penultimate game of the season away to Arsenal, both games finished in goalless draws. His third and final appearance for the Reds came against Bolton Wanderers on 18 March 1922, where Liverpool lost 2-0 in their successful season that saw them crowned League Champions. He was killed on 28 June 1934 while working down in a mine in Shilbottle Colliery in Northumberland.

## DABBS, Benjamin
*Full-back defender*
**Born:** *1909 Oakengates, Shropshire* **Died:** 2000
**Playing career:** *Liverpool F.C, Watford (1926-1940)*
Although he spent five years with Liverpool, Benjamin Dabbs failed to cement a regular spot in the first team. He made his debut for the opening game of the 1933/34 season but failed to play a single league game for the remainder of the season! Two years later and he enjoyed a lengthy sequence of games. He was however, shunned out of the team after conceding a needless penalty against Everton in 1937. This mistake would bring an end to his five year stay with Liverpool before he moved to Watford shortly before the Second World War. His mother and former England captain Billy Wright's grandmother were sisters. After retiring as a player, he became a coach with Rickmansworth Town.

King Kenny

## Dalglish, Kenny
*Forward*
**Born:** *1951 Glasgow, Scotland*
**Playing career:** *Celtic, Liverpool. (1967-1989).*
When Kevin Keegan left Liverpool in the Summer of 1977 bound for S.V. Hamburg, Kenny Dalglish was purchased from Celtic. With him he brought a magnificent record of almost a goal a game from over 200 matches. Dalglish has won almost every honour possible in Scotland, England and Europe. His move into management at Anfield was equally as successful, picking up three championship titles and two F.A. Cup wins before deciding to quit the game for a less stressful existence. However, it was not long before he was tempted back, to take the helm at Blackburn Rovers, whom he shaped into a Championship winning side. He relinquished team duties in June 1995 to take on the new role of Director of Football but was fired in August 1996. He took an extensive period of time away from management but was tempted back by Liverpool during the 2011/2012 season before stepping down for the final time. He has since focused on charitable concerns, founding The Marina Dalglish Appeal with his wife to raise money for breast cancer. He is also a patron of Marine FC. He was Capped 102 times by Scotland and scored 30 goals, both are records that stay intact today – although he shares the scoring record with Denis Law.

## DALGLISH, Paul
*Forward*
**Born:** *1977 Glasgow, Scotland*
**Playing career:** *Celtic, Liverpool, Newcastle United, Bury (loan), Wigan Athletic (loan), Blakpool, Linfield, Livingston, Hibernian (1997-2008)*
Kenny's son Paul started at Celtic and was on the books at Anfield but did not make a first team appearance for either club. He then went on to effectively have two playing careers. The first took in stops at nine clubs, many on loan, before retiring in 2003. A career in the media then seemed to be opening up before he was offered the chance to play again, this time for Livingston in Scotland. This second coming finally came to an end in 2008 before moving into management with American teams including: Tampa Bay, Austin Aztec, Real Salt Lake and Miami FC.

Philipp Degan

## DEGAN, Philipp
*Right-back/right winger*
**Born:** *1983 Liestal, Switzerland*
**Playing career:** *FC Basel, Borussia Dortmund, Liverpool, VfB Stuttgart (loan), FC Basel (1987-2016)*
Prior to his move to Anfield in 2008, Phillip Degan had won the league title twice with Basel in his native country before moving to Borussia Dortmund in 2005. Injuries hindered his time with the German team and after his contract expired in the summer of 2008 he had joined Liverpool on a free transfer. The start of his Liverpool career was quite unlucky, as injuries affected his playing time. He broke two ribs on his debut for the club in a League Cup tie against Crewe in September 2009 and he then injured his foot in his following game against Tottenham. During the 2009/10 season, he only featured in 11 of Liverpool's 56 competitive games and was sent off against Fulham in October. His lack of opportunities at Liverpool influenced a move to Stuttgart on loan in the summer of 2010 and his contract was nullified by both parties the following year. He returned to Basel but his contributions were minimal as the Swiss team continued to dominate domestically. He retired as a player in 2016 because of injuries and he set up in business as a football agent.

## DeMANGE, Ken

*Midfielder*

**Born:** *1964 Dublin, Republic of Ireland*
**Playing career:** *Home Farm, Liverpool, Scunthorpe United (loan), Leeds United, Hull City, Cardiff City (loan), Limerick, Ards, Bohemians, Dundalk, Crusaders (1978-1996)*

Ken DeMange arrived at Anfield in August 1993, alongside Brian Mooney. He spent four seasons on Merseyside but failed to make a single appearance for the senior side. He was, however, influential for the reserve team who won two consecutive Central League titles in 1984 and 1985. During the latter, he was top scorer for the side with 12 goals. He also had a successful short-term loan spell with Scunthorpe, scoring twice in three games. He made his international debut for Ireland whilst playing for the reserves at Liverpool. He moved to Leeds in 1987 and then Hull the following year before returning to Ireland. He was believed to have worked at Heathrow Airport after retiring from football.

## DEVLIN, Tom

*Inside-forward*

**Born:** *1903 Bellshill, Scotland* **Died:** *1936*
**Playing career:** *Birmingham, Preston North End, Liverpool, Swindon Town, Brooklyn Wanderers, Aberdeen, Walsall, Fall River, FC Zurich, Oldham Athletic, RC Roubaix, Fleetwood Town (1922-1936)*

Tom Devlin had played for many clubs but failed to make too much of an impact at any of them. He was signed for Liverpool from Preston North End for £250 in 1927 but did not make one first team appearance and moved to Swindon the following year. His brother, William Devlin also signed for Liverpool in the same window. He died in his native Scotland at the age of 33 and the same year he retired from football.

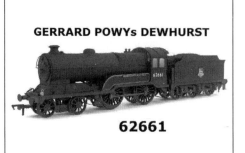

**GERRARD POWYs DEWHURST**

**62661**

## DEWHURST, Gerard

*Inside-forward*

**Born:** *1872 London* **Died:** *1956*
**Playing career:** *Liverpool Ramblers, Corinthian, Liverpool (1892-1895)*

Gerard Dewhurst came from a wealthy family and enjoyed playing football as a hobby. He won one cap with Liverpool and vowed to dress similar to the professionals at the time. He was also capped by England once during a game against Wales in 1895. He later joined his family cotton trading company, Geo. & R. Dewhurst Ltd where he became the managing director. After leaving the cotton business he became the director of the Royal Bank of Scotland. His family home housed himself, his wife, two sons and ten servants. He spent time as the director of Great Central Railway and had a steam engine train named after him in 1920.

## DIAO, Salif

*Defensive midfielder*

**Born:** *1977 Kedougou, Senegal*
**Playing career:** *Monaco, Sedan, Liverpool, Birmingham City, Portsmouth, Stoke City (1996-2012)*

Salif Diao was a part of Monaco's academy in Senegal when he impressed the team and was flown over to France to play for the senior side in 1995. He signed for Liverpool after the 2002 World Cup – where he scored and was sent off in the group stages. He arrived at Anfield with a lot of hope, but sadly could not quite make the break in the Premiership. He made 22 starts and 18 substitute appearances during his debut season with the club and his highlight was a goal against Leeds that took Liverpool to the summit of the table. Steven Gerrard wrote in his autobiography about Diao: "With Salif, I knew after a week of training that he wasn't going to be good enough". When Houllier departed for Rafael Benitez, Diao was loaned out to Birmingham and then Portsmouth. However, injuries started to take their toll and neither club wanted to sign him. He moved to Stoke in 2007 but failed to cement a regular place in the side. He eventually worked for the club as an ambassador to improve their links with African countries. He left Stoke when he was 35 and turned down an offer to join the coaching staff. He founded the non-profit organisation Sport4Africa and continues to be involved with Caap-Afrika.

## DIARRA, Alou
*Defensive midfielder*
**Born:** *1981 Villepinte, France*
**Playing career:** *Louhans-Cuiseaux, Bayern Munich II, Bayern Munich, Liverpool, Le Havre (loan), Bastia (loan), Lens (loan), Lens, Lyon, Bordeaux, Marseille, West Ham United, Rennes (loan), Charlton Athletic, Nancy (1987-2017)*

Alou Diarra arrived at Anfield on 9 July 2002 after an unsuccessful spell with German giants Bayern Munich. The French midfielder had spent two years in Germany but never made a senior appearance for the club. Prior to arriving at Liverpool, Gerard Houllier likened the player to Patrick Vieira, which naturally instilled excitement into the club's fans. He signed on a five-year deal and made his debut against Le Havre during pre-season. Strangely, the day after the match it was reported that Diarra was linked to a loan move with yesterday's opposition - on 1 August the move was confirmed. He was loaned to Lens following Rafael Benitez's appointment and that move was made permanent the following window. The Frenchman failed to make a single competitive appearance for Liverpool. He briefly returned to England to feature for West Ham and Charlton before finishing his career with Nancy. He won 44 caps for France and is currently a youth team coach at Lens.

## DICK, Douglas
*Striker*
**Born:** *1868 Kirktonholm, Scotland*
**Died:** 1940
**Playing career:** *Greenock Morton, Rangers, Liverpool, Greenock Morton (1891-1896)*

Douglas Dick was part of the Liverpool team to feature in the inaugural season of the Football League in 1893/94. Prior to signing for the club, he was the first player in the Scottish League to score a penalty when he was playing for Greenock Morton. He played seven consecutive games for Liverpool during late October to early December of that season but only represented the team from the bench four more times before leaving the following year. He returned to Scotland after retiring, where he ran a motor company and was a director of Kilmarnock FC before his death on 24 June 1940.

## DICKS, Julien
*Defender*
**Born:** *1968 Bristol*
**Playing career:** *Birmingham City, West Ham United, Liverpool, Canvey Island (1985-2002)*

Julien Dicks was Graeme Souness' last signing for Liverpool. The Scotsman wanted to add steel to Liverpool's back-line, which influenced the signing of Dicks who was twice voted 'Hammer of the Year' by West Ham supporters. He had a lethal left foot from dead-ball scenarios and added another attacking element for the team. Unfortunately, he struggled with his fitness levels, which frustrated Souness' successor Roy Evans, and he was sold back to West Ham the following season. He made a further 103 appearances for the London-based team before finishing his career with non-league outfit Canvey Island. When he retired he became a publican in Essex before moving to Spain. He did return to the non-league scene in January 2009 when he was appointed Wivenhoe Town manager, but left at the end of the season. He had a stint of coaching at West ham under Slaven Bilic but both left the club in 2017. In July 2019 he joined the coaching staff at West Brom and remains there today.

Julian Dicks

## DINES, Joseph
*Centre-half*
**Born:** *1886 King's Lynn, Norfolk*
**Died:** 1918
**Playing career:** *Kings Lynn, Liverpool*
Prior to signing forms at Liverpool, Joseph Dines was a schoolteacher who had won the gold medal at the 1912 Olympics as part of Great Britain's football team. He was also capped 27 times for England's amateur side. He made one appearance for the club prior to World War I, away to Chelsea when Liverpool won 2-1. He was described as: 'the smiling footballer' throughout his career. Dines served as a Second Lieutenant in the King's Liverpool Regiment and was killed in Pas de Calais on 27 September 1918. He is buried in the Grand Ravine Cemetery in France.

Bernard Diomede

## Diomede, Bernard
*Winger*
**Born:** *1974 Saint-Doulchard, France*
**Playing career:** *Auxerre, Liverpool, Ajaccio, Creteil, Cleremont Foot (1992-2006)*
Despite his £3 million move form Auxerre, Bernard Diomede only featured in the league on two occasions. He swiftly moved back to France to play for Ajaccio. He retired from football in 2008 after two more stints with French clubs. He was capped eight times for France and was a part of the 1998 World Cup winning squad, starting three times. He currently runs the Bernard Diomede Football Academy in the south of Paris.

## DIOUF, El Hadji
*Winger/Forward*
**Born:** *1981 Dakar, Senegal*
**Playing career:** *Sochaux, Rennes, Lens, Liverpool, Bolton Wanderers (loan), Sunderland, Blackburn Rovers, Rangers (loan), Doncaster Rovers, Leeds United, Sabah FA (1998-2015)*
A controversial character at Liverpool who seemingly caused more trouble than pleasure during his three years with the club. He played in 55 league matches but only managed to score three goals. He later came out and stated that his move to Liverpool was a mistake and he wished he joined Manchester United instead! Sadly, he will be remembered for incidents of spiting and being unprofessional. After retiring from football, Diouf moved back to Senegal and has since worked as a government goodwill ambassador and advisor on sport to president Macky Sall. He has also ran his own sports newspaper and opened his own gymnasium.

## DOIG, Ned
*Goalkeeper*
**Born:** *1866 Arbroath, Scotland*
**Died:** 1919
**Playing career:** *Arbroath, Blackburn Rovers, Sunderland, Liverpool, (1885-1910)*
Ned Doig is arguably Sunderland's greatest ever player – certainly their most successful goalkeeper. He had spent 14 years with the club and played in 417 league matches. He arrived at Anfield on 12 August 1904 for a fee of £150 after the clubs spent two months arguing over the transfer!

El Hadji Diouf

It was claimed that he was built more similar to a boxer than a football player! He scored the only goal of the match on his debut against Chelsea but the outbreak of the war resulted in that being the final competitive fixture for many years. The goal he scored was later nullified as the only three matches of that season were expunged from Football League records. He was, however, in prolific form in wartime games for Liverpool and scored 147 goals in 137 games! When the Football League resumed after the war, Done's ten goals helped Liverpool win the 1946/47 League Championship. He later moved to Tranmere after dropping down the pecking order with Liverpool and scored 61 goals in 87 league games. His final professional club was Port Vale and he returned to haunt Liverpool when his new team beat them 4-3 – with all four goals coming from the man himself. When he retired he worked raising awareness for a cancer charity and died on 24 February 1993, the same day as Bobby Moore.

## DONI, Alexander

*Goalkeeper*
**Born:** *1979 Jundiai, Sao Paulo, Brazil*
**Playing career:** *Botafogo-SP, Corinthians, Santos, Cruzeiro, Juventude, Roma, Liverpool, Botafogo Futebol Clube (SP) (1999-2013)*

Alexander Doni was relatively inexperienced when he signed for Roma, but he quickly established himself as their number one and even won the Coppa Italia in both 2007 and 2008 with the club. He won his first cap with Brazil in 2007 and won the Copa America with the country in the same year, saving two penalties in the shoot-out against Uruguay in the semi-final. However, when he came to Liverpool he was used as cover for Pepe Reina and only featured on four occasions. It has been reported that he played a big part in Liverpool's capture of Allison Becker as he advised goalkeeping coach, John Achterberg, to keep an eye on the Brazilian international. In total he was capped 10 times by Brazil but he was forced to retire in 2013 due to previous cardiac problems. Since retiring he has become an entrepreneur in different business sectors which includes the sports and entertainment sector. He currently resides in Florida with his family.

Liverpool had been previously relegated so it was up to the Scotsman to help the side attain First Division status. He became the oldest player to make a debut for the club at the age of 37 and 307 days on 1 September 1904. Liverpool won the title in his first season, where Doig only conceded 25 goals in 34 matches - keeping 16 clean sheets in the process. He lost his place the following season as Liverpool won their second League Championship. Liverpool told the 'keeper that his career with the club had ended via a postcard, which his 6-year-old son handed to his father. This prompted a rage by Doig as he completely smashed up his kitchen! He played for St Helens Recreational for two seasons before finally retiring in the summer of 1910. Throughout his 25-year career, he played in at least 1,055 games of football! He died on 7 November 1919 from Spanish flu.

## DONE, Cyril

*Centre-forward*
**Born:** *1920 Liverpool*
**Died:** 1993
**Playing career:** *Liverpool, Tranmere Rovers, Port Vale (1938-1959)*

Prior to World War II, Liverpool had signed strong centre-forward Cyril Done, who struck fear into opposition defences.

# **D**

## **DOSSENA, Andrea**
*Left winger/Left-back*
**Born:** *1981 Lodi, Italy*
**Playing career:** *Verona, Treviso, Udinese, Liverpool, Napoli, Palermo (loan), Sunderland, Leyton Orient, Chiasso, Piacenza (1995-2017)*

The Italian full-back was viewed as a potential replacement for the recently departed John Arne Riise and was brought to Anfield in the summer of 2008 for £7 million. Unfortunately for Liverpool, the Italian looked woefully out of depth in his debut season but he did confess that he was struggling to play further up field, a much different playstyle to when he was playing in Italy. However, he did shine for two games when he was used as a substitute against Manchester United and Real Madrid, scoring in both matches. In the summer of 2009 he was linked to a move back home with either Juventus or Napoli but stayed and vowed to fight for his place. He moved to Napoli in the following January transfer window. He spent three years in Naples before returning to England to play for Sunderland prior to joining Leyton Orient for a season. His last registered club was Piacenza but he left in 2017. Despite failing to find a club since then, he has not formally retired from the game and still operates as a free agent.

Stewart Downing

## **DOWNING, Stewart**
*Winger/Attacking midfielder*
**Born:** *1984 Middlesbrough*
**Playing career:** *Middlesbrough, Sunderland (loan), Aston Villa, Liverpool, West Ham United, Middlesbrough (2001-2015)*

Prior to Stewart Downing joining Liverpool in 2011, there were strong rumours that the club had initially tried to lure the winger to Anfield in 2009. After Middlesbrough were relegated, both Liverpool and Aston Villa were after the England international and he chose the latter. Liverpool fans did not have to wait long to see him in a red shirt though, as he joined the club in July 2011 for £18.5 million.

However, his first season for the club could hardly being viewed as a success. In his 36 Premier League matches that he appeared in, he failed to register a single goal or assist. Brendan Rodgers was looking to sell him in 2012 but after a heart-to-heart discussion, Downing vowed to win back the manager's trust. The conversation certainly helped as Downing had a better season that saw him play in 83% of Liverpool's competitive matches that year. He completed a move to West Ham in August 2013 and became a big part of the team. He returned to his boyhood club Middlesbrough for three years before being released in 2019 and joined Blackburn Rovers on a free transfer.

## DRUMMOND, John
*Midfielder*
**Born:** *1869 Edinburgh* **Died:** 1947
**Playing career:** *Partick Thistle, Preston North End, Sheffield United, Liverpool (1889-1897)*

Sheffield United's decision to sign John Drummond in 1891 paid dividends when his goal in the test match at the end of the 1892/93 season against Accrington saw his side promoted to the First Division for the first time in their history. The playing pitch was in a pitiful state and Drummond was the only player who was able to stay on his feet after painting the soles of his boots with black lead to prevent his boots from sticking into the mud! He scored 24 times in 89 matches before joining Liverpool in the summer of 1894. He played in 14 of Liverpool's 30 First Division matches the following season but the team failed to cope with the quality that was in the top tier and they were relegated immediately. His only goal for the club came in a FA Cup first round replay against Barnsley St. Peter's, where Liverpool won 4-0. Drummond had been an apprentice shipyard carpenter as a youth and returned to work in the Dumbarton Shipyards after his retirement from football.

## DUDEK, Jerzy
*Goalkeeper*
**Born:** *1973 Rybnik, Poland*
**Playing career:** *Concordia Knurow, Sokol Tychy, Feyenoord, Liverpool, Real Madrid (1991-2011)*

Jerzy Dudek's career started to accelerate when he joined Dutch side Feyenoord in 1996.

Jerzy Dudek

He was voted the best 'keeper in the Dutch league the following season and was awarded the 'Golden Shoe' in his final year in Holland, which rewards the best player. He almost joined Arsenal over Liverpool but thankfully for fans of the club the move fell through as he was simply outstanding in his debut season at Anfield when the Reds finished second in the league. He failed to emulate similar performances the following season. He occasionally lost his place to Chris Kirkland over the next few years but he certified his legendary status on that historic night in Istanbul after numerous penalty saves! The arrival of Pepe Reina spelt the end of Dudek's time at Liverpool and he curiously chose Real Madrid as his next destination – despite moving on for more first team opportunities. His final game in club football was on 21 May 2011 when he was substituted in the 77th minute to a guard of honour from his Real Madrid teammates. Since retiring, he has been named as an ambassador for the 2012 UEFA European Championships and the 2015 UEFA Europa League final in Warsaw. In 2014, he completed in his first full season in the Volkswagen Castrol Cup which is a racing championship held in circuits around Eastern Europe during summer months.

# DUNBAVIN, Ian
*Goalkeeper*
**Born:** *1980 Huyton*
**Playing career:** *Liverpool, Shrewsbury Town, Morecambe (loan), Halifax Town, Scarborough (loan), Accrington Stanley (1998-2014)*

Ian Dunbavin started his professional career with Liverpool but failed to make a single appearance for the club during his two year stay at Anfield. He moved to Shrewsbury Town in 2000 before joining several other clubs in the following six years. He finally found a home in Accrington Stanley and spent eight years of his career with the club, before retiring in 2014. In January 2009 he was arrested on suspicion of assault and affray by Merseyside Police, as a result of a bar brawl for which Steven Gerrard had previously been arrested for. He was sentenced to 18 weeks in prison, suspended for a year, for his part in the altercation. He now coaches young goalkeepers in the 9-17 age bracket and returned to Liverpool first on a part-time basis in 2014 before being turned into full-time in October 2016.

# DUNDEE, Sean
*Striker*
**Born:** *1972 Durban, South Africa*
**Playing career:** *Karlsruher SC, Liverpool, VfB Stuttgart, FK Austria Vienna, Kickers Offenbach, AmaZulu (1992-2009)*

When Sean Dundee arrived at Anfield in 1998, he had made quite the impact in Germany. He was so impressive there, the Germans put pressure on him to become a citizen so that he could play for their national team! Once he did become a German citizen, he was never selected to play for the team. Dundee is often remembered as being one of the worst strikers in Liverpool's recent history. He signed for £1.8 million in 1998 and only made three appearances before moving back to Germany. Roy Evans recalled his time working with Dundee at Liverpool: "one player I do regret signing was Sean Dundee, he was terrible on and off the pitch. He didn't take any notice of me, did what he wanted and lacked discipline. He certainly shouldn't have joined Liverpool". He joined Stuttgart in 1999 before moving to the Austrian league and finishing his career in South Africa in 2009. He now works as an expert commentator for the Bundesliga.

# DUNLOP, Billy
*Left-back*
**Born:** *1874 Hurlford, Scotland* **Died:** 1941
**Playing career:** *Kilmarnock, Liverpool (1892-1909)*

Billy Dunlop signed for Liverpool in 1895 for a fee of £35. A good investment considering that the Scotsman would go on to play in over 350 matches for the club spanning over 15 years! Dunlop broke into the team near the climax of his debut season but featured more the following year. He had spent time away from the senior team after an injury but won back his place during the 1896/97 season and featured regularly for the next decade. He was appointed the team's captain from 1899-1900. He won the Second Division twice and two First Division titles with Liverpool during his time with the club. After retiring he was appointed as assistant trainer at Sunderland in 1911. He died 28 November 1941.

# DURNIN, John
*Midfielder/Striker*
**Born:** *1965 Bootle*
**Playing career:** *Liverpool, West Bromwich Albion (loan), Oxford United, Portsmouth, Blackpool (loan), Carlisle United, Port Vale, Accrington S (1986-2004)*

John Durnin started his career with Liverpool when he signed from non-league side Waterloo Duck for a fee of £500. However, he never broke into the senior side and moved to Oxford United where he spent four years before moving to the south coast to feature for Portsmouth for another seven. He finished his career with a sole season at Accrington Stanley before he retired in 2004. He linked up with the coaching staff at Southport in July 2006 but left in October of that year. He did return to the club in May 2017 but departed only three months later. He later became a regular for the Liverpool Masters team, playing in many competitions for the side. In 2019, he was convicted of assault after he attacked a pensioner, this was prior to two assault charges the previous year.

## "DID YOU KNOW?"

*"The Kop is named after a hill called Spion Kop in South Africa where many soldiers lost their lives during the Boer War"*

## EDMED, Dick
*Outside-right*
**Born:** *1904 Gillingham, Kent* **Died:** 1984
**Playing career:** *Gillingham, Liverpool, Bolton Wanderers (1923-1933)*

Liverpool captured Dick Edmed from Gillingham for a fee of £1800. The money would prove worthy after he spent six years for Liverpool and made 170 appearances. During that time he scored 46 goals. He had previously continued to work at the Chatham Dockyards whilst he was playing for Gillingham. A cartilage injury reduced his playing time with Liverpool which influenced his move to Bolton Wanderers. Ironically, Edmed scored on his debut for Bolton, against Liverpool! He died on his 80th birthday.

## ENGLISH, Sam
*Striker*
**Born:** *1908 Crevolea, Northern Ireland* **Died:** 1967
**Playing career:** *Rangers, Liverpool (1929-1938)*

Sam English's career started in Scotland with Rangers but he was forced to move south following an unfortunate incident that took place during a match in 1931.
He innocently went for a loose ball in the opponents' penalty area but clashed with Celtic's keeper of the time, John Thomson. Unfortunately, Thomson died in hospital just a few hours later and despite being cleared of all blame, English never really recovered either. He was barracked by Scottish crowds and a move to Liverpool in 1933 did nothing to help the situation. He retired at the age of 28 and died in 1967 after a battle with motor neurone disease.

## EVANS, Alun
*Striker*
**Born:** *1949 Kidderminster*
**Playing career:** *Wolverhampton Wanderers, Los Angeles Wolves (guest), Liverpool, Aston Villa, Walsall, South Melbourne (1964-1983)*

When Alun Evans joined Liverpool for £100,000, he became Britain's most expensive teenage footballer in the process. He had plenty of potential but failed to reach the heights that were expected of him. Evans made a promising start to his Liverpool career, netting within ten minutes of his debut before returning to Molineux to help himself to two more as his former side went down 6-0. He played in every league game from his debut to the end of the season for a very good team who were undergoing a transitional period. Evans made a bright start to the 1970/71 season after scoring 5 in 6 games but after this he struggled. He was attacked at a nightclub in Wolverhampton that left him badly scarred on the face. In addition to the attack, he was injured in a UEFA Cup game that kept him on the side lines for four months. The highlight of Evans' time at Liverpool came on 10 March 1971 after he scored a hat-trick against Bayern Munich at Anfield in Fairs Cup. By the start of the 1971/72 season Evans was only 23 but a new rising star by the name of Kevin Keegan was on the scene. He moved to Aston Villa before moving to Australia. After his career finished, he moved back to Melbourne and settled there.

Alun Evans

Roy Evans

## EVANS, John

*Striker*

**Born:** *1929 Tilbury* **Died:** 2004
**Playing career:** *Charlton Athletic, Liverpool, Colchester United, Romford, Ford United (1949-1960)*

John Evans made his name at Charlton, where he scored 38 times in 90 First Division appearances for the club. He was notably even more prolific against Liverpool, scoring seven times in only five matches! Liverpool were edging closer to relegation before Evans joined the club and although the inclusion of the striker bolstered the overall quality of the team, it was not enough to survive the drop. He only missed four league matches in 1954/55 and scored 29 times. He was the first Liverpool player to score five goals in one match – only four other players have managed to equal this in the club's history. He wasn't as successful the following season but still contributed with 13 league goals before moving to Colchester United in November 1957. He briefly managed Grays Athletic after retiring as a player and continued to work in the non-league until his death in 2004.

## EVANS CBE, Roy

*Left-half*

**Born:** *1948 Bootle*
**Playing career:** *Liverpool (1969-1973).*

Roy Evans joined Liverpool straight from school and made his debut in 1970. However, he only made a total of 11 appearances in nine seasons. Although he never represented England at senior level, he did play for England schoolboys when he was younger. In 1974 at the age of 25, Evans became reserve team coach - a post at which he excelled earning him promotion to Assistant Manager at the end of the 1992/3 season. Took over as Manager in January 1994, following the departure of Graham Souness. Awarded a CBE in 2005 for services to football, he currently acts as a co-commentator for live audio broadcasts of Liverpool matches on www.liverpoolfc.tv.

## FAGAN, Willie

*Forward*

**Born:** *1917 Musselburgh, Scotland*
**Died:** 1992
**Playing career:** *Wellesley Juniors, Celtic, Preston North End, Liverpool, Distillery, Weymouth (1934-1955)*

A promising teenager who crossed the border at the age of 19. Both him and Bill Shankly played for Preston when they lost the 1937 FA Cup final to Sunderland. The following October, Fagan moved to Liverpool and certainly justified his £8000 price tag after featuring 182 times and scoring 57 goals. He had ambitions to be an opera singer as a youngster so it may come as a surprise that he ended up in prison after retiring from football! He did not commit any offence however, as he was employed as a senior officer in a young offender's prison. He retired from work in 1982 and enjoyed ten years of retirement before dying in Northampton.

## FAIRCLOUGH, David

*Liverpool*

**Born:** *1957 Liverpool*
**Playing career:** *Liverpool, Norwich City, Oldham Athletic, Tranmere Rovers, Wigan. (1975-1990)*

'Supersub' now lives in Formby, Liverpool. He played in two European Cups during his time with Liverpool and notched 34 goals in 98 league appearances for the team. After eight years with Liverpool he moved to several teams throughout England. He now works as a freelance journalist, having successfully completed a course for the National Council Training Journalists during his playing days.

David Fairclough

## FAIRCLOUGH, Paul

*Midfielder*
**Born:** *1950 Litherland, Lancashire*
**Playing career:** *Liverpool, Wigan Athletic, Witton Albion, Wealdstone, St Albans City (1975-1984)*
Although being on Liverpool's and Wigan's books, he never made a league appearance for either team. He did however play for Wealdstone for five years. Despite not making a name for himself as a player, he did go into management. It turns out he was pretty good at it, too. He has managed Barnet on four separate occasions and is the current manager of England C – where he has been since 2003.

## FAIRFOUL, Tom

*Half-back*
**Born:** *1881 West Calder, Scotland* **Died:** 1952
**Playing career:** *Third Lanark, Liverpool (1899-1915)*
Tom Fairfoul had an interesting career with Liverpool. He played for them 71 times and was part of the 1914 FA Cup losing team. In 1915, he was suspended by the FA for his involvement in the 1915 betting scandal. Players of both teams were reprimanded as it was deemed to have been corrupted in Manchester United's favour. He was reinstated after the First World War after his service to his country. Despite this, he did not return to football and died in his native Scotland at the age of 71.

## FARLEY, Adam

*Central defender*
**Born:** *1980 Liverpool*
**Playing career:** *Everton, Altrincham, Droylsden, Witton Albion, Marine, Leigh Genesis, Formby, Burscough, AFC Liverpool (1994-2011)*
Adam Farley joined Everton whilst in school and won the 1998 FA Youth Cup with the team. He was awarded man of the match for the second leg of the tie. He was capped three times by Everton's first team before he broke his cheekbone and was released in 2000. He then spent the remainder of his career playing non-league football and is still currently on the books at AFC Liverpool.

## FELTON, Roy

*Full-back*
**Born:** *1918 Gateshead* **Died:** 1982
**Playing career:** *Everton, Port Vale, Crystal Palace, South Liverpool, Nottingham Forest, Northwich Victoria (1938-1947)*
He came through the youth ranks at Everton but was not offered a professional contract with the club. Port Vale picked him up but similar to many others on this list, the Second World War disrupted his career. He was called up for military training in August 1939. He had trials at Crystal Palace and was awarded a professional contract but only managed to play in one league fixture. Nottingham Forest also invited him for a trial but nothing materialised with the club. He died on 24 April 1982.

## FERRI, Jean-Michel

*Defender/midfielder*
**Born:** *1969 Lyon, France*
**Playing career:** *FC Nantes, Istanbulspor A.S, Liverpool, Sochaux (1987-2000)*
Another Gerard Houlier signing, another disappointment. Having been brought to Liverpool for £1.5 million, Jean-Michael Ferri played a total of 47 minutes for the club from two substitute appearances – a stark contrast to his 288 league appearances for former side FC Nantes. He left Istanbulspor after a dispute over pay. He picked up an injury and the chairman of the club told the manager to leave the Frenchman out, so he didn't need to pay him! He moved on to Sochaux for a similar fee and has become one of many forgotten men at Anfield. Capped five times by France. He has since gone on to do media work in France.

Steve Finnan

## FINNAN, Steve

*Right-back*

**Born:** *1976 Limerick, Ireland*
**Playing career:** *Wimbledon, Welling United, Birmingham City, Notts County, Fulham, Liverpool, Espanyol, Portsmouth (1990-2010)*

One of the more memorable full-backs in the recent history of Liverpool Football Club. The Irishman played 217 times for the Reds, scoring one goal. Steve Finnan struggled to find a club as a youngster and was rejected by Wimbledon at the age of 16. He was brought into the team for £3.5 million. His introduction to the side pushed Jamie Carragher away, who jokingly said to Sky Sports: "There's nothing you can do, except impress the manager in training and in games. Or find out Finnan's address and send the boys round!". He was a good servant for Rafael Benitez and was part of the starting XI on that special night in Istanbul. His performances at Liverpool won him 53 caps with his country. Just after the Champions League final, Finnan was arrested for running over an 81-year-old and killing him. He never faced charges despite the man dying and the Irishman travelling at twice the speed of the limit. He now lives in London and works as a property developer.

## FITZPATRICK, Harold

*Striker*

**Born:** *1880 Everton* **Died:** 1942
**Playing career:** *Gordon Highlanders, Liverpool, Luton Town, Chesterfield (1897-1909)*

Harold Fitzpatrick's father was a goalkeeper and he dreamt of a career in football similar to his dad. He scored the only goal of the game on his debut in 1907. In December 1915, Liverpool's board received a letter informing them that Fitzpatrick was a prisoner of war. The club bought two parcels of groceries in an attempt to negotiate his safe return. After the war, he was a coach at Zandaam FC in Holland before moving back to Liverpool and was living in Skerries Road prior to his death in 1942.

### "DID YOU KNOW?"

*"The first ever match on the BBC's Match of the Day featured Liverpool against Arsenal"*

## FITZPATRICK, Paul

*Central defender*

**Born:** *1965 Liverpool*
**Playing career:** *Liverpool, Tranmere Rovers, Bolton Wanderers, Bristol City, Carlisle United, Leicester City, Birmingham City, Bury (loan), Northampton Town, Shenzhen (1985-1999)*

Having started his career with the youth academy, he was soon released and welcomed into Tranmere's youth setup. He played for 13 clubs throughout his senior career and spent time on loan with two others. After retiring as a player, he became assistant manager at both Gresley Rovers and Workington.

## FLEMING, George

*Defender*

**Born:** *1869 Bannockburn, Scotland* **Died:** 1922
**Playing career:** *Liverpool, East Stirlingshire, Wolverhampton Wanderers (1894-1906)*

He made his name with Wolves and featured in 187 matches for the club between 1894-1901. His impressive ability to adapt to several positions greatly assisted Liverpool in regaining First Division status after a shock relegation the season before. After losing his place in the team, he became assistant trainer with the club. He remained in this role until his death and was buried at Anfield Cemetery. His daughter Helen, spent a week in jail for feeding pigeons outside of their property.

## FORSHAW, Dick

*Striker*

**Born:** *1895 Preston*
**Died:** 1963
**Playing career:** *Liverpool, Everton, Wolves, Hednesford Town, Rhyl Athletic (1919-1931)*

A player who enjoyed eight years with Liverpool. He featured in 288 games and scored 123 goals. His move to Everton was controversial in 1927 but he picked up his third league championship after winning his first two with Liverpool. In April 1932, he was charged for theft after an altercation during the Royal Hunt Cup at Ascot. The court heard of Forshaw's struggle after retirement from football as he had been a failed commission agent and co-ran a fish and chip shop with his wife. He was sentenced to 12 months' hard labour after he illegally amended a winning betting slip from a £2 return to £20.

## FOSTER, Ian

*Striker*

**Born:** *1976 Whiston, Merseyside*
**Playing career:** *Liverpool, Hereford United, Barrow, Chester-City, Kidderminster Harriers, Galway United (1996-2008)*

Ian Foster Spent time with Liverpool's youth academy before being released and playing non-league football throughout his career. Although he failed to make a big impact as a player, he does hold the UEFA Pro Licence - which is the highest coaching badge available throughout the continent. He has been the manager of Galway United and Dundalk in the past and is currently working with The FA as a specialist coach with England's youth teams.

## FOWLER, Robbie

*Striker*

**Born:** *1975 Toxteth, Liverpool*
**Playing career:** *Liverpool, Leeds United, Manchester City, Cardiff City, Blackburn Rovers (1984-2012)*

Robbie Fowler is born and raised in Toxteth in Liverpool, an area where unemployment is rife. He was an Everton supporter as a child, so it's ironic that he would become one of Liverpool's greatest players ever.

Brad Friedel

He scored all five goals in Liverpool's match against Fulham in 1993 and scored a hat-trick against Arsenal in only four minutes and 33 seconds – which remained a Premier League record until Sadio Mane beat it in 2015. In total, Fowler spent 14 years at Anfield, scored 183 goals before moving to several English clubs and finishing his career Australia and Thailand. He had worked in media roles after retiring and returned to coaching becoming Brisbane Roar's head coach in 2019.

## FRIARS, Sean

*Forward*

**Born:** *1979 Derry, Northern Ireland*
**Playing career:** *Foyle Harps, Liverpool, Ipswich Town (1995-2012)*

Sean Friars Started his career with Liverpool's youth academy but struggled to find himself as a footballer. He was signed by Ipswich in 1998 but only made one league appearance before being released. He captained the Northern Ireland U-21 team and showed great promise as a youngster but homesickness stagnated his potential. Friars' story is a sad one. He struggled to accept his failure in football and turned to alcohol, gambling and prescription drugs to numb the pain. However, he was offered a coaching role with a semi-professional team in Ireland in 2016 and is still employed by the club.

## FRIEDEL, Brad

*Goalkeeper*

**Born:** *1971 Lakewood, Ohio, United States*
**Playing career:** *USSF, Newcastle United (loan), Brv®ndby (loan), Galatasaray, Columbus Crew, Liverpool, Blackburn Rovers, Aston Villa, Tottenham Hotspur (1990-2015)*

One of the most recognisable players to come from America, Brad Friedel is an absolute giant of American soccer. He was capped 82 times by his country and enjoyed spells with Liverpool, Blackburn Rovers, Aston Villa and Tottenham Hotspur in England. It took him four years to make his debut for Liverpool and it became apparent that he would never be considered as first choice between the sticks. He has since been involved with media duties and managerial positions. He was part of the BBC's 2014 World Cup team and he has managed the United States' junior national teams.

Robbie Fowler

## FRODSHAM, Ian
*Midfielder*
**Born:** *1975 England* **Died:** 1995
**Playing career:** *Liverpool (1987-1995)*
Ian Frodsham was destined to become a
good servant for Liverpool before disaster
struck in 1995. He spent seven years in
Liverpool's academy before being awarded
with a professional contract. Sadly at the
age of 19 he died from a spinal tumour.
To commemorate the former player, the
indoor training arena at Liverpool Football
Academy is named the Ian Frodsham Indoor
Arena. In addition to this, there is an annual
football tournament held there for school
children in the local area that is called the
Ian Frodsham Memorial Cup.

## FROST, Arthur
*forward*
**Born:** *1915 Liverpool* **Died:** 1998
**Playing career:** *Liverpool, South Lancashire
Regiment, Newcastle United, Southport, South
Liverpool (1938-1947)*
Liverpool signed Arthur Frost after seeing
him play football in the army where he was
part of the South Lancashire Regiment. He
did not feature for Liverpool but eventually
signed for Newcastle United for a fee of
£2500. Once again the Second World War
disrupted his progress. After the conflict
concluded he finished his career as a
player-manager with South Liverpool for the
1946/47 season.

## FURNELL, Jim
*Goalkeeper*
**Born:** *1937 Clitheroe*
**Playing career:** *Burnley, Liverpool, Arsenal,
Rotherham United & Plymouth Argyle*
A goalkeeper who played in the Football
League between 1954-76. He started his
career with Burnley but only made two
appearances for them in eight seasons.
He then joined Liverpool but is best
remembered for his time with Arsenal and
his last club Plymouth Argyle - where he
played until he was 39. He then became a
coach with them but moved to Blackburn
Rovers when manager Bobby Saxton
relocated there. He was appointed reserve
team coach and later took the position of
youth development officer before retiring
in 1998. He lives in retirement at Wilpshire
near Blackburn.

## GALLAGHER, Joe
*Centre-half*
**Born:** *1955 Liverpool*
**Playing career:** *Liverpool, Birmingham City,
Wolverhampton Wanderers, West Ham United,
Burnley (1970-1995)*
Joe Gallagher started his footballing journey
with Liverpool's youth academy but was
released in 1970 before being picked up by
Birmingham. He spent two years in their
set up before being awarded a professional
contract in 1972. He had nine years with the
club as a professional and featured in over
300 games. His last Football League club
was Burnley before he dropped down into
the non-leagues during the twilight years of
his career. He moved into management with
Atherstone United and Kings heath before
retiring from the game in 1995. He became
community liaison officer with Birmingham
City and he later worked for Land Rover
before providing statistics for the Press
Association. He is currently involved
in corporate hospitality at Birmingham
matches.

## GARCIA, Luis
*Winger/Attacking midfielder*
**Born:** *1978 Badalona, Spain*
**Playing career:** *Sant Gabriel, Barcelona, Barcelona
B, Valladolid (loan), Toledo , Tenerife (loan), Valladolid
(loan), Atletico Madrid, Liverpool (1994-2016)*
Luis Garcia was a good servant for Liverpool
that spent seven years in Barcelona's La
Masia. His goal against Chelsea in the
2004/05 Champions League semi-final had
been awarded despite the ball not crossing
the line. Thus, the term 'ghost goal' was
coined. This crucial decision ensured
Liverpool would feature in the final and
arguably the greatest football comeback of
all time would take place. He later played
in India and became a marquee player for
the Central Coast Miners. After retiring,
he was part of beIN Sports pundit team
for their coverage of the UEFA European
Championships in 2016 and has since
returned in a similar role for BT Sport.

### "DID YOU KNOW?"

*"Kenny Dalglish was the first ever
player-manager in English League
football"*

## GARDNER, Tommy
*Wing-half*
**Born:** *1910 Huyton* **Died:** 1970
**Playing career:** *Liverpool, Grimsby Town, Hull City, Aston Villa, Burnley, Wrexham (1929-1947)*

Tommy Gardner signed for Liverpool on an amateur basis in 1928. He struggled to cement a regular spot in the senior team and featured five times for the club. His performances for Aston Villa however, won him two England caps. Gardner was a long-throw expert and even won a Daily Mail competition by throwing 32 yards. His great-granddaughter Hannah Keryakoplis played international football for Wales.

## GAYLE, Howard
*Forward/winger*
**Born:** *1958 Toxteth, Liverpool*
**Playing career:** *Liverpool, Fulham (loan), Newcastle United (loan), Birmingham City, Sunderland, Stoke City, Blackburn Rovers, Halifax Town (1974-1993)*

Howard Gayle made history for Liverpool by becoming the first black player to play for the club in 1981. Having come through the youth academy, he was awarded with a professional contract but only played in five games during his six years with the club. He often received racial abuse from opposing supporters and had to endure bananas being thrown at him and 70,000 Bayern Munich fans chanting and performing the Nazi salute. In 2016, he released his autobiography, '*61 Minutes In Munich*'. It was also reported that Gayle turned down a nomination for an MBE for his work with racism in football as he believed it would be a betrayal to all the Africans who lost their lives or have suffered from a result of the Empire.

Howard Gayle

## GAYLE, Mark
*Goalkeeper*
**Born:** *1969 Bromsgrove*
**Playing career:** *Leicester City, Blackpool, Worcester City, Walsall, Crewe Alexandra, Liverpool (loan), Birmingham City (loan), Hereford United (loan), Chesterfield (loan), Luton Town (loan), Rushden & Diamonds, Chesterfield, Hednesford Town, Solihull Borough, Hereford United, Halesowen Town, Solihull Borough, Tamworth, Halesowen Town, Rushall Olympic (1988-2007)*

A well-travelled goalkeeper who failed to settle at a professional club. His longest stint in the English Football League was with Crewe Alexandra, where he spent five years for the club. He was sent on loan to Liverpool during this time but he never made an appearance – he was an unused substitute on three occasions. After his playing career, Gayle moved into coaching and was employed by Leamington. He has since worked as a financial analyst and is the CEO of TCP Tings, which sell Jamaican creative products.

## GEARY, Fred
*Centre-forward*
**Born:** *1868 Hyson Green*
**Died:** 1955
**Playing career:** *Notts Rangers, Notts County, Grimsby Town, Everton, Liverpool (1886-1896)*

Fred Geary was petite and powerful and is the smallest man to every play for Liverpool at the height of 5 ft. 2ins (157 cm). He was phenomenal for Everton during the Victorian era from 1889-1895, scoring 85 goals in only 99 games! When the Blues won the 1890/91 League Championship he was the club's top scorer with 20 goals. He was also the first man to score a goal after a net was put between the frames of the goal – an invention by Liverpudlian Jon Alexander Brodie, who was also the designer of the Mersey Tunnel. Sadly, Geary lost his first child before having four more. When he was 27 he joined neighbours Liverpool when they were relegated to the Second Division. He made his debut against Notts County on the opening day of the 1895/96 season but only played 19 more times that season. He eventually lost his pace - which was his key asset - and he spent two years with the reserves. Alongside his footballing journey, Geary owned a pub and when his career finished he became the groundsman at Goodison Park.

Steve Gerrard

## GERHARDI, Hugh

*Defender*

**Born:** *1933 Johannesburg, South Africa* **Died:** 1985

**Playing career:** *Thistle., Liverpool (1950-1953)*

Hugh Gerhardi is one of the tallest players to ever play for Liverpool at 6'4. He played in six league matches before homesickness took over and he moved back to South Africa after just one season with the club. He committed suicide in 1985 after mistakenly believing he had a brain tumour. His blood pressure became high and he was forced to give up coaching, which is what influenced his decision according to his wife.

## GERRARD, Steven

*Midfielder*

**Born:** *1980 Whiston*

**Playing career:** *Liverpool, LA Galaxy (1987-2015)*

Steven Gerrard was the ultimate leader who really carried Liverpool for many years. He was strong in tackling, could hit the ball at ferocious speed, had brilliant vision, scored incredible goals, made superb passes and quite simply, had every single feature that was needed in a world-class footballer. There is no doubt that he is one of the greatest players in the club's history. Gerrard was not selected to play at Lilleshall, the national football and sports centre, due to his lack of height. When he was 15, he was the same height as Michael Owen but a late growth spurt caused problems in his back which restricted him to only playing 20 games from the age of 14 to 16. He was finally given his first opportunity when Jamie Redknapp got inured in 1998. In his first Merseyside derby he played as right-back and two goal line clearances demonstrated that he was going to be something special. He got his first goal for the club against Sheffield Wednesday on 5 December 1999 and would later go on to display his versatility by playing at left-back, right-back, defensive and offensive midfield as well as a right-winger! On 31 May 2000, Gerrard made his international debut at the age of 20 years and one day – England won the match 2-0 against Ukraine at Wembley. After Liverpool finished runners-up to Arsenal during the 2001/02 season, they started to decline. However, Gerrard was the complete opposite as he continued to grow and was awarded the captaincy on 15 October 2003.

His header nine minutes into the second half of the 2005 Champions League final inspired the club's greatest ever comeback. He was awarded the England captaincy in 2010 for the upcoming World Cup, but the national team would have an underwhelming tournament. The elusive Premier League winner's medal was the only silverware missing from Gerrard's sensational time at Liverpool before he moved to LA Galaxy in the summer of 2015. He announced his retirement from football on 24th November 2016 and returned to Liverpool as coach of the under 18s. He left this role in May 2018 when he was appointed in his first managerial position with Rangers, where he remains to this day.

## GIDMAN, John

*Right-back*

**Born:** *1954 Liverpool*

**Playing career:** *Liverpool, Aston Villa, Everton, Manchester United, Manchester City, Stoke City, Darlington (1970-1989)*

John Gidman came through the youth set up at Liverpool but was deemed surplus to requirements and Aston Villa signed the full-back - where he stayed for eight years before demanding better terms on his contract which spelt the end of his stay at Villa Park. Eventually signed for Manchester United and became a fan favourite but a string of injuries hampered his true potential with the club. He did, however, help the club win the FA Cup in both 1983 and 1985. When his final club Darlington were relegated to the Football Conference in 1989 he hung up his boots. He made one cap for England against Luxembourg in March 1977. Prior to his move to Villa, Bill Shankly called the then 16-year-old into his office to let him know he has been informed that he was 'Sh*te' and that the club would be releasing him! He moved into management with Jings Lynn and moved to Marbella on the Costa del Sol in 1990 where he still resides.

### "DID YOU KNOW?"

*"The Merseyside derby may be known as 'The Friendly Derby' but it has still produced more red cards than any other league fixture"*

## GILLESPIE, Gary

*Defender*
**Born:** *1960 Stirling, Scotland*
**Playing career:** *Falkirk, Coventry City, Liverpool, Celtic, Coventry City (1977-1997)*

Gary Gillespie was appointed Falkirk's captain in the Scottish Second Division at only 17 - the youngest captain in Scottish League history. He signed for Liverpool in 1983 for £325,000 but had his work cut out for him if he wished to split up the successful partnership of Mark Lawrenson and Alan Hansen. He spent his first year primarily in the reserves. He was used frequently the following season as he came in as replacement for the injured Lawrenson and occasionally played as a midfielder. He came on as a 3rd minute substitute for Lawrenson during the 1985 European Cup final. However, when Graeme Souness was appointed manager, the Scotsman fell out of favour and moved to Celtic for three years before returning to England for a sole season with former side Coventry. When he retired as a player he was appointed in a coaching role with the Sky Blues before moving to Stockport City under Dave Jones. Since then he has been involved with Radio Merseyside in addition to Liverpool's official TV Channel.

## GILLIGAN, Sam

*Centre-forward*
**Born:** *1882 Dundee, Scotland* **Died:** 1965
**Playing career:** *Dundee, Celtic, Bristol City, Liverpool, Gillingham, Forfar Athletic (1902-1915)*

Sam Gilligan made his name with Celtic, which influenced the decision for Bristol City to sign the Scotsman. Six impressive years with City caught the eye of Liverpool, who signed the forward in 1910. He made a scoring debut for Liverpool on 24 September 1910 and became the club's hero two years later when he scored the winner against Oldham in what was effectively a must-win to stay in the First Division. He left for Gillingham the following season and remained there as player-manager for two years. He later moved to America and worked for the 'Republican Iron and Steel Company' whilst playing for a local non-professional soccer team. He died in Ohio on 17 June 1965.

## GLOVER, John

*Right-back*
**Born:** *1876 West Bromwich* **Died:** 1955
**Playing career:** *West Bromwich Albion, Blackburn Rovers, New Brompton, Liverpool (1896-1910)*

John Glover was a small but tough full-back that spent three years at Anfield. He was banned from football for four months at the end of the 1902/03 season after he accepted illegal payments from Portsmouth to sign for the club - he was also banned for life for signing for the south coast club. When his ban was lifted he was offered the maximum wage for a new contract from Liverpool but he declined the offer and moved to Small Heath (now Birmingham Football Club) before retiring after their relegation in the 1907/08 season. He later ran a pub in Dudley and represented Shropshire at bowls.

## GODDARD, Arthur

*Winger*
**Born:** *1876 Heaton Norris, Stockport* **Died:** 1956
**Playing career:** *Stockport County, Glossop North End, Liverpool, Cardiff City (1895-1914)*

Arthur Goddard was not only a brilliant servant to Liverpool Football Club, he is also a worthy member of the club's official Hall of Fame. A consistent winger who knew where the goal was, he was an integral player for Liverpool for 15 years. Goddard joined Liverpool in 1902 for £460 – a great investment considering the longevity of his time at Anfield. Jack Cox was moved to the left-wing to accommodate the arrival of Goddard and the two provided a brilliant partnership. He was appointed captain of the side during the 1909/10 season. The 1913/14 campaign proved to be his final in a Liverpool shirt as he lost his place in the autumn and his contract was not renewed, paving the way for a free transfer to Cardiff City. He was chosen twice for England trials at both Liverpool and Glossop but was never selected. He did, however, represent the English League which beat the Irish League 9-0 in 1901. He was granted a testimonial match which raised a monumental sum of £250 that would help him to start up a business. On 29 May 1956 it was reported by the Liverpool Echo that the former player had died after being in ill health for some time. Although no exact date was given about his death, his funeral took place on 31 May at Anfield Cemetery.

## GOLDIE, Archie
*Right-back*
**Born:** *1874 Hurlford, Ayrshire, Scotland* **Died:** 1953
**Playing career:** *Clyde, Liverpool, Small Heath, Crewe Alexandra (1892-1905)*

Archie Goldie was just one of many Scotsman who represented Liverpool during their early years. Although he was slow in pace, his passing and vision certainly made up for it. He was purchased to strengthen the team that had been relegated in 1895 and immediately assisted with Liverpool's successful attempt to regain First Division status. His brother Bill joined him for the second half of his time at Anfield as Liverpool established themselves in the top tier of English football.

## GOLDIE, William
*Left-half*
**Born:** *1878 Hurlford, Ayrshire, Scotland* **Died:** 1952
**Playing career:** *Hurlford Thistle, Clyde, Liverpool, Fulham, Leicester Fosse (1895-1911)*

William Goldie is the brother of Archie and enjoyed seven years in Merseyside. He was an ever-present member of the squad during the 1899-1903 seasons and played in 129 consecutive games from 23 December 1899 until 27 April 1903! He was part of the 1900/01 League Championship winning team. At the end of the 1902/03 season, Goldie was caught accepting illegal payments from Portsmouth to sign for them in the Southern League. As a consequence, he was banned from football until 31 December 1903. After the suspension was over, he joined Fulham in January 1904 and won two Southern League Championships with the London-based club. He joined Leicester for a sole season before retiring in 1911. He ran a pub after retiring whilst occasionally playing for amateurs Leicester Imperial. Goldie's Scottish accent was so difficult to understand that that the FA were forced to employ an interpreter during his playing days!

### "DID YOU KNOW?"

*"Robbie Fowler's record for the fastest Premier League hat-trick was taken away from him by another Red, Sadio Mane"*

## GONZALEZ, Mark
*Winger*
**Born:** *1984 Durban, South Africa*
**Playing career:** *Albacete, Liverpool, Real Sociedad (loan), Betis, CSKA Moscow, Sport Recife, Colo-Colo, Megallanes (2002-)*

Mark Gonzalez was born to Chilean parents and, ironically, was on the books at Everton - a Chilean club named Everton de Vina del Mar. Liverpool's first team coach Paco Herrera was decisive in the decision to bring him to Anfield but it was not straightforward. As Chile were outside the top 70 countries in the FIFA Rankings, it took six months for the work permit to be approved. During this time he enjoyed a loan spell with Real Sociedad before returning to Liverpool. He started his Liverpool career well, scoring the winner against Maccabi Haifa in the home leg of the Champions League qualifier. Despite this, he struggled at Liverpool and was primarily used as an impact substitution before moving to Russia. He was capped 56 times by Chile and is currently plying his trade with Chilean football club Magallanes.

## GOODALL, Archie
*Half-back/Forward*
**Born:** *1865 Belfast, Ireland* **Died:** 1929
**Playing career:** *Liverpool Stanley, Everton, St Jude's, Preston North End, Aston Villa, Derby County, Glossop, Wolverhampton Wanderers (1887-1905)*

Archie Goodall moved to several teams before settling at Derby County and spending 14 years with the club. During his career, he set three age records. He was the oldest player to score an international goal in the 19th century, the oldest player to score for Ireland and the oldest player to ever play for Wolves. He was, however, a controversial character. He once refused to play an extra 30 minutes for West Brom because he believed his contract ended after 90 minutes! He was also caught trying to sell on extra FA Cup final tickets to a ticket tout. His older brother John also played football – including England. Despite both being Scottish, they were ineligible to play for the country due to their birthplace. They became the first brothers in world football to play for two different national teams. After retiring he travelled around America and Europe as part of a strongman act before settling in London for the remainder of his life.

## GORE, Tommy
*Midfielder*
**Born:** *1953 Liverpool*
**Playing career:** *Liverpool, Tranmere Rovers, Wigan Athletic, Bury, Port Vale (1974-1984)*

Tommy Gore started his career in Liverpool's youth academy before being released and snapped up by neighbours Tranmere. He signed his first professional contract with Wigan and would remain with the club for six years. During his first season, he was shipped out to Dallas Tornado on loan before proving his worth to the northern club. After retiring in 1984, he owned and ran a snooker club in Wigan. He now lives in Billinge and manages a cleaning company providing services on board ships. A talented golfer, he became the club captain at Dean Wood Golf Club.

## GRACIE, Tom
*Centre-forward*
**Born:** *1889 Glasgow, Scotland* **Died:** 1915
**Playing career:** *Morton, Everton, Liverpool, Heart of Midlothian (1907-1916)*

Tom Gracie had been highly rated in Scotland before his move to Everton but he struggled in Merseyside – scoring one goal in 13 league appearances spread across two years. He moved to Liverpool in February 1912 alongside teammate Bill Lacey for a combined fee of £300 with Harold Uren going the opposite way. It did not take the Scotsman long to find the net for his new team as he scored on his debut against Bury on 24 February 1912. However, a goal drought followed which prevented him adding to his tally for the remainder of the season. He would only score three more goals from his last 23 games with the club. He returned to Scotland with Hearts in 1914 and was the joint-leading scorer in the Scottish League during the 1914/15 season with 29 goals. In addition to his footballing duties, he served as Corporal with the 16th Royal Scots and was promoted to Sergeant in May 1915. Tragically, he was diagnosed with leukaemia in March 1915 but continued to soldier on in an act of pure bravery – only the manager of Hearts knew of his severe illness. He passed away at Stobhill hospital in Glasgow on 23 October 1915, only 26 years old. His brother had died less than a month prior in the great offensive at Loos in France.

## GRAY, Jimmy
*defender*
**Born:** *1900 Glasgow, Scotland* **Died:** 1978
**Playing career:** *Transvaal, Liverpool, Exeter City (1921-1936)*

Jimmy Gray started his career with South African Transvaal before joining Liverpool in 1926. He only made one appearance for his new side before moving to Exeter and becoming a club legend, playing 221 games in six years. He was given a testimonial match when Exeter and Liverpool faced each other in 1935. After his playing days, Gray was working in Liverpool for a telephone exchange company. He had to have a lung removed in 1954 before living the remainder of his days in South Africa.

## GRAYER, Frank
*Full-back*
**Born:** *1890 Brighton* **Died:** 1961
**Playing career:** *St Mary's Athletic (Southampton), Southampton, Liverpool (1908-1915)*

Liverpool picked up Frank Grayer from Southampton for £100. He was eager to move as he was getting limited game time at Southampton. Unfortunately the trend would continue and he only played once for Liverpool's first team during a three-year stay. Grayer was so badly injured during the war that it was impossible to go back to football as a career. Once the war had finished he found employment with a furniture company called Shepherd & Hedger until his retirement in 1955.

## GRIFFITHS, Bryan
*Full-back*
**Born:** *1939 Litherland*
**Playing career:** *Everton, Southport, Formby, Burscough, South Liverpool, Southport, Mossley, Morecambe, Witton Albion, Bangor City, Chorley, Kendal Town, Congleton Town, Rossendale United (1958-2002)*

Bryan Griffiths started his career with Everton but found limited opportunities with the First Division club. He moved to Southport and spent three years being an integral player and one of the first names on the team sheet. He later moved into management and has enjoyed 35 years managing non-league teams around England. He is currently the manager of Rossendale United who play in the North West Counties League.

## GROBBELAAR, Bruce

*Goalkeeper*

**Born:** 1957 Durban, South Africa
**Playing career:** Highlanders FC, Durban City, Vancouver Whitecaps, Crewe Alexandra, Liverpool, Stoke City, Southampton, Plymouth Argyle, Oxford United, Sheffield Wednesday, Oldham Athletic, Chesham United, Bury, Lincoln City, Northwich Victoria, Glasshoughton Welfare (1976-2007)

Arguably one of Liverpool's greatest ever goalkeepers – if not the greatest! South African-born Grobbelaar signed for Liverpool on 17 March 1981 for a fee of £250,000. Although he was initially brought into the club as a reserve 'keeper, within a year he had firmly established himself as Liverpool's number one. He made his debut against Wolves in a league match where both Mark Lawrenson and Craig Johnston featured for the first time for the club. He would spend 14 years with Liverpool and make nearly 500 appearances for the club - a young David James spelt the end for the South African and he would move to Southampton mid-1994. During his time with Liverpool, he had won six league titles, three FA Cups, three Football League Cups and a European Cup. His time on the south coast was dripped in controversy as there was alleged match-fixing accusations aimed at the stopper. Despite this, he won his libel case against the Sun newspaper and was originally awarded £85,000. However, the publication appealed and the charge was cut significantly to just £1 and Grobbelaar was ordered to pay the Sun's legal fees, which amassed over £500,000. He was forced to declare bankruptcy as he was unable to pay the fees. After his playing days he returned to South Africa and coached several teams with some success. He took Seven Stars from the relegation zone to finish in the top four and in 2001 he took over at Hellenic and saved them from relegation – he even played in the final match of the season but was forced to bring himself off after cracking his ribs only 20 minutes into the showdown! He also featured in Sky One's *The Match* in both 2004 and 2006, where he kept two clean sheets. More recently, he became the goalkeeping coach for the Matabeleland football team and even started in goal for one match in June 2018! No matter what happens, Grobbelaar just cannot stay away from playing the game that he loves.

## HAIGH, Jack

*Inside-forward*

**Born:** 1928 Rotherham    **Died:** 2007
**Playing career:** Bolton Wanderers, Gainsborough Trinity, Liverpool, Scunthorpe United, Doncaster Rovers, Buxton (1949-1965)

Jack Haigh was a Yorkshireman who signed for Liverpool at the age of 21. He made his debut on Boxing Day 1950 and enjoyed a short stint in the starting XI. He eventually lost his place after Don Welsh had replaced George Kay as manager. He was later shipped to Scunthorpe United where he became one of the club's greatest servants. He played 362 games and scored 72 goals for Scunthorpe that stretched over eight years. His most memorable performance was a 3-1 FA Cup fourth round victory over Newcastle. He was knocked out during the match and badly injured but refused to be substituted and went on to score.

## HAINES, Jack

*Inside-forward*

**Born:** 1920 Evesham    **Died:** 1987
**Playing career:** Cheltenham Town, Liverpool, Swansea Town, Leicester City, West Bromwich Albion, Bradford Park Avenue, Rochdale, Chester-City, Wellington United, Kidderminster Harriers, Evesham Town (1937-1956)

Jack Haines spent his youth career with Cheltenham Town before signing professional papers with Liverpool in 1937. Despite spending nine years with the club, he failed to make a single appearance that was largely influenced by the advent of the Second World War. After the conclusion of the war, he moved to Swansea where he spent a sole season with the Welsh club. His post-war performances saw him awarded with an England cap where he scored twice! He was never selected for the national side again. After retiring as a player, he moved into coaching and coached at Bishops Cleeve Secondary School during the 1960's. He also managed local teams in the Cheltenham and Evesham area.

## "DID YOU KNOW?"

*"Anfield was named after Annefield in Wexford, Ireland by the then Irish mayor of Liverpool who bought the land where the ground now sits"*

LIFE IN A JUNGLE

MY AUTOBIOGRAPHY

**BRUCE GROBBELAAR**

## HALL, Brian

*Midfielder*
**Born:** 1946, Glasgow, Scotland **Died:** 2015
**Playing career:** *Liverpool, Plymouth Argyle, Burnley. (1968-1980).*

All Brian Hall wanted in his life was to go to Liverpool. He did not want to play football – he wanted to study at the university! He studied mathematics and graduated with a Bachelor of Science degree. Away from academia and Hall was a fantastic servant for Liverpool Football Club. Although small in stature, he was clever and efficient. He was an important member of the team that Bill Shankly rebuilt during the early 1970s. He was, however, forced to wait for his opportunity after spending his first three years at Liverpool in the reserves. Ian Callaghan's injury in September 1970 gave hall his breakthrough and he performed so well that when the former returned, he placed in him in central midfield to accommodate both players! Hall's most memorable moment came during the 1970/71 season when the Scotsman netted a dramatic winning goal in the FA Cup semi-final against Everton which took his side to Wembley for the first time since 1965. Unfortunately, they lost the final but would finally lift the cup three years later against Newcastle. In total, Hall won one

League Championship, one FA Cup and two UEFA Cups. He eventually lost his place to Jimmy Case midway through the 1975/76 season and moved to Plymouth Argyle the following summer before finishing his career with Burnley. He took on teaching and was a schoolmaster for a while but he returned to Anfield in 1991 to head the club's public relations department, a post he held until 2011 where he was forced to retire due to his battle with leukemia. Hall passed away on 16 July 2015 from the illness.

## HALLIDAY, Fred

*Full-back*
**Born:** *1880 Chester* **Died:** 1953
**Playing career:** *Liverpool, Everton, Bolton Wanderers, Bradford City, Chester, Bradford PA (1898-1908)*

Fred Halliday started his career with amateur club Chester before impressing in a friendly against Liverpool that subsequently ended with his signature for the side. He failed to make a first team appearance and was released two years later where he joined Everton – although never played for the senior team. He eventually settled at Bradford City and stayed with the club for four years. Halliday moved into management with Bradford Park Avenue and even had to play once as an emergency goalkeeper after regular stopper Tom Baddersley missed his train! He then had three spells with Brentford and in total managed the club for 334 matches.

## HALSALL, Mick

*Midfield*
**Born:** *1961 Bootle*
**Playing career:** *Liverpool, Birmingham City, Carlisle United, Grimsby Town, Peterborough United (1979-1993)*

Mick Halsall started his career in Liverpool's youth academy before being offered professional papers in 1979. Despite staying with the club for four years, he never represented the senior side. He moved to Birmingham in 1983 before joining Carlisle and Grimsby.

### "DID YOU KNOW?"

*"The first Liverpool match attracted a crowd of only 100. The stadium had the capacity to hold 20,000"*

He eventually settled with Peterborough United and even captained the club to promotion from the Fourth Division in the 1990/91 season. In his last season as a Peterborough player he became involved in the coaching side and was appointed assistant manager to Chris Turner in January 1994. He left his role in 1996 and worked for a private football academy before becoming assistant to John Still at Barnet. He was caretaker manager at Walsall for a while before taking an eight-year hiatus from coaching duties. He returned in 2014 to become the interim manager of Notts County and had another spell with them in 2015/16 before taking on the role as Head of Coaching at the Coventry City academy.

## HALSALL, Wally

*Wing-half*
**Born:** *1912 Liverpool* **Died:** 1996
**Playing career:** *Bootle Celtic, Liverpool, Marine, Burscough Rangers, Bolton Wanderers, Blackburn Rovers, Birmingham, Chesterfield (1932-1946)*
Wally Halsall was born in Liverpool and as a young man he played as an amateur for various clubs in the Lancashire area. He reached the FA Amateur Cup in 1932 with Marine but lost 7-1 in the final to Dulwich Hamlet. In December 1932 he signed for Blackburn rovers as an amateur, turning professional a few months later. He eventually lost his place to Charlie Calladine and was released, subsequently signing for Birmingham before finishing his career with Chesterfield. Although Halsall was contracted to his final club for seven years, he failed to make a league appearance for them as World War II broke out. After the war he became a commercial traveller until his death in Sefton South in March 1996.

Dietmar Hamann

## HAMANN, Dietmar

*Defensive midfielder*
**Born:** *1973 Waldsassen, West Germany*
**Playing career:** *Bayern Munich, Newcastle United, Liverpool, Bolton Wanderers, Manchester City, Milton Keynes Dons, Wacker Munchen (1978-1992)*
Dietmar Hamann was snapped up by German giants Bayern Munich when he was just 16 years old. He enjoyed success with the team, winning two Bundesliga titles, the UEFA Cup, the German Cup and the German League Cup. After impressing in the 1998 World Cup he was brought to Newcastle for £5.5 million. When he arrived at Anfield he was one of four new signings announced by Gerard Houllier during the summer of 1999. He made his debut on the opening day of the 1999/00 season but would only last 24 minutes after he ruptured his ankle ligaments. Fortunately, he recovered quickly and was only out for seven weeks before featuring in 29 more matches that season. He missed very few games over the next few seasons as he became the preferred defensive-midfielder for Liverpool. During the 2000/01 season he won the FA Cup, UEFA Cup and League Cup. In 2003, he wanted to give his second League Cup winner's medal to one of the younger players who played in the earlier rounds of the tournament as he believed: "valuing everyone who had made an effort for us was more important to me than personal gratification". His most memorable moment in a Liverpool shirt came when he as brought on as a half-time substitute during the 2005 Champion's League final, which saw Liverpool come back from 3-0 down. He took his penalty in the shootout with a fractured foot and scored! The next season it was clear that Hamann was no longer part of the plan and he had agreed a free transfer to Bolton. However, within 24 hours of signing for the team he joined Manchester City for £400,000 – the most expensive free transfer of all time! He spent three years in Manchester before finishing his playing career with Milton Keynes Dons in 2011 as player-manager. He continued with the managerial route and managed both Leicester City and Stockport County. He has since been involved with the media industry and has covered two World Cups, a UEFA Euro Championships and appeared on Sky Sports and Match of the Day 2.

Andrew Hannah

moved out of Anfield and a new team were established by the name of Liverpool, he was lured back to England one final time. He received a £150 signing-on fee and was paid £5 a week for his services. He became the first captain for Liverpool Football Club and played in 24 of the 28 matches in their debut season, winning promotion from the Second Division. Unfortunately, they were relegated the following season as a string of injuries kept the Scotsman out of the team during the latter half of the season. He left at the end of the disappointing season for a sole year back in Scotland before calling it time on his incredible footballing career. He died on 29 May 1940 and was buried in an unmarked grave. That was until the efforts of the Everton Heritage Society and Everton Football Club successfully managed to rededicate the grave and ensure that his achievements will forever be remembered.

## HANNAH, Andrew

*Right-back*
**Born:** *1864 Dumbartonshire* **Died:** 1940
**Playing career:** *Renton, West Bromwich Albion, Renton, Everton, Liverpool, Rob Roy (1883-1897)*

Andrew Hannah is the only man to captain both Everton and Liverpool but started his journey in his native Scotland as captain of Renton. They won the 1888 Scottish Cup final and played English Cup winners West Brom in what was dubbed as the 'Championship of the United Kingdom and the World'. Renton ran out as 4-1 winners and placed a sign on the door of their pavilion that read: "Renton FC, Champions of the World". Alongside playing right-back for his team, Hannah worked as a shipyard detective and also owned a milk business in the village. West Brom were so impressed with his performance against them they signed him for the inaugural season of the Football League. However, he failed to settle in the Midlands and moved back to Scotland after only a year. His second spell south of the border came with Everton which saw the team finish runners-up during the 1889/90 season before going one better and winning their first league title the subsequent year. That following summer, however, he returned to Scotland for a third spell with Renton. Once Everton

## HANSEN, Alan

*Centre-back*
**Born:** *1955 Sauchie, Clackmannanshire, Scotland*
**Playing career:** *Partick T, Liverpool, (1973-1989).*

Alan Hansen was the complete sportsman. Not only did he represent his club and country at the highest level in football, he was good enough to play golf, volleyball and squash for Scotland during his junior years! After watching his brother's Partick Thistle side beat firm favourites Glasgow Celtic in a Scottish League Cup final, Alan was playing for the team two years later. He helped Partick win promotion to the Scottish Premier League in 1976 and featured over 100 times for the side. Hansen arrived at Anfield for £100,000 in May 1977 and made his debut against Derby County at the end of September the same year – where he was awarded man of the match. He was known for his elegant style of dribbling past attackers instead of hoofing it up field, which didn't always please manager Bob Paisley who said: "he has given me more heart attacks than any other player I have ever known". Hansen won absolutely every piece of silverware available to Liverpool during his time there. Eight League Championships, two FA Cups, three League Cups and three European Cups! He played in 620 games for the club – which spanned across 13 years – and scored 14 goals.

Injuries finally caught up with him at the age of 34 and he was warned by specialists that if he wanted to walk pain free for the remainder of his life, it would be wise to give up the sport he adored. He was offered a coaching role with the club but he informed them he didn't feel comfortable and wanted a clean break away from the game. Thus, he announced his retirement in March 1991 and although he was heavily tipped to take over from the recently departed Kenny Dalglish, he knew management was not for him. He did, however, go on to become a knowledgeable football analyst with the BBC as a regular member of their 'Match of The Day' team up until 2014. Hansen was one of the greatest footballers to ever play for Liverpool and although he only won 26 international caps, there are very few more successful club players than the Scotsman.

## "DID YOU KNOW?"

*"In 1915, one of the earliest betting scandals resulted in four Liverpool players being banned."*

## HANSON, Alf
*Outside-left*
**Born:** *1912 Bootle*  **Died:** 1993
**Playing career:** *Liverpool, Chelsea, Gloucester City, Shelbourne, South Liverpool (1931-1950)*

Alf Hanson repaid Liverpool with six years of loyal service after he was brought to Anfield following one season playing in Everton's A-team. He had to be patient as he spent his first year in red in the reserves before he was called up into the senior side midway through the 1932/33 season. He performed well and frequently for Liverpool until injuries kept him out for the majority of the 1935/36 season. When he finally departed, Chelsea paid a club transfer record of £7,500 to secure the wingers services in the summer of 1938. He scored 9 goals in 46 games for the Blues but his career came to an end with the outbreak of World War II. After the conflict had concluded, he became player-manager for several amateur teams including South Liverpool, Shelbourne and Ellesmere Port Town. He featured in 16 wartime games for Liverpool where he was forced to hide his Christian name – Adolph! He also represented England in baseball and was a plumber after his sporting career.

Alan Hansen

## HARDY, Sam

*Goalkeeper*
**Born:** *1882 Chesterfield*
**Died:** 1966
**Playing career:** *Chesterfield, Liverpool, Aston Villa, Nottingham Forest (1898-1925)*

Co-founder of the Football Writers' Association, Charlie Buchan, stated that Sam Hardy is the finest goalkeeper he ever played against. His positioning, awareness and intelligent footballing brain meant that scoring just once against him was an achievement – let alone winning the game! The goalkeeper spent two years with Chesterfield before Liverpool came knocking in 1905. He signed for £340 and would stay with the club for seven years, playing 240 times. Hardy replaced Ned Doig who had been the preferred 'keeper but Liverpool were struggling for consistency. They then won their next four games with Hardy in goal, including a 3-2 win against champions Newcastle. A ten-year-old fan of the club was so impressed with his displays that he wrote a poem that was published in the Liverpool Echo in April 1906: "I know a good goalie Called Hardy, and when the ball comes he's not tardy, he belongs to the 'Pool, and he's been to school, has that jolly good goalie called Hardy". In total, Hardy was Liverpool's number one for seven years, up until the age of 30 when he was replaced by Scotsman Ken Campbell, ten years his junior. The 'keeper became a member of the Professional Footballer's Association when he retired and ran his own billiard hall in Derbyshire. He died on 24 October 1966.

## HARKNESS, Steve

*Left-back*
**Born:** *1971 Carlisle, Cumberland*
**Playing career:** *Carlisle United, Huddersfield Town, Southend United, Blackburn Rovers, Sheffield Wednesday, Chester-City, Liverpool (1989-2002)*

Steve Harkness had only played in 13 league matches for Carlisle before Liverpool purchased the full-back for £75,000 in 1989. Although traditionally a right-back, when playing in Liverpool's reserves a string of injuries forced him to play on the left, which is where he was primarily used during his time in the senior side too. He failed to settle in during the first five years but an injury crisis at the club allowed him one final chance to prove his worth.

His performances were awarded with a new three-year contract and he was first-choice for the first half of the 1995/96 season. Unfortunately, in January 1996 he lost his place after picking up too many bookings and Liverpool seemed to be stronger without him. Stan Collymore accused Harkness of racially abusing him at Villa Park in February 1998 after his former teammate supposedly promised to properly break his legs this time. The two sides met again nine months later and a horror tackle by Collymore forced Harkness to leave the field via a stretcher. The arrival of Gerard Houllier spelt the end for the full-back who then reconnected with Graeme Souness at Benfica. He was banned from the first team after arguing with the club's president following the sacking of Souness. He moved back to England to play for Blackburn and Sheffield Wednesday before finishing his career with non-league side Chester City due to a plight of injuries. In September 2019, he admitted to driving whilst disqualified and uninsured. He was sentenced to a three-year driving ban, a nine-week jail term suspended for two years and 100 hours of community service.

## HARLEY, Jim

*Full-back*
**Born:** *1917 Methil, Fife, Scotland* **Died:** 1989
**Playing career:** *Liverpool (1932-1949)*

Jim Harley was one of the toughest men to play for Liverpool, if not the toughest! He would often come into training with cuts and bruises all over his face and knuckles. It was obvious that he had been out fighting the night before but not with just one man. Harley would prefer to fight three, four or even five men at once! He established himself in the side during the 1937/38 season after being on the fringes of the senior side for a couple of seasons. His professional career was cut short with the outbreak of World War II and during wartime he won Scotland international honours and the Royal Navy Commando was also decorated for his role at Dunkirk as he was bringing soldiers in the armed forces home while under fire from German planes. When the footballing calendar resumed after the conflict, he made 17 appearances for the club that secured their fifth First Division title.

However, he had passed his thirtieth birthday at that point and would only stay for one final year at Anfield. He was also an exceptional sprinter and at 18 he won the famous Powderhall Handicap, a New Year sprint in Scotland that originated in 1870. He competed under the name 'J H Mitchell' so Liverpool would not find out about this! He retired from the game when his contract with Liverpool expired in 1948.

## HARPER, Alan
*Defender/midfield*
**Born:** *1960 Liverpool, Merseyside*
**Playing career:** *Liverpool, Everton, Sheffield Wednesday, Manchester City, Luton Town, Burnley,Cardiff City (loan) (1978-1995)*
Having graduated through Liverpool's youth system and signed professional papers, it's slightly ironic that Alan Harper would play for Everton and become a good servant to the club. He played for several English clubs but failed to settle at any – excluding the five years he had with Everton. After retiring, he returned to the Toffees as a youth team coach before leaving in 2005. He has since worked for Bolton Wanderers as a scout and is currently employed by Liverpool as head scout.

## HARRIS, Andy
*Midfielder*
**Born:** *1977 Springs, Gauteng, South Africa*
**Playing career:** *Liverpool, Southend United, Leyton Orient, Chester-City, Forest Green Rovers (loan), Weymouth, Eastleigh (1993-2009)*
Andy Harris came through the academy at Liverpool and signed professionally before moving to Southend without making a single appearance for the first team. He then spent four years with Leyton Orient before dropping into the non-leagues of English football. Harris later moved into teaching and taught a National Football Studies course at Kingston Maurward College in Dorset. He is also a member of Mensa International, which is the largest and oldest high IQ society in the world. He appeared on the ITV1 programme Britain's Brainiest Footballers in 2002 and possesses an IQ of 153. He is also the chairman of Weymouth Cougars Youth Football Club.

## HARRISON, Paul

*Goalkeeper*
**Born:** *1984 Liverpool*
**Playing career:** *Liverpool, Leeds United (loan), Wolverhampton Wanderers, Chester-City, Hereford United, Southport, The New Saints (2003-2007)*

Paul Harrison is another attendee of Liverpool's youth academy who failed to make a single appearance for the club – which demonstrates the difficulty in cutting it as a professional. He did, however, make the bench on three occasions. When he left Liverpool he struggled to find a home and recorded only 23 league appearances during his first four years in professional football. However, that changed when he signed for The New Saints and he is heavily regarded as a club legend for the Welsh football team. He is still under contract there and has set a Welsh Premier League record for the most successive starts with 190+ dating back to 2007. He has won six Welsh Premier League titles and four Welsh Cups with the side.

## HARRISON, Wayne

*Striker*
**Born:** *1967 Stockport*
**Died:** 2013
**Playing career:** *Oldham Athletic, Liverpool, Crewe Alexandra. (1984-1991)*

When Wayne Harrison moved from Oldham to Liverpool in 1985, he became the most expensive 17-year-old in the world. He signed for Liverpool for a phenomenal fee of £250,000 which truly portrayed the belief the club had in the youngster. Unfortunately, a blight of injuries cost him dearly and despite spending six years on Liverpool's books, he failed to make a single appearance for the senior side. He was loaned back to Oldham and Crewe three years later before being forced to retire in 1991 due to an irreparable knee injury. In total, he made 10 league appearances in his four years as a professional footballer. The injury was so bad he was forced to miss his testimonial games at Boundary Park in 1992 between Oldham and Liverpool. Whilst at Liverpool, he fell through a greenhouse and almost died due to the massive blood loss he endured. After his retiring, he played Sunday League football and worked as an HGV driver for a local brewery. He died on 25 December 2013 at the age of 46, after suffering from pancreatic illness.

Jimmy Harrop

## HARROP, Jimmy

*Defender*
**Born:** *1884 Sheffield, Yorkshire* **Died:** 1958
**Playing career:** *Ranmoor Wesleyans, Sheffield Wednesday, Denaby United, Rotherham Town, Liverpool, Aston Villa,Sheffield United, Burton All Saints (1900-1924)*

Jimmy Harrop started off as a forward but was quickly transitioned into a centre-half whilst at Rotherham, where he was appointed captain. When Liverpool signed the Yorkshireman they were looking for a replacement to the well-respected Alec Raisbeck – and that's exactly what they found in Harrop in 1908. His performances in a Liverpool shirt were brilliant, with his delicate footwork and strong defending winning many of the Kop over. He would stay in the heart of the club's defence for the next four years. Liverpool finished in the bottom half of the First Division for the first three seasons but finished runners-up to Aston Villa in his final year. Ironically, both Harrop and Sam Hardy left for Villa in the summer and won the FA Cup in their debut season with the Midlands-based club. He remained contracted with the club until 1921 and played in 170 league and cup matches for the team.

### "DID YOU KNOW?"

*"In 1974, a local factory threatened to go on strike when Bill Shankly said that he would be resigning."*

## HARROWER, Jimmy

*Inside-forward*

**Born:** *1935 Alva, Clackmannanshire* **Died:** 2006
**Playing career:** *Sauchie, Kilsyth Rangers, Bo'ness United, Hibernian, Liverpool, Newcastle United, Falkirk, St Johnstone, Albion Rovers (1954-1966)*

Jimmy Harrower was a talented winger who averaged a goal less than every five games. At times, he would demonstrate capabilities that very few players possessed playing in the English leagues. If he could have remained consistent, he would have surely had a longer career at Anfield. He signed for Liverpool in January 1958 when he was 22 years old but the club had tried to sign him two years prior to no avail. He played in 12 games during his debut season and found the net twice but it was the following campaign where he truly began to shine. He only missed five games of the successive year but the arrival of Bill Shankly spelt the end for Harrower as Jimmy Melia was the preferred man for the inside-left position. He moved to Newcastle before returning to Scotland. He passed away on 29 August 2006 and was well remembered by Liverpool fans on forums, where they recollected their memories of the fiery winger.

## HARSTON, Ted

*Centre-forward*

**Born:** *1907 Monk Bretton* **Died:** 1971
**Playing career:** *Sheffield Wed, Barnsley, Reading, Bristol City, Mansfield Town, Liverpool (1928-1939)*

Liverpool showed interest in Ted Harston after he scored 81 goals in only 70 league matches for Mansfield Town. Incredibly, he scored 55 of Mansfield's 91 goals in the 1936/37 season! However, Harston only played for Liverpool on five occasions during the first half of the 1937/38 campaign. He scored after only 13 minutes into his debut at Chelsea but Liverpool were comprehensively beaten 6-1. He scored twice in the following game against Portsmouth but lost his place to Fed Howe after four matches of the new season. His final appearance came from the bench as he replaced Howe away to Blackpool towards the end of November. He unfortunately broke his leg the following year which finished his professional footballing career. He joined amateurs Shorts Football Club in August 1939. He died in Rochester, Kent in 1971.

## HARTLEY, Abe

*Right-back/Centre-forward*

**Born:** *1872 Dumbarton, Scotland* **Died:** 1909
**Playing career:** *Dumbarton, Everton, Liverpool, Southampton, Woolwich Arsenal, Burnley (1892-1900)*

Abe Hartley scored 5 goals in 8 games for Dumbarton (who at the time won the Scottish Football League in successive years), which encouraged Everton to tempt him south. Whilst never establishing himself as a first-choice striker he did bag 25 goals in his 50 appearances before crossing the city to sign for Liverpool. Around this time, the Association Footballers Union was fighting to gain better terms for their members and after just one season at Anfield, Hartley had the opportunity to earn more money by signing for Southampton. They were members of the Southern League and therefore free to pay more than their Football League counterparts and their investment paid off - Abe scored 25 times in 50 appearances and helped them win the title. He died in 1909, nine years after retiring from the game and still only 37 years old. He had taken up employment with the London and South West Railway but collapsed and died outside their pay office. During his playing days, it was claimed that he used to put a roll-up (cigarette) behind his ear before kick-off and smoke it at half time!

Abe Hartley

Steve Heighway

### HATELEY, Tony

*Striker*

**Born:** *1941 Derby*  **Died:** 2014

**Playing career:** *Notts County, Aston Villa, Chelsea, Liverpool, Coventry City, Birmingham City, Notts County, Oldham Athletic. (1958-1973).*

When Tony Hateley arrived at Anfield in 1967, he was the club's record signing for a fee of £96,000 after he swapped the blue side of London for Merseyside. He scored an incredible 27 times in his first season with the club but failed to emulate that success going forward. His final appearance came against Leeds on the final day of August 1968 and he moved to Coventry. Despite his impressive goal tally for the club, the striker moved away from Liverpool as he did not suit their style of play. Prior to the signing, Liverpool liked to move the ball quickly and find spaces with the sheer pace of the current side. However, when Hateley joined they found themselves playing the long-ball too frequently and failing to control games. In total, he played 429 league appearances throughout his career and scored 209 goals. The combined amount of all of his transfer fees broke the record for an individual English player at the time. He died at the age of 72 on 1 February 2014 after a long battle against illness.

Vegard Heggam

### HEGGEM, Vegard

*Right-back*

**Born:** *1975 Trondheim, Norway*

**Playing career:** *Rennebu IL, Orkdal IL, Rosenborg, Liverpool (1982-2003)*

Vegard Heggem scored the winning goal for Rosenborg that ensured the Norwegian team would qualify ahead of Italian giant's AC Milan during the 1996/97 Champions League. He was brought to Liverpool and spent five years with the club but failed to make a single appearance during the final three years of his contract and was forced to retire at the age of 28 after a plight of successive injuries. After retiring from the game, he set up a salmon fishing business on the river Orkla. He is an official patron of A.F.C Liverpool, who are an independent football club owned and governed by Liverpool supporters. He is a regular attendee of Liverpool home matches and he was present at the 2005 Champions League Final.

### HEIGHWAY, Steve

*Winger*

**Born:** *1947 Dublin, Ireland*

**Playing career:** *Skelmersdale United, Liverpool, Minnesota Kicks, Philadelphia Fever (indoor) (1970-1982)*

Steve Heighway had the ability that many professionals would kill for. He could evade tackles, demonstrate perfect ball-control, deliver great passes and, of course, find the back of net consistently. He is undoubtedly one of the trickiest players to ever pull on the Liverpool shirt. He signed for Bill Shankly's Liverpool in May 1970 and would stay with the club for 11 years. He was a university graduate with a degree in economics - a stark contrast to his career in professional football. Bobby Graham broke his leg in a match against Chelsea in early October which gave way for a long run in the senior team for Heighway which lasted virtually a decade! He introduced himself to the Kop when Liverpool were trailing the Merseyside derby 2-0 in November 1970. He picked up the ball on the left-wing, beat numerous players and squeezed the ball into the bottom corner past Andy Ranking in the Everton goal. Seven minutes later, his accurate cross was headed home by John Toshack before Chris Lawler got a dramatic winner. (Cont'd)

Heighway won four League Championships, one FA Cup, two European Cups and two UEFA Cups whilst at Liverpool. He eventually fell down the pecking order at Anfield and moved to American club Minnesota Kicks. He enjoyed life in the States and developed his coaching skills at Umbro which led to a position at the Clearwater Chargers Youth Soccer Club, where he was appointed in the role of Director of Coaching in the United States. In 1989 Kenny Dalglish appointed Heighway to youth development officer at Anfield and he was at the forefront of Liverpool's academy. He remained in this role until his retirement in 2007 and helped bring through stars such as Robbie Fowler, Steven Gerrard and Michael Owen.

Stephane Henchoz

## HENCHOZ, Stephane

*Defender*

**Born:** *1974 Billens, Switzerland*
**Playing career:** *Bulle, Neuchatel Xamax, Hamburger SV, Blackburn Rovers , Liverpool, Celtic, Wigan Athletic, Blackburn Rovers (1989-2008)*

When Liverpool made a move for Stephane Henchoz, many criticised the club. There was a clause in his contract with Blackburn Rovers that enabled the Swiss star to leave for a fee of £3.5 million if Rovers were relegated, which is exactly what happened. Henchoz was a fantastic man-marker, would time his tackles superbly and had a brilliant temperament. He started off as a midfielder with Neuchatel Xamax and made his debut at the Bernabeu against Real Madrid at the age of 17 after coming off the bench. He was offered a contract at Manchester United in the summer of 1997 but negotiations fell through after United doubted his fitness levels. He joined Liverpool in 1999 but missed the first few months of the season following a groin injury. However, he quickly settled into the team and would often go into hotel rooms at 10:30 pm to make sure all the players were in the correct place! Liverpool had a fantastic season during Henchoz's second year with the club and his controversial moment during the FA Cup final – where he used his hand to prevent the ball going into the net – earnt him the nickname of 'Handchoz'. He eventually fell out of favour at Anfield and the appointment of Rafael Benitez spelt the end for him at Liverpool and he moved to Celtic before returning to England to play for Wigan and Blackburn. Since retiring as a player, he has moved into management and resigned from his role with FC Sion in 2019.

## TAYLOR, Phil

*Wing-half*

**Born:** *1917 Bristol* **Died:** 2012
**Playing career:** *Bristol Rovers, Liverpool (1935-1954)*

Having started his career with local club Bristol Rovers as an attacking player, Phil Taylor was later developed into a defensive wing-half during his time with Liverpool. Taylor spent a staggering 18 years with Liverpool and played in 312 league games for the club. He was also a keen cricketer, even being selected by Gloucestershire's first team in 1938 before playing in several second XI matches for the county.

After retiring from playing, he became Liverpool manager in 1956. He was ambitious and vowed to get Liverpool 'back where they belonged'. Ironically, after four years of attempting promotion, he resigned from his role. Before his death in 2012, he was believed to have been the oldest player who represented England prior to the Second World War to still be living.

## HESKEY, Emile

*Striker*
**Born:** *1978 Leicester*
**Playing career:** *Leicester City, Liverpool, Birmingham City, Wigan Athletic, Aston Villa, Newcastle Jets, Bolton Wanderers (1987-2014)*

Emile Heskey signed for Liverpool for £11 million from Leicester City in 2000 and spent four years with the club. During this time, he netted 60 times in 223 games. His signature set the then transfer record for Liverpool. During his first season with the club, Heskey won the FA Cup, League Cup and UEFA Cup treble. In 2002, he made a six-figure donation to aid a consortium led by Gary Lineker that was to assist with the purchase of Leicester City, who were struggling financially at the time. The signing of Milan Baros effectively ended his Anfield career and he later moved to Birmingham City. He was capped 62 times for England and scored 7 goals for his country. He started his coaching career at Cheshire League One club Egerton in 2017.

Emile Heskey

## HEWITT, Charlie

*Darlington/England*
**Born:** *1884 Greatham, County Durham* **Died:** 1966
**Playing career:** *Middlesbrough, Tottenham Hotspur, Liverpool, West Bromwich Albion, Spennymoor United, Crystal Palace (1904-1919)*

Charlie Hewitt signed for Tottenham from Middlesbrough in 1906, which left the footballing world confused. He was expected to sign for Liverpool but did not hear of their bid until he signed for Spurs! He attempted to force his way to the Merseyside club but the FA ruled that he had to honour his one-year contract with the north London club. After the season was finished, he immediately signed for Liverpool but only spent one year with the club as he failed to settle into their style of play. After his playing days, he experienced success as a manager. He promoted Chester to the Football League and took Millwall out of the Third Division South in 1938 – he also got them to the FA Cup semi-finals in 1937. He was known as 'captain' by his teammates as he previously spent time as a naval skipper. Throughout his life, it has been reported that Hewitt saved a total of 11 lives, which was recognised with Human Society Medals.

## HEYDON, John

*Half-back*
**Born:** *1928 Birkenhead* **Died:** 2012
**Playing career:** *Everton, Liverpool, Millwall, Tranmere Rovers (1946-1961)*

John Heydon signed for Liverpool in January 1949 after he had lost patience being stuck in Everton's reserve team for three years. However, he had to wait until October 1950 before making his senior side debut and played a total of 13 times during the 1950/51 season where he was primarily used as cover for Phil Taylor. His hard work finally paid off and he was rewarded with an extended run in the side from November 1951 to January 1952 before he indefinitely lost his place in the side. He eventually moved to Millwall in May 1953 and stayed with the London club for a few years before returning to Merseyside to finish his career with Tranmere – becoming one of the three players who played for all three clubs in the area. After he retired he became a bookmaker and died in September 2012.

## HICKSON, Dave

*Striker*
**Born:** *1929 Salford*
**Died:** 2013
**Playing career:** *Everton, Aston Villa, Huddersfield Town, Everton, Liverpool, Bury, Tranmere Rovers. (1951-1963).*

Dave Hickson established himself as a quality player whilst at Everton. Both sets of supporters were horrified with the signing as Everton fans were disgusted he joined Liverpool and the latter's supporters were furious that the board would even contemplate signing a player from the blue side of Merseyside. Alas, he crossed Stanley Park and was a useful player for Liverpool. Ironically, Hickson's final game for Everton was at Anfield where the visitors won 2-0 in the Floodlight Cup. He was given a big kiss on his Liverpool debut by a fan for good luck and he scored both goals as Liverpool beat Aston Villa 2-1. He scored 15 goals in 15 games to end the season but Liverpool failed to achieve First Division status. He was less effective in his second season and the arrival of Ian St John in 1961 signalled the end for Hickson's Liverpool career. He is also one of the trio who played for all three professional Merseyside clubs! After his playing career finished, he went to Ireland as player-manager of Ballymena, then took a job as a bricklayer and later worked in a pub. He also spent time living in Ellesmere Port where he worked for the Local Authority. During the final years of his life he returned to Everton and despite being older than 80, he worked as a tour guide for the club.

## HINNIGAN, Joe

*Defender*
**Born:** *1955 Liverpool*
**Playing career:** *South Liverpool, Wigan Athletic, Sunderland, Preston North End, Gillingham, Wrexham, Chester-City (1975-1990)*

Having impressed with non-league South Liverpool, Joe Hinnigan joint Wigan and spent five years with the club as a prominent player. His playing career spanned 18 years and he played for six professional clubs. After retiring, he stayed within the football industry and worked as a physio at Wigan, Rochdale, Chester and Bury – all under manager Graham Barrow. He is currently the physio at Accrington Stanley and has held that role since 2008.

## HOARE, Joe

*Full-buck*
**Born:** *1881 Southampton*
**Died:** 1947
**Playing career:** *Southampton Oxford, Southampton, Liverpool, Southampton, Bitterne Guild, Salisbury City, Woolston (1902-1912)*

Joe Hoare was born in Southampton and trained as a carpenter and joiner whilst playing amateur football with Southampton Oxford Football Club. He joined Southampton Football Club in 1902 and became understudy to England star George Molyneux. Although he only played in four league matches for the Saints, he had offers from both Reading and Liverpool – he chose the latter and signed in 1903. He made seven league appearances during his sole season with Liverpool before moving back to the south coast to re-join Southampton. He retired from professional football in 1905 and became the proprietor of a tobacconist's shop in Woolston. He then returned to the sport on an amateur basis – although he did momentarily come out of retirement to feature for Saints in the 1907 Southern Charity Cup Final. He died at West End, Hampshire on 24 March 1947.

## HOBSON, Alf

*goalkeeper*
**Born:** *1913 Leamside, Country Durham*
**Died:** 2004
**Playing career:** *Ferryhill Athletic, Shildon Colliery, Chester City, Liverpool, South Liverpool (1938-1947)*

Alf Hobson featured heavily during the initial half of the 1936/37 season but a disastrous two months between December and January saw him dropped as Liverpool picked up one point and he conceded 17! He made one appearance the following season before the Second World War disrupted the usual football season. He did, however, feature 170 times for Liverpool in wartime. Liverpool TV had made contact with the Hobson family to interview Hobson, but he sadly passed away before he could reminisce on a topsy-turvy Liverpool career.

### "DID YOU KNOW?"

*"The Pink Floyd song 'Fearless' features Liverpool fans singing 'You'll Never Walk Alone'."*

## HODGSON, Dave

*Striker*

**Born:** *1960 Gateshead*
**Playing career:** *Middlesbrough, Liverpool, Sunderland, Norwich City, Middlesbrough, Sheffield Wednesday, Swansea City. (1978-1991)*

Arriving from Middlesbrough as an England U- 21 international, there was a lot of promise around Dave Hodgson's signature. Unfortunately, his potential wasn't displayed enough and he had to settle for being a bit-part player. Ultimately, this influenced him to sign for Sunderland where he was likely to get more games, despite current manager, Joe Fagan, pleading with the Englishman to speak to him before signing any papers. After retiring as a player, Hodgson had three spells with Darlington United as manager and even wrote a book titled: *'Three Times A Quaker: My World of Football and Passion for Darlington F.C.'*. He is currently the director of sport at Blackett Hart and Prat LLP.

## HODGSON, Gordon

*Forward*

**Born:** *1904 Johannesburg, South Africa*
**Died:** 1951
**Playing career:** *Benoni, Rustenburg, Pretoria, Transvaal, Liverpool, Aston Villa, Leeds United (1919-1939)*

Gordon Hodgson is not only one of Liverpool's greatest ever strikers, but one of the best to ever grace the Football League. He played 377 times for Liverpool and scored an incredible 241 goals – a goal every 1.56 games. Despite being born in South Africa, Hodgson represented England and was awarded with a Liverpool contract in December 1925. In total, Hodgson scored 17 hat-tricks – which remains a club record in 2019. After 11 brilliant years in a red shirt he moved to Aston Villa in January 1936 at the age of 31. In addition to his incredible footballing ability, he also featured for Lancashire Cricket Club and played in 56 first-class matches. Whilst playing as an amateur he once took all ten wickets against Liverpool Police for just 13 runs! He managed Port Vale for five years and was even interviewed for the Liverpool position but narrowly lost out to Don Welsh. He died only a few months after that interview from cancer on 14 June 1951.

## HOOPER, Mike

*Goalkeeper*

**Born:** *1964 Bristol*
**Playing career:** *Bristol City, Wrexham, Liverpool, Leicester City, Newcastle U, Sunderland (1983-1995)*

Mike Hooper impressed with Fourth Division Wrexham, in addition to receiving a degree in English literature at Swansea University before Liverpool came knocking. He was told that he would be used as cover for Bruce Grobbelaar who hadn't missed a game for the previous four years! Hooper's longest run in the team was 25 consecutive matches in 1988/89. Although he showed signs of brilliance at times, it was widely accepted that he was not good enough to be Liverpool's number one. He moved to Newcastle in 1993 but remained as second choice and hung up his gloves in the summer of 1996 at the age of only 32. Hooper found work as a security bouncer in Chetser-Le-Street after his playing days. He is also an avid bird watcher who holds expansive knowledge about the animals.

## HOPKIN, Fred

*Outside-left*
**Born:** *1895 Dewsbury*
**Died:** 1970
**Playing career:** *Tottenham Hotspur (guest), Manchester United, Liverpool, Darlington (1912-1932)*

Fred Hopkin was signed by Liverpool from Manchester United in 1921. United were given a fine of £350 at the time for paying Hopkin more than the maximum wage and for promising him a cut of his transfer fee which was illegal. Hopkin was an absolute menace from the left-wing and would regularly send defenders the wrong way. He won two League Championships with the club in successive seasons of 1921/22 and 1922/23. Although he did not find the back of the net too often, he was known for his creativity in producing assists for his teammates. He was also a fantastic hurdler who won hurdling competitions. He finished his career with Darlington and retired in 1932. He died 5 March 1970.

## HOUGHTON, Ray

*Midfielder*
**Born:** *1962 Glasgow, Scotland*
**Playing career:** *West Ham United, Fulham, Oxford United, Liverpool, Aston Villa, Crystal Palace, Reading. (1981-1999)*

Ray Houghton was use to rejection as West Ham released him after only one game and U-18 Scotland manager, Andy Roxburgh, said he wasn't good enough for Scotland. He went on to star for Ireland and

scored the winner in the 1988 European Championships group game against England. He was snapped up by Fulham after being rejected by the Hammers and made 145 appearances across a four-year spell with the west-London club. He joined Oxford United and won the League Cup in his debut season. He was viewed as the final piece of the Kenny Dalglish jigsaw and he was brought to Anfield for £825,000 in 1987. He scored two minutes after coming off the bench on his debut for Liverpool and generally slotted in smoothly to give the manager even more options. He won two league titles and two FA Cups with Liverpool before moving forward with Aston Villa and eventually finishing his career with Reading. He embarked on a media career after his playing days and has worked for outlets such as: RTÉ, Sky Sports, TalkSPORT and LFC TV.

## HOWE, Fred

*Striker*
**Born:** *1912 Bredbury, Cheshire* **Died:** 1984
**Playing career:** *Wilmslow,Hyde United,Stockport County,Hyde United,Liverpool,Manchester City,Grimsby Town,Oldham Athletic (1929-1947)*

Fred Howe was recommended to Liverpool by former star Tommy Johnson, who saw the striker feature for Hyde United. He joined the 'Pool in 1935 for a fee of £400 and made his debut against Derby before going on to play in six of the final seven league games that year.

Ray Houghton

**Fred Howe**

He was a consistent player and only missed four domestic games the following season as Liverpool finished second to Aston Villa. He had one more solid season with the club before age finally caught up with him and he was sold to Preston. When he retired from football, he remained in the city of his final club and worked as a labourer and a night watchman. During his final years, he was in poor health and went blind towards the end of 1936. He died on 21 July 1937 at the age of 69.

## HUGHES, Emlyn

*Defender/Midfielder*
**Born:** *1947 Barrow-in-Furness, Lancashire*
**Died:** 2004
**Playing career:** *Blackpool, Liverpool, Wolverhampton Wanderers, Rotherham United, Hull City, Swansea City. (1965-1983)*

It is hard to pinpoint a man more passionate about the Liverpool jersey than Emlyn Hughes. Billy Shankly saw him playing in one of his first games for Blackpool and immediately offered £25,000 for him. However, Blackpool were not keen on selling the versatile player but Liverpool were promised first refusal if the player ever became available – Shankly then rang Hughes every Sunday to tell him he would become a Liverpool player soon! Hughes recalled how the weekly event had stuck with him his entire life: "Today, thirty years later, I still associate the smell of bacon frying with the telephone ringing at 8.30 sharp on a Sunday morning". Shanks finally got his man on 27 February 1967 but had to part with £65,000 in order to secure his services. He was thrown straight into the side and quickly got the nickname 'Crazy Horse' after he rugby-tackled Newcastle's forward Albert Bennett to the floor! In total, Hughes would spend 11 years at Anfield and win almost every honour available with the club: four League Championships, one FA Cup, two European Cups and one UEFA Cup. He played in 665 matches and contributed with 49 goals. When he hung up his boots, he managed Rotherham for two years before becoming a nationally recognised celebrity – regularly appearing on television and radio. He died in November 2004 after a 14-year battle with a brain tumour.

He scored in three successive matches against Aston Villa, Stoke City and Chelsea. Howe would be the club's leading goal scorer for the next two seasons with 17 goals in 36 during the 1925/26 campaign and 17 from 36 the following year. His biggest moment for the Reds came when he scored four against Everton in the club's biggest win over their eternal rivals. Prior to this, only three other players had scored hat-tricks against their local opponents: Harry Chambers in 1922, Dick Forshaw in 1925 and Harold Barton in 1933. 77 years had to pass before a fourth member was added to that list – Steven Gerrard. However, no one has matched Howe's quadruple which keeps him in the history books at Liverpool!

## HOWELL, Rab

*Right-Half-back*
**Born:** *1867 Dore Moor, Sheffield* **Died:** 1937
**Playing career:** *Rotherham Swifts, Sheffield United, Liverpool, Preston North End (1887-1903)*

Rab Howell was the first gypsy to represent both Liverpool and England in football. He was born in a Romany caravan in Wincobank, Sheffield. He played in 24 of Sheffield United's 30 league games before arriving at Anfield and playing the final game of the 1897/98 season.

## HUGHES, John

*Defender*

**Born:** *1887 Flintshire, Wales* **Died:** 1950
**Playing career:** *Aberdare Athletic, Liverpool,
Plymouth Argyle (1900-1906)*

John Hughes was born in Wales but moved
to Liverpool quite young with his parents
so he could be termed a local player. Fellow
Welshman and current Liverpool player
Maurice Parry, recommended Hughes for a
trial at the club and he must have impressed
as he was signed not too long after. He only
missed three games of his only season and
played primarily at half-back. Unfortunately,
it was an unsuccessful campaign that
ended in Liverpool being relegated; the
club finished 17th but won the title only
three years prior. He was shipped off to
Plymouth in the summer but only made
one appearance for his new club as he was
still carrying an injury from his time with
Liverpool and he retired from football in
January 1907. In addition to his footballing
ability, Hughes was also a lightweight
boxing champion. He was an extraordinary
brave man who saved four people from
drowning! Two were rescued from the River
Mersey, including a child who had fallen
into a clay pit.

## HUGHES, Laurie

*Defender*

**Born:** *1924 Liverpool* **Died:** 2011
**Playing career:** *Liverpool (1943-1950)*

Laurie Hughes asked both Everton and
Liverpool for trials during his junior years
but both clubs refused as they worried that
his lack of height would prevent him from
playing at the highest level – how wrong
they both originally were. Hughes spent 6
years with the 'Pool and represented the
club 326 times. He started his career playing
as an inside-forward but as he grew taller
he was shifted to the centre-half position.
He signed for Liverpool in February 1943
and played in the remainder of the Reds'
wartime matches. Liverpool won the First
Division title during the opening season
after the conclusion of the war but further
success never came. He was the first
Liverpool player to feature in the World
Cup finals when he was selected for the 1950
tournament. Hughes played his final game
in October 1959, a couple of months before
Bill Shankly arrived. When he retired as a
player he ran a grocery store. However, he
was fined £20 for selling stolen food from
Woolworths! He died at his home on 9
September 2011, aged 87.

Emlyn Hughes

## HUNT, Roger
*Striker*
**Born:** *1938 Glazebury, Cheshire*
**Playing career:** *Liverpool, Bolton W (1959-1971).*
Roger Hunt was spotted by Liverpool
whilst playing for Stockton Heath in the
Mid-Cheshire league and was subsequently
signed. He had only featured in six reserve
games before he got his chance in the
senior side, making his debut against
Scunthorpe in the absence of Billy Liddell
in September 1959. He scored on his debut
and demonstrated his talent in front of the
adoring Kop. As he played in more games
he continued to show off his pace, strength,
skill and powerful shot that he possessed.
When Hunt had joined, Liverpool fell short
four consecutive times in their attempt to
regain promotion to the topflight of English
football. They were eventually promoted
during the 1961/62 season where the striker
scored 41 goals in 41 games – including
five hat-tricks! Over the next four seasons,
he would score 129 times in only 160
appearances as Liverpool won the League
Championship in 1964 and the 1965 FA Cup.
Hunt was Liverpool's top scorer for eight
successive seasons and in 1967 he broke
Gordon Hodgson's goalscoring record at the
club by netting his 242nd goal for Liverpool.
Despite his incredible eye for goal, he
received a weekly letter from one fan who
clearly didn't like him:

Roger Hunt

"Dear Over-the-bar-Hunt. I see you missed
another couple of sitters on Saturday". In
March 1969 the normally cool Hunt lost
his temper when he was substituted and
he threw his jersey in the direction of the
dugout. He eventually lost his place in the
following Autumn and signed for Bolton
in December 1969. Ian Rush broke Hunt's
overall goalscoring record on 18 October
1992, but he still holds the record for the
most league goals with 244. He was awarded
an MBE in 2000. When he retired in 1972 he
joined the family's haulage company and in
1975 he became a member of the Pools Panel.
He is now retired and lives in Warrington.

## HUNTER, John
*Centre-forward*
**Born:** *1878 Johnstone, Scotland* **Died:** 1966
**Playing career:** *Abercorn, Liverpool, Heart of
Midlothian, Woolwich Arsenal, Portsmouth, Dundee,
Clyde (1896-1911)*
John 'Sailor' Hunter played as an inside-
forward and scored five times from 20
First Division appearances in the 1899/00
campaign, before netting three further goals
the following year when Liverpool won their
first-ever League Championship. He played
one final time towards the end of March
1902 before returning to Scotland to play for
Hearts. He had one final spell in England
with Woolwich Arsenal and Portsmouth
before returning to his homeland to
finish his career. His finest season was
with Dundee, when he scored 28 goals
in 31 league matches. He was appointed
manager of Motherwell in 1911 at the age
of 32. It was the club's first-ever season and
incredibly, he would remain in this role for
35 years! He only left this position because
his eyesight was failing. The club, however,
accommodated one of their greatest legends
in an administrative role from 1946-1959
until he was 80 years old. Unsurprisingly, he
is the club's longest serving manager, seeing
out 1,064 games and winning the 1932
Scottish League after his team scored 199
goals in only 38 league games!

## "DID YOU KNOW?"

*"The famous 'This is Anfield' sign
was Bill Shankly's way of striking
fear into the opposition."*

Don Hutchison

## HUTCHISON, Don

*Midfielder*

**Born:** *1971 Gateshead*
**Playing career:** *Hartlepool United, Liverpool, West Ham United, Sheffield United, Everton, Sunderland, Millwall, Coventry City, Luton Town (1989-2008)*

Don Hutchison enjoyed a long spell in Liverpool's team during the 1992/93 campaign, playing in 42 games and scoring ten goals. He was a fine passer of the ball, a competitive player and had enough ability to cause any opposition trouble. However, his immature attitude and off-field antics cost him his time at Liverpool – revealing his 'crown jewels' in a city centre bar was the last straw. He did, however, represent Scotland after he left Liverpool in 1994. In the summer of 2009 he participated in the 'Celebrity Soccer Six' tournament at Stamford Bridge. This angered fans of the club as the Sun were present and it fell on the twentieth anniversary of the Hillsborough disaster. He now works as a match summariser for TalkSPORT.

## HYSEN, Glenn

*Defender*

**Born:** *1959 Gothenburg, Sweden*
**Playing career:** *IFK Goteborg, PSV Eindhoven, Fiorentina, Liverpool, GAIS, IF Warta (1978-1994)*

Prior to joining Liverpool, Glenn Hysen was well travelled as he had played in Sweden, Germany and Holland. He came to light during his displays against England in two 1990 World Cup qualifying matches that inspired interest from multiple English clubs. He had verbally agreed to join Manchester United before Liverpool stole the defender right under their noses. When he arrived at Anfield he was already well respected throughout Europe, captain of the Swedish international side and won the 1987 Golden Ball.

He was awarded man of the match on his debut in the 1989 Charity Shield against Arsenal and had an excellent season when the club won the League Championship in 1990. It was the arrival of Graeme Souness that spelt the end for Hysen at Anfield, as he was only chosen five times to start during the 1991/92 season. He returned to Sweden in 1992 and signed for GAIS as the club had promised to build him a house in return. Unfortunately, they were in deep financial trouble and went down – the fans blamed Hysen for the relegation and the trouble at the club. He hung up his boots in 1994 and is one of Sweden's most well-known and respected sportsman. When he retired he worked in television media and as a coach in Sweden. He was, however, involved in a violent incident at Frankfurt airport after a male had groped him in the toilets.

Glenn Hysen

#ÅRETSFAN

## HYYPIA, Sami

*Defender*

**Born:** *1973 Porvoo, Finland*
**Playing career:** *PaPe, Kumu, MyPa, Willem II,*
*Liverpool, Bayer Leverkusen (1977-2011)*

Sami Hyppia was a sensational player
for Liverpool, where he reminded fans of
the legendary giant Ron Yeats - who was
Bill Shankly's talisman defender. Hyppia
himself was a strong pillar in defence firstly
for Gerard Houllier before Rafael Benitez.
He was strong, intelligent and certainly
led by example. He signed for his local
club Kumu, at the age of 17 and decided to
undertake his National Service earlier rather
than later - as he knew it could be a problem
if he was going to play football away from
Finland. After 11 months of army training,
he impressed MyPa's scouts and joined
the topflight of Finnish football. He spent
four years with the club before he moved
to Holland to join Willem II. He was also
invited to two trials with Newcastle but
nothing materialised. Liverpool brought
the Finn to the club thanks to a cameraman
who alerted former Chief Executive Peter
Robinson about the young lad plying his
trade in the Dutch league. Scouts were sent
out and Hyppia was subsequently signed to
the club in May 1999 for a fee of £2.5 million.

Football under Roy Evans was inconsistent
to say the least. Yes, Liverpool scored many
goals – but they also leaked a lot. Hyppia
was brought in to stabilise the defence, and
he did just that. He stayed with the club for
11 years and won two FA Cups, one League
Cup, one UEFA Cup and the biggest of
them all, the 2005 Champions League. He
represented the club more than 450 times
and scored 35 goals. He eventually left for
Bayer Leverkusen in 2009 and hung up his
boots in 2011. He moved into management
after his playing days and had spells with
the Finland international team, Bayer
Leverkusen, Brighton and FC Zurich –
where he was sacked on 12 May 2016 after
he had lost a vote of no confidence from the
Swiss team.

### "DID YOU KNOW?"

*"Danish goalkeeper Michael
Stensgaard must rank as the holder
of the strangest injury award. He
dislocated a shoulder when setting
up an ironing board at home."*

Sami Hyppia

Paul Ince

## INCE, Paul

*Midfielder*

**Born:** *1967 Ilford, London*
**Playing career:** *West Ham United, Manchester United, Inter Milan, Liverpool, Middlesbrough, Wolverhampton Wanderers, Swindon Town, Macclesfield Town (1984-2007)*

Paul Ince was the complete midfielder who had the ability to pass, score and tackle. Having infuriated West Ham fans by posing in a Manchester United top prior to the announcement of the signing, Ince spent six years with the club and won every trophy on offer with the footballing giants. He moved to Italy for two years before surprisingly lending his services to Liverpool. In his debut season, only Michael Owen and Steven McManaman made more appearances than Ince's 40. During his two years with the club, Ince performed averagely. He was neither poor nor fantastic, he just done his job. Liverpool were trophy-less in both seasons but a personal highpoint was when he scored a late equaliser against Manchester United and celebrated emphatically in front of the Kop. A huge bust-up with then manager Gerard Houllier spelt the end for Ince at Liverpool and he subsequently moved to Middlesbrough. He won 52 caps for England and became the first black person to captain the English national side.

After his playing days he moved into management and had relative success with Mk Dons as he won the Football League Trophy on 31 March 2008 and then won promotion to League One after the Dons became League Two champions. In 2015 Ince passed his UEFA Pro Licence which is the highest managerial qualification in football and allows him to manage any team in Europe. However, he currently works as a match analyst for BBC and BT Sport.

## IRVINE, Alan

*Striker*

**Born:** *1962 Broxburn, Scotland*
**Playing career:** *Blackburn United, Hibernian, Falkirk, Liverpool, Dundee United, Shrewsbury Town, Mazda, St Mirren, Portadown, East Fife (1979-1995)*

Alan Irvine was a Scottish striker who failed to establish himself as part of Liverpool's senior team. He made four appearances – all from the bench – and failed to score a goal for the club. He was, however, the victim of a cruel practical joke. Liverpool's FA Cup match against Luton Town was called off and he was the only member of the team unaware. Kenny Dalglish then asked Irvine if he'd be comfortable playing in central-defence for the game. Reluctant to play so out of position, both Dalglish and Irvine settled on the Scotsman playing central-midfield. All of the players were told to leave the dressing room and Irvine sat solely by himself until it clicked that the game had been called off!

## IRWIN, Colin

*Defender*

**Born:** *1957 Liverpool*
**Playing career:** *Liverpool, Swansea City. (1979-1984)*

Colin Irwin was primarily used as cover for Alan Hansen or Phil Thompson at the centre of Liverpool's defence, as well as demonstrating his versatility by playing at left-back. He came through the youth academy and made his debut in August 1979. He scored in his second match for the club, but Liverpool fell 3-2 away to Southampton. He then lost his place in the side and would not feature for another six months. He almost made his debut a few years prior, while working as an electrician, as he was on standby for the 1977 FA Cup semi-final against Everton if veteran Tommy Smith had failed a fitness test.

He didn't, and he helped the side beat their dearest rivals 3-0. His best performance for the Reds came against Bayern Munich in second leg of the European cup semi-final but lost his starting position for the final against Real Madrid. The arrival of Mark Lawrenson pushed Irwin further afield and he joined Swansea for a club record fee of £340,000. In total, he won two European Cups and a League Championship whilst at Anfield. He retired from the game in 1984 and had two years as Bolton's assistant manager before leaving the game for good. He emigrated to Australia in 1987 and worked as a distribution manager for a wine and spirits wholesaler.

## ITANDJE, Charles

*Goalkeeper*
**Born:** *1982 Bobigny, France*
**Playing career:** *Red Star, Lens, Liverpool, Kavala (loan), Atromitos, PAOK, Konyaspor (loan), caykur Rizespor, Gaziantepspor, Adanaspor, Versailles (1997-)*

Charles Itandje impressed Liverpool whilst at Lens and the departure of Jerzy Dudek to Real Madrid influenced Liverpool's move for the French-born goalkeeper. However, with Pepe Reina as Liverpool's firm first-choice keeper, his senior team opportunities were limited. He played in all seven cup games during the 2008/09 season but his performances were questionable. The final straw came during the 20th anniversary of the Hillsborough disaster where Itandje was snickering and bothering Damien Plessis who sat next to him during the service. Although he was capped three times by France's U-21 team, he opted to play for Cameroon – where his parents were born – and played in the 2014 World Cup held in Brazil. Currently back in France playing for Versailles.

## JACKSON, Brian

*Outside-right*
**Born:** *1933 Walton-on-Thames*
**Playing career:** *Leyton Orient, Liverpool, Port Vale, Peterborough United, Lincoln City, Burton Albion, Boston United (1950-1966)*

Brian Jackson started his career in the Arsenal youth setup but was sold to Leyton Orient before making it as a professional in north-London. His performances there gathered lots of interest from top clubs, including Liverpool. When Liverpool made contact he was serving in the army completing his National Service but his commander granted his release. Liverpool parted with £6,500 and Donal Woan to secure his services in 1951. He netted on his debut for the club against Bolton but that was the only goal in 15 league appearances he would score. Although he stayed with the club for seven years, he was never a firm favourite at Anfield, making only 27 appearances as his highest in a singular campaign. He moved to Port Vale in July 1958, playing 178 games and scoring 34 goals before signing for Peterborough and finishing his Football League career with Lincoln City.

## JACKSON, James

*Full-back*
**Born:** *1900 Newcastle* **Died:** 1976
**Playing career:** *Queen's Park, Motherwell, Aberdeen, Liverpool (1918-1933)*

James Jackson joined Aberdeen in June 1923 for a club record transfer fee of £2,000 from Motherwell. After seven years in Scotland, Liverpool signed the full-back on controversial terms. Aberdeen's original asking fee was £4,500 but Liverpool were not financially ready to part with the money. Jackson then requested a transfer to the Merseyside club and Aberdeen finally agreed to a fee of £1,750 – less than half of the asking price! He had to wait two years before he was given an opportunity at Anfield but he certainly cemented his starting place by playing in 122 of 126 First Division games from August 1927 to May 1930. He was also made captain of the team during this time. He was given the nickname 'The Parson' whilst at Liverpool in reference to his religious beliefs. His father, named James also, was Arsenal's captain of their inaugural First Division season, so his son was very popular with their fanbase. It was said that he got the biggest standing ovation whenever Liverpool played at Highbury. He finished his university studies of Philosophy and Greek at Cambridge whilst playing for Liverpool - this forced him to miss three months of the 1932/33 season. After he had left the club he was ordained as a minister on 29 June 1933 and in May 1946 he was appointed president of the Liverpool Free Church Council. He eventually settled in Dorset, where he died on January 1 1977.

## JAMES, David
*Goalkeeper*
**Born:** *1970 Welwyn Garden City*
**Playing career:** *Watford, Liverpool, Aston Villa, West Ham United, Manchester City, Portsmouth, Bristol City, Bournemouth, iBV Vestmannaeyjar , Kerala Blasters (1986-2014)*

When David James arrived at Anfield he had the mightiest of tasks ahead of him – force Bruce Grobbelaar out of the team. Granted, the South African was ageing, but he was an absolute hero to the Kop. He made his debut in a 1-0 home loss to Nottingham Forest and after conceding 20 goals in 11 matches he was dropped. He did return to the side in January that saw him save a penalty against Paul Merson as Liverpool ran out 1-0 victors against Arsenal. During James' time with the club, he was nicknamed as a member of the 'Spice Boys', where it was deemed that several Liverpool players preferred the exclusive lifestyle of footballers as opposed to winning trophies. He made frequent mistakes for Liverpool and he was even labelled 'Calamity James'. The 'keeper blamed his love for video games on his mistakes. He did, however, win the 1995 League Cup with Liverpool but the arrival of American Brad Friedel paved the way for James to join Aston Villa after 277 games for Liverpool. After bouncing between many clubs, he retired from playing in 2014 and he won 53 caps for England. He has since moved into management and has managed Indian football team Kerala Blasters as player-manager in 2014 and then manager in 2018. In 2012, he famously stated that football had no issue with racism - in regard to employing black managers - and they were not offered jobs due to lack of qualifications. He now works primarily as a pundit for BT Sport.

## JEWELL, Paul
*Striker*
**Born:** *1964 Liverpool*
**Playing career:** *Liverpool, Wigan Athletic, Bradford City, Grimsby Town (loan) (1982-1995)*

Paul Jewell started his long footballing journey in the youth academy at Liverpool, but he was released without signing professional forms. Wigan, however, signed the striker and he spent four relatively-successful years with the club. He moved to Bradford in 1988 and stayed there for the remainder of his career, adding 56 more goals to his overall tally. When he retired as a player in 1998 he took over as manager of Bradford before being sacked in 2000.

David James

He returned to Wigan in 2001 and spent six years with the club before moving to Championship teams Derby and Ipswich. He was out of work for five years before returning to the fold in 2017 as Oldham's assistant manager, although he left his post in 2018. His son is a Yorkshire County golfer and his dad was a trade union activist in Liverpool. He currently resides in Witney.

## JOHNSON, David

*Striker*
**Born:** *1951 Liverpool*
**Playing career:** *Everton, Ipswich Town, Liverpool, Everton, Barnsley, Manchester City, Tulsa Roughnecks, Preston North End (1970-1984).*

Prior to joining Liverpool, 24-year-old David Johnson was already an England international having scored 46 goals for both Everton and Ipswich. The boyhood Liverpool supporter started his career with their rivals – which came as a "great shock" to his family who were all Reds! He scored the winning goal as a 20-year-old against the 'Pool which certainly got their attention. Bill Shankly enquired about bringing the forward to the club twice whilst at Everton, but nothing materialised. It wasn't until he was at Ipswich when Liverpool finally got their man. He was viewed as a long-term replacement for John Toshack but had to spend a large proportion of his debut season on the bench. He was forced to watch Liverpool triumph in the 1977 European Cup final from the bench. He finally established himself in the team

during the latter half of the 1978/79 season and his best year in red was the following year when he scored 27 goals. He won four League Championships, one League Cup and two European Cups whilst at Liverpool. The arrival of Ian Rush influenced a move back to Everton in August 1992 and he remained with the Toffees for a couple of years before trying his luck in America. He was nicknamed 'Doc' as he would always carry cough sweets as he constantly had a bad throat. He now lives in Liverpool and previously worked for an insurance company. He currently hosts corporate fans at Anfield and works as a radio pundit.

## JOHNSON, Dick

*Forward*
**Born:** *1895 Gateshead* **Died:** 1933
**Playing career:** *Liverpool, Felling Colliery, Stoke City, New Brighton, Connah's Quay (1919-1933)*

Dick Johnson certainly knew where the goal was situated and he averaged a goal every other game during his debut season with Liverpool. However, the following season he sustained a nasty injury that forced him to watch his team win their third League Championship from the side lines in 1922/23. Despite the setback, he returned in fine form, netting 14 more goals and only missing five league games the following campaign. He was only used twice in the following year as a serious knee injury kept him out for a large majority of the season. He left for Stoke in February 1925 to round off a topsy-turvy time with Liverpool. He was still playing football for Connah's Quay when his death took place on 3 January 1933, at the age of 38.

## JOHNSON, Glen

*Right-back*
**Born:** *1984 Greenwich*
**Playing career:** *West Ham United, Millwall, Chelsea, Portsmouth, Liverpool, Stoke City (1993-2019)*

Glen Johnson started his career playing for Harry Redknapp's West Ham but after only 16 appearances, he became the first signing for Chelsea owner Roman Abramovich in 2003 for £6 million. He made his debut for the Blues against Liverpool on 17 August 2003 as his side ran out as 2-1 winners. He eventually lost his place at Stamford Bridge and was loaned out to Portsmouth for the entirety of the 2006/07 season.

David Johnson

Glen Johnson

He joined Portsmouth permanently before moving to Anfield for £17.5 million in the summer of 2009. His first season was average for the Reds, although he featured in 35 of the club's 56 competitive fixtures. He began to star for Liverpool in the following few seasons and was rewarded with starting every fixture of the 2010 World Cup. His contract expired in 2015 after exactly 200 appearances and he won the 2012 League Cup whilst at Anfield. He joined Stoke and stayed with the club for three years before bringing the curtain down on his playing career in 2018. He now works for a pundit on TalkSPORT and continues his work with the Johnson Soccer School alongside former West Ham player Sam Taylor. In January 2007 Johnson was forced to pay a £80 fine as B&Q believed he had stolen bathroom fittings from their store!

The police were called and he was given an option to either pay an £80 fine or fight the charges in court. In total, the cost of the fitting was £2.35 but B&Q would not allow the footballer to pay the small amount. He opted for the fine.

## JOHNSON, Tommy
*Striker*
**Born:** *1901 Dalton-in-Furness*
**Died:** 1973
**Playing career:** *Dalton Athletic , Dalton Casuals, Manchester City, Everton, Liverpool, Darwen (1919-1939)*

Tommy Johnson is a Manchester City legend who enjoyed brief spells with both Everton and Liverpool. In total, he scored 158 goals for City in 328 league appearances. His record of 38 goals in 39 first division matches still stands. When he left City for Everton, it sparked a huge reaction by the fans and their attendance dropped by a staggering 7,000! After retiring, Johnson ran a pub in Stockport called the Woodman Inn before he took over the Crown Inn in Gorton. In 1977, a street near Maine Road was named Tommy Johnson Walk in his honour.

## JOHNSTON, Craig
*Midfielder*
**Born:** *1960 Johannesburg, South Africa*
**Playing career:** *Middlesbro, Liverpool. (1977-1987).*

Craig Johnston was the workhorse that helped Liverpool be so successful in the 1980's. Born in South Africa but raised in Australia, the midfielder was so confident in his ability that he handwrote letters to several English clubs asking for a trial as a 15-year-old! Middlesbrough were the only team that responded and he borrowed the £632 return air fare from his father. He was signed by the club after a four-month trial. However, it could have been completely different as he suffered a bone disease when he was only six after being kicked in the leg. The doctor recommended an amputation of the left leg but an American specialist saved it. Johnston signed for Liverpool in April 1981, still only 20 years old but with over 60 domestic appearance to his name. He was largely overlooked during his first year at Anfield but a visit from Arsenal changed that completely. His first goal for the club in extra time took Liverpool to the quarter-final of the League Cup.

The Kop quickly got behind their new man as it became apparent he would continue to run until he had absolutely nothing left to give! In total, the South African spent seven years with Liverpool and won five League Championships, one FA Cup, two League Cups and a European Cup. His sister nearly died in a gassing accident that was caused in her hotel room which resulted in him taking time away from football. When he returned, a plight of injuries kept him out and he eventually retired from playing in 1988. He embarked on a business career after football and helped design and create the Predator football boot for Adidas. When the Hillsborough disaster took place he returned from Australia and attended the funerals of the victims. He has since gone back to Australia and now works as a photographer.

## JONES, Bill
*Defender*
**Born:** *1921 Whaley Bridge, Derbyshire* **Died:** 2010
**Playing career:** *Hayfield St Matthews, Liverpool (1938-1954)*
Bill Jones joined Liverpool as an 18-year-old in 1938 but the advent of World War II stole many years of competitive football away from the youngster. However, when the Football League resumed in August he was 24 and he immediately made up for lost time by helping his club win the League Championship. Although that success would not be emulated for over 20 years, he was a consistent figure in Liverpool's team for the next seven years.

He was an extremely versatile player who could play well in several positions. Jones featured in Liverpool's first Wembley cup final against Arsenal in the 1950 FA Cup but had to settle for a runners-up medal. The club's form gradually worsened over the coming years and in Jones' last season the club were relegated. He went on to become player-manager at Ellesmore Port before returning to Liverpool as a scout in the 1960s. His grandson, Rob Jones, featured for Liverpool and England too. On 26 December 2010, he died from natural causes at the Countess of Chester Hospital.

## JONES, Brad
*Goalkeeper*
**Born:** *1982 Armadale, Perth, Australia*
**Playing career:** *Bayswater City, Middlesbrough, Liverpool, Bradford City, NEC, Feyenoord, Al-Nassr*
When Brad Jones joined Liverpool in 2010, he knew that he was going to be primarily used as cover for the well-established Pepe Reina. He played for a couple of years in Australia as a teenager before joining the youth academy at Middlesbrough. He was rewarded with a professional contract on his seventeenth birthday in March 1999. However, he was forced to wait five years before he was given a chance to play in the club's senior side. When Mark Scwarzer moved to Fulham, Jones was brought into the team and was tasked with saving Middlesbrough's topflight status – the club went down and failed in their promotion push the following year.

Hi, I'm Kelly Forshaw, here with Red Touch Media, joined with Craig Johnston.

Brad Jones

assist for Liverpool's goal. Nevertheless, he became the first Welshman to win a European Cup when his team beat Borussia Monchengladbach 3-1 in the final. The following campaign there were limited opportunities and he moved on in 1978 after exactly 100 appearances for the Reds. Briefly managed Wrexham after he retired, but had to undergo heart surgery in 2002. However, he remains a coach with the club in 2019. He completed his autobiography in 2005 and it was Sky Sports' News *book of the week* in February 2006.

## JONES, Lee
*Striker*
**Born:** *1973 Wrexham, Wales*
**Playing career:** *Wrexham, Liverpool, Tranmere Rovers, Barnsley (1991-2013)*

Lee Jones signed from Wrexham for £300,000 in 1992 after a brilliant year with his local team. He scored a number of goals for the youth team and the reserves at Liverpool despite breaking his leg twice! He only appeared four times for the senior side – all from bench. He was sold to Tranmere and enjoyed three successful years with the Merseyside club before returning to Wrexham for a final time. He then played and managed NEWI Cefn Druids in the Welsh league. He retired in 2008 after a knee injury failed to recover. In the summer of 2016, Jones was appointed Tranmere Rovers' new academy manager and head of recruitment.

He was named in Australia's World Cup squad in 2010 but had to withdraw as his young son had been tragically diagnosed with cancer. When he moved to Liverpool in that summer it is unsurprising that he was only used on two occasions for the season, as Pepe Reina was the firm first-choice 'keeper. Despite this, he stayed with the club for four years and played in 27 matches. He grew up a Liverpool supporter so it was certainly a dream come true for the Australian. He moved to Bradford before having a brief spell in Holland. He headed to Saudi Arabia in 2018 and is still contracted with Al-Nassr.

## JONES, Joey
*Left-back*
**Born:** *1955 Llandudno, Wales*
**Playing career:** *Wrexham, Liverpool, Wrexham, Chelsea, Huddersfield Town, Wrexham. (1972-1991).*

It should come as little surprise that Joey Jones left Wrexham for Liverpool – he had a Liverbird tattoo on his forearm which is the mythical creature of the city of Liverpool. He joined in July 1975 for a fee of £110,000. Unfortunately, he missed out on a championship medal as he failed to play in enough games throughout the successful season of 1975/76. He was part of the treble-chasing team of 1977 but lost in the FA Cup final 2-1 to Manchester United - although the full-back did provide the

## JONES, Paul
*Goalkeeper*
**Born:** *1967 Chirk, Wrexham, Wales*
**Playing career:** *Kidderminster Harriers, Stockport County, Southampton, Liverpool, Wolverhampton Wanderers, Watford, Millwall, QPR, Bognor Regis Town (1986-2008)*

Paul Jones was an established international 'keeper when he arrived at Liverpool on loan in January 2004. He was requested as an emergency as both Chris Kirkland and Jersey Dudek were injured. He made two appearances for the Reds and he became the oldest player to make their debut for the club since World War II! After he retired as a player he played for Liverpool Legends team in 2012 as they toured Thailand. On his 50th appearance for Wales, he marked the occasion with shaving 50 into his hair.

Unfortunately, Wales lost 5-1 and it was their worst home defeat for 98 years as he was beaten from range on three occasions! Whilst at Southampton, he received a FA Cup runners-up medal after Arsenal beat the Saints 1-0. He retired from the game in 2008 and his most recent involvement with football was training Southampton's youth goalkeepers. Jones is also available to be booked out as a guest speaker/dinner host.

## JONES, Rob
*Right-back*
**Born:** *1971 Wrexham, Wales*
**Playing career:** *Crewe Alexandra, Liverpool, West Ham United (1987-1999)*
Following in his grandfather's footsteps, Rob Jones was a red since the day his grandad signed for the club. He was an integral player for Liverpool during the 90s and stayed for seven years in total. Regrettably, injuries took their toll on the Welshman and he was forced to retire in 1999. Graeme Souness believes that Jones was one of the best, if not the best signings he made at Liverpool. He now runs a chain of children's nurseries that have branches as far as the United Arab Emirates! In October 2013, Jones took up a coaching role with Liverpool, where his eldest son Declan was a part of the youth team.

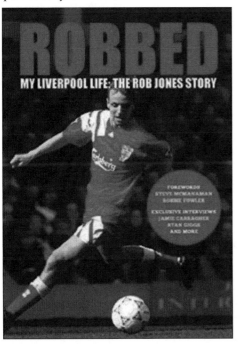

## JOVANOVIC, Milan
*Forward/Winger*
**Born:** *1981 Bajina Basta, SFR Yugoslavia*
**Playing career:** *Buducnost Valjevo, Vojvodina, Shakhtar Donetsk, Lokomotiv Moscow, Standard Li-ège, Liverpool, Anderlecht (1999-2013)*
Milan Jovanovic had agreed to join Liverpool prior to Rafael Benitez's departure in 2010 and still went through with the transfer. Annoyingly for the striker, Roy Hodgson did not show much belief in the Serbian and he had to settle as a squad player. His frustration later led to his move away from Anfield the following summer. Throughout his career he was capped 41 times by Serbia and retired from football in 2013. Strangely, Jovanovic was mentioned in Australian soap Neighbours where he was referred to as 'one of the greatest footballers in the world'.

## KEANE, Robbie
*Striker*
**Born:** *1980 Dublin, Ireland*
**Playing career:** *Wolves, Coventry City, Inter Milan, Leeds United, Tottenham Hotspur, Liverpool, Tottenham Hotspur, Celtic (loan), West Ham United (loan), LA Galaxy, Aston Villa (loan) (1995-2012)*
Robbie Keane was a fantastic player who would score for fun. His smart finishes would usually be followed by his acrobatic trademark celebration. He is the current record goal scorer for the Republic of Ireland. He was also Britain's most expensive teenager when Coventry paid Wolves £6 million in 1999 and has amassed over £74 million in transfer fees throughout his career. He had special memories at Tottenham, where he was the top scorer for the club in his first four seasons. He arrived at Anfield in the summer of 2008 for £19 million and great things were expected of the Irishman. Annoyingly, he couldn't quite cut it at Liverpool and after 18 months in Merseyside, he returned to Spurs. His second spell was nowhere near as successful as his first and he eventually departed for LA Galaxy in America. He was a vital part of their team and scored 83 goals in 125 league matches before finishing his career in India. He moved into management after his playing days and he became the assistant manager of the Republic of Ireland in 2018 before joining as an assistant at Middlesbrough.

## KEECH, Bill

*Defender*

**Born:** *1872 Irthlingborough, Northamptonshire*
**Died:** 1948
**Playing career:** *Liverpool, Barnsley St. Peters, Blackpool, Leicester Fosse, Loughborough, QPR, Brentford, Kensal (1895-1904)*

Bill Keech played six times for Liverpool during the 1895/96 season – which was only Liverpool's third year as official members of the Football League. Despite winning the Second Division championship the previous year, the side were constantly chopped and changed which resulted in Liverpool failing to find any consistency. He later moved to Leicester and became a forward. He was an all-round sportsman and won honours for skating and boxing. When he retired from playing football he became a coach with Queens Park Rangers. He died on 6 September 1948 in Paddington, London.

## KEEGAN, Kevin

*Forward*

**Born:** *1951 Armthorpe, Doncaster*
**Playing career:** *Scunthorpe United, Liverpool, Southampton, Newcastle United. (1968-1983).*

One of the most iconic in not only English football, but world football. Having joined Scunthorpe as an apprentice in 1968, he made the move to Anfield in 1971 and would play over 300 times for the club. He scored 12 minutes into his debut against Nottingham Forest. Bill Shankly famously told Keegan that he would play for England 18 months before his first call up. His first major honour with the club came during the 1972/73 season where Liverpool won the First Division – they won the UEFA Cup in the same year. In total, he would win three First Division titles, one FA Cup, Two FA Charity Shields, one European Cup and two UEFA Cups whilst at Liverpool. After six years in Merseyside he moved to Germany before finishing off his professional playing career with Newcastle United. He was capped 63 times by England and he scored 21 goals. In April 1991 he was attacked whilst sleeping in his Range Rover on the M25. The attackers stated they had no idea who they were attempting to rob and needed the money to pay off a drug debt. When he retired as a player he moved into management and he was equally effective along the side-lines. His first position was with former club Newcastle, where they pushed Manchester United all the way during the 1995/96 Premiership season. His quote: "I would love it if we beat them! Love it!" was actually voted the *Quote of the Decade* by Premier League 10 Seasons Awards in April 2003.

Kevin Keegan

He was eventually give the opportunity to manage England in 1999, a tenure that would last only a year. Despite being popular initially, he came under pressure for his decision making and they crashed out of the 2000 Euro campaign after a 3-2 loss to Romania – despite beating Germany in the previous game. He returned to Newcastle one final time but tensions from the board and the man himself grew to a toxic level and he was forced to walk away from the club again – this was Keegan's last involvement in professional football. After this, he briefly worked as a pundit for ITV for the 2010 World Cup and he was also part of ESPN's 2011, 2012 and 2013 FA Cup final media team. He eventually moved to Costa del Sol to enjoy a very well-deserved retirement.

## KEENAN, Gerry

*Right-back*
**Born:** *1954 Liverpool*
**Playing career:** *Liverpool, Skelmersdale United, Bury, Port Vale, Rochdale, Accrington Stanley, Ashton United, Rossendale United, Rossendale United, Bacup Borough, St. Joseph's (1975-1984)*

Gerry Keenan started his footballing journey on the books at Liverpool's youth academy but he was later released without making it professionally with the club. Bury snapped up the youngster and he spent three years with the club. He then moved to Port Vale before joining Bury's bitter rivals Rochdale! He eventually dropped into the non-professional leagues of English football before retiring. When he hung up his boots, he became a gas fitter but continued to work with former club Port Vale as a matchday ambassador.

## KELVIN, Arthur

*Outside-left*
**Born:** *1869 Kilmarnock, Scotland*
**Died:** 1911
**Playing career:** *Liverpool, Kilmarnock (1892-)*

A consistent Scottish attacker who lacked opportunity during his time with Liverpool. He was acknowledged for having 'the speed of a deer and dogged persistency to score'. His greatest individual achievement came when Kilmarnock beat Hurlford 7-1 and he scored five of the goals! He died shortly after retiring at the age of 42.

Alan Kennedy

## KENNEDY, Alan

*Left-back*
**Born:** *1954 Sunderland*
**Playing career:** *Newcastle United, Liverpool, Sunderland, Hartlepool United, Wigan Athletic, Wrexham. (1972-1990).*

Alan Kennedy was a fantastic full-back who had a special ability to score very important goals that brought unprecedented levels of success for the club. Without a doubt, the most important moment of his career was when he netted the winning goal in the 1981 European Cup final to down Real Madrid. Prior to Kennedy's arrival at the club, the left-back position was the one awkward position that no man exclusively held. That all changed when he arrived, however. He made his debut against Queens Park Rangers and although Liverpool won 2-1, he didn't have the best of games. "Early on I miskicked with my right foot and knocked a policeman's helmet off," summarises it best by the player himself! Obviously nervous after that first half performance, he was looking for reassurance from Bob Paisley who said: "I think that they shot the wrong Kennedy!". However, he did eventually settle and continued to thrive as he won the League Championship five times, League Cup four times and two European Cups. In total, he would play 359 times for Liverpool and score 20 goals. He left Liverpool in 1986 and played for several clubs before calling it quits on his time as a professional footballer in 1994. He now lives in Ormskirk and runs his own soccer schools. He writes a column for a Liverpool fans' website and is a regular on radio and television. He is also available to hire as an after dinner guest.

## Kennedy, Mark

*Left-back/Left winger*
**Born:** *1976 Dublin, Republic of Ireland*
**Playing career:** *St.Mochta's FC , Belvedere, Millwall, Liverpool, QPR (loan), Wimbledon, Manchester City, Wolverhampton Wanderers, Crystal Palace, Cardiff City, Ipswich Town (1992-2012)*

When 16-year-old Mark Kennedy arrived to join Mick McCarthy's Millwall, he had already been rejected by several English clubs as they believed he was too light in weight to make it as a professional footballer. However, he was about to prove them all wrong by scoring a goal in the game where the Lions knocked Arsenal out of the FA Cup in January 1995. He was heavily praised for his performance and would become the most expensive teenager in British history when he signed for £1.5 million in March 1995. He made the first XI four times during his first season with the club and almost scored a wonder goal against Leeds but his effort bounced off the bar. However, he was only given one more chance from a starting position over the next three years – with many questioning why Liverpool spent so much money on a player they seemingly didn't believe in.

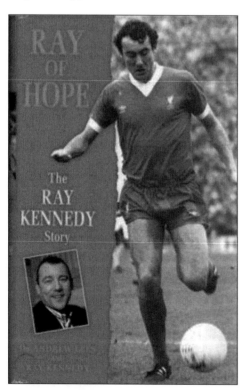

He left in 1998 and struggled to impress in the Premier League with Manchester City and Wimbledon so he dropped down a division with Wolves and flourished. He finished his career with Ipswich Town in 2012 and was appointed in a coaching role with the club.

## KENNEDY, Ray

*Midfielder/Centre-forward*
**Born:** *1951 Seaton Delaval*
**Playing career:** *Arsenal, Liverpool, Swansea City, Hartlepool United. (1969-1983).*

Ray Kennedy made his name with Arsenal, where he scored 71 goals in 212 games. He was also a vital player in the triumphant side that won the League and FA Cup double in his debut season in 1970/71. His move to Anfield on 12 July 1974 was largely overshadowed by the unexpected news that Bill Shankly was to stand down as Liverpool manager with immediate effect. However, he assured the press that his final signing for the club would be a brilliant addition to the squad – and he was completely correct. Kennedy was physically strong and held the ball well, in addition to having a keen eye for goal. He scored in all three of his first games for Liverpool and was forming quite the partnership with partner Phil Boersma. However, he struggled over the next year and was left out of the side due to a lack of form. This, however, changed when he netted two goals against Real Sociedad. One of the most important goals he ever scored came in the semi-final of the 1981 European Cup when Liverpool needed a goal he stood up and found the back of the net seven minutes from time – confirming their place in the final. He was incredibly successful at Liverpool and won five League Championships, one League Cup, three European Cups and a UEFA Cup. He played 393 times for the club and scored 72 goals. He left for Swansea in 1982 before heading to Cyprus for a sole year. He retired in 1985 but was diagnosed with Parkinson's disease in November 1986. In 1991 his loyalty to both Arsenal and Liverpool was rewarded with a well-attended testimonial match which was undoubtedly an emotional experience for him and his family. He became a publican in Northumberland but as his condition worsened, he had to leave his role.

## KETTLE, Brian
*Left-back*
**Born:** *1956 Prescot*
**Playing career:** *Liverpool, Dallas Tornado (loan), Houston Hurricane (loan), Wigan Athletic, Burscough, Barrow (1973-1981)*

Brian Kettle was Liverpool's reserve team captain for three years, winning the Central League on several occasions. However, he was never able to push Joey Jones, Alan Kennedy or Alec Lindsay out of the first team and had to settle for four senior appearances. He was sold to Wigan in 1980 where he played 14 more games before dropping into non-league football. He did, however, ask Bob Paisley what his future at the club was when he was 21 years old. Paisley responded with: "Your future? You're only 21! Who do you think I am – Patrick flaming Moore?". He moved into management after his playing days and he had a long successful run with Southport which saw him take the club to an unprecedented level. However, he unexpectedly handed in his resignation for personal reasons after six years with the club. In 2010, he joined A.F.C Liverpool as assistant reserve team manager.

## KEWELL, Harry
*Winger /Attacking midfielder*
**Born:** *1978 Sydney, New South Wales, Australia*
**Playing career:** *Leeds United, Liverpool, Galatasaray, Melbourne Victory, Al-Gharafa (1990-2014)*

Harry Kewell was on tour with an Australian soccer academy in England when he was spotted by Howard Wilkinson who contacted Leeds. Only three months later, he was playing his first Premiership match for the club at the age of 18. He was voted Young Player of the Year during the 1999/00 campaign and helped his team reach the Champions League semi-finals the following season. Unfortunately, Leeds suffered financial problems and were forced to sell off several of their best players – including Kewell. He had more lucrative offers elsewhere but he turned them all down in favour to join Liverpool in 2003. He started his career at Anfield off well, playing in 49 competitive games and scoring 11 goals throughout his debut season. When Rafael Benitez took over, Kewell suffered a string of injuries that kept him away from the first team, leaving his manager frustrated.

Harry Kewell

Kewell's time at Liverpool can be best judged as unlucky – proved by the fact he was substituted in three successive finals whilst playing for the 'Pool. His contract expired in 2008 and he left for Turkish champions Galatasaray. He did, however, win the FA Cup and Champions League whilst at Liverpool. He finished his career in Australia with Melbourne heat and retired in 2014. He moved into management the following year and had spells with Watford's youth teams, Crawley Town and lastly with Notts County, where he was sacked on 13 November 2018.

## KEWLEY, Kevin
*Liverpool/England*
**Born:** *1955 Liverpool*
**Playing career:** *Liverpool, Dallas Tornado (loan), Dallas Tornado, Wichita Wings (1970-1989)*

Kevin Kewley made only one substitute appearance for Liverpool during his six years with the club – against Middlesbrough at Anfield before he emigrated to America for good. He joined Dallas Tornado – where he spent two summer loans prior – and stayed with the club until 1979. He then went into the Major Indoor Soccer League with Wichita Wings for ten years. When he hung up his boots he remained in Wichita and was involved with college soccer coaching.

## Kippe, Frode

*Defender*
**Born:** *1978 Oslo, Norway*
**Playing career:** *Lillestrom, Stoke City (loan), Liverpool (1997-2002)*

Frode Kippe was Gerard Houllier's second signing after Jean Michael Ferri. He was tall and athletic but lacked the pace to succeed in the Premier League. He was loaned to Stoke in two successive years and seemed to have found his level playing in the Second Division. However, he was released back to Lillestrom in 2002 after only two appearances for Liverpool. He was appointed captain of the team and was voted as 'Defender of the Year' in 2007 in the Norwegian top division. In 2018, he celebrated his 40th birthday and he completed his seventeenth successive season with the club – he was also helped them win two cups.

## KIRKLAND, Chris

*Goalkeeper*
**Born:** *1981 Barwell*
**Playing career:** *Coventry City, Liverpool, West Bromwich Albion (loan), Wigan Athletic (loan),Wigan Athletic, Leicester City (loan), Doncaster Rovers (loan), Sheffield Wednesday, Preston North End (1998-2015)*

Chris Kirkland was a tall goalkeeper who graduated from the youth academy at Coventry City and was voted Young Player of the Year by their fans. It only took 28 appearances for Coventry before Liverpool made their move and signed the Englishman for £6 million in 2001. Kirkland only started four games of his debut season but after a mistake from Jerzy Dudek against Manchester United, he was given an extended run in the side. He restored the faith his manager had in him and helped Liverpool get to the League Cup final before suffering a nasty injury that effectively gifted Dudek his starting position back. However, another poor performance by Dudek once again against United handed Kirkland an additional chance. Similarly, he found himself injured and at one time both Liverpool stoppers were injured which forced the club to get an emergency replacement in! When he was given his final chance a number of errors led to not only his removal from the team, but his time at Liverpool. He moved to Wigan before finishing his career at Bury in 2016.

Chris Kirkland

Whilst at his penultimate club Preston, he opened up about suffering with depression but has since overcome the illness. In January 2017 he took a coaching role with Port Vale but returned to Liverpool in the summer of 2018 as part of the women's team coaching set up.

## KONCHESKY, Paul

*Left-back*
**Born:** *1981 Barking, London*
**Playing career:** *West Ham United, Charlton Athletic, Fulham, Liverpool, Notts Forest (loan), Leicester City, QPR (loan), Tottenham Hotspur (loan) (1997-2015)*

Prior to arriving at Anfield in 2010, Paul Konchesky spent the entirety of his footballing career playing in London – with four different clubs in the capital. He was part of the Fulham side that made it to the Europa League Final in 2010 but they were beaten 2-1 by Atletico Madrid in Hamburg. Liverpool paid £3.5 million for his services when Roy Hodgson brought him to the club. It was evident by many of the supporters that he was not of Liverpool quality. Konchesky received so much abuse that his mum took to Facebook to complain about the team, stating: "To all you Liverpool scouse scum, take a real look at your team. Stop living in the past. The team are crap. Never should have left Fulham".

## KOZMA, Istvan

*Midfielder*

**Born:** *1964 Paszto, Hungary*
**Playing career:** *Salgotarjani TC, ujpesti Dozsa, Girondins Bordeaux, Dunfermline Athletic, Liverpool, ujpest FC, APOEL, ujpest FC, Videoton, Tatabanya, (1983-2001)*

Istvan Kozma was brought to Anfield under the management of Graeme Souness, which was another baffling transfer that the Scotsman made. Michael Platini actually dropped into Souness' office to recommend a player who had been having trouble in France but was a very talented footballer. Souness decided to ignore the advice of the Frenchman and so Eric Cantona signed for Manchester United and not Liverpool! Even more frustrating, Souness opted for Kozma instead of the fiery forward! He did, however, have one good moment in a Liverpool shirt. He contributed with two assists that helped Liverpool salvage a 4-4 draw from 3-0 down against Chesterfield in the second round of the League Cup. Kozma did not play enough games to be granted a new work permit in England and he returned to Hungary after two seasons at Anfield. He is considered a legend of Dunfermline Athletic and made 267 league appearances for Ujpesti in four different spells with the club. When he retired he went into coaching in Hungary.

## KROMKAMP, Jan

*Right-back*

**Born:** *1980 Makkinga, Netherlands*
**Playing career:** *AGOVV, Go Ahead Eagles, AZ, Villarreal, Liverpool, PSV, Go Ahead Eagles (1998-2013)*

Jan Kromkamp started out as a midfielder with Go Ahead Eagles in the Dutch Second Division but was soon sold to AZ Alkmaar and was transitioned into a full-back. This proved to be a shrewd move. When AZ reached the semi-finals of the UEFA Cup in 2005 he had started to attract admirers from all across Europe. After negotiations fell through with Portuguese giants Porto he joined Villarreal. He struggled for form in Spain and after only 11 games and five months into his five-year contract, he swapped sunny Spain for murky England by joining Liverpool. Although he was never able to push Steve Finnan out of the team, he did come on as a substitute during Liverpool's 2006 FA Cup final win. However, home sickness grew and he returned to Holland without making any real impact at Liverpool. He won the Eredivise in two successive years with PSV before finishing his career with first club Eagles. He retired in June 2013 and is currently coaching the U-19 side of Go Ahead Eagles.

Dirk Kuyt

## KUYT, Dirk

*Forward/Winger/Wing-back*
**Born:** *1980 Katwijk aan Zee, Netherlands*
**Playing career:** *Utrecht, Feyenoord, Liverpool, Fenerbahce, Feyenoord (1985-2015)*

Dirk Kuyt was the son of a fisherman and when he was 12 years old he was left with an ultimatum where he would either become a fisherman or a footballer – thankfully, he chose the latter. Kuyt was never picked up by any of the big professional clubs in Holland and slowly started to lose faith in his dream. He had a new dream, and that was to play for the first team of his amateur side. However, he did sign for Utrecht and became a household name through the Netherlands as he scored 20 goals in 34 games for the club. He was later transferred to Feyenoord and scored 83 goals in 122 games for his new side. Liverpool signed the Dutchman for £9 million in 2006 and he hit the ground running in his debut season scoring 14 goals.

However, his second year was not to the same standard - although he lost his beloved father which would have undoubtedly played a part in his erratic form in front of goal. He rediscovered his best days during the latter half of the season and continued to pop up with important goals. Kuyt spent six years with Liverpool and played in 285 games for the club, scoring 71 goals. He joined Turkish side Fenerbahce after leaving Anfield before returning to Holland and retiring with first club Quick Boys in 2018. Since retiring he and his wife have carried out extensive charity work away from the football pitch and have raised millions for good causes.

## KVARME, Bjorn

*Defender*
**Born:** *1972 Trondheim, Norway*
**Playing career:** *Utleira, Rosenborg, Liverpool, AS Saint-etienne, Real Sociedad, Bastia, (1991-2008)*

Bjorn Kvarme impressed at Rosenborg - who reached the quarter-finals of the Champions League during the 1996/97 season. The defender was available on a Bosman transfer in January 1997 when Liverpool swept in from nowhere and brought the Norwegian to Anfield. He started off his career in red well and was a prominent figure of the team for the latter half of the season that he joined in – with the exclusion of being cup-tied thanks to his heroics for Rosenborg. His form started to dip after he struggled in a derby match at Goodison Park. Danny Cadamarteri completely ran rings around the defender. He kept his place but another high-profile mistake against Manchester United kept him out of the side for some time. He had one final game against Coventry in the FA Cup in January 1998 and this appeared to be the final straw for Kvarme who was never a regular for the first team again and left the club at the start of the 1999/00 season. He played in France and Italy before re-joining Rosenborg in 2005. He retired mid-season in 2008 and has not been involved in football since.

## "DID YOU KNOW?"

*"The distinctive Liver Bird only became part of the badge in 1901."*

## KYRGIAKOS, Sotirios
*Centre-back*
**Born:** *1979 Trikala, Greece*
**Playing career:** *Panathinaikos, Rangers, Eintracht Frankfurt, AEK Athens, Liverpool, Wolfsburg, Sunderland (loan), Sydney Olympic (1996-2014)*

By the time Sotirios Kyrgiakos arrived at Liverpool, he had been an experienced Greek international. He was signed after Sami Hyppia left for Leverkusen and both Martin Skrtel and Daniel Agger had injury concerns. Unfortunately, he missed Greece's 2004 European Championship shock win with a knee injury. There were three central-defenders ahead of him in the pecking order, so it will come as little surprise that he was only called upon 21 times during his debut season with the club. When he was selected though, he was a commanding presence who was extremely vocal on the pitch. The only negative for his opening season was when he was sent off against Everton after being voted the club's Player of the Month the previous one. However, as his time with Liverpool elongated, it was clear that his lack of pace had the potential to really hurt the team. He was given a 12-month extension on his Liverpool contract in June 2011 but he left for Wolfsburg only a couple of months after. He returned to England on loan with Sunderland before finishing his career in Australia in 2014. He has led a fairly reclusive life since leaving the game as a player and has kept his personal life private.

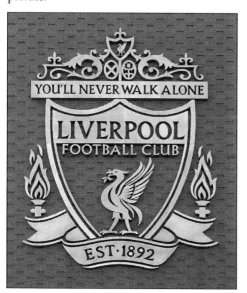

## LACEY, Bill
*Defender/Midfielder/Forward*
**Born:** *1889 Wexford, Ireland* **Died:** 1969
**Playing career:** *Shelbourne, Everton, Linfield (guest), Liverpool, New Brighton, Shelbourne, Cork Bohemians (player coach) (1906-1931)*

Bill Lacey impressed in Ireland with Shelbourne before he was brought to Merseyside – to play for Everton in 1908! He had to wait two years before he was given an opportunity with the club but he repaid the manager's trust by scoring eight goals in 24 matches. However, he was left out of the side completely the following season and Liverpool bought the player for £300. He was instantly placed into the starting XI at Anfield and played in the final 11 fixtures of the season. Although he was never known for his goalscoring ability, his creativity allowed others to shine. He helped the team reach their first cup final but lost narrowly to Burnley in the final. However, he did win two successive League Championships in 1922 and 1923. In total, he played 260 times and scored 29 goals. He eventually returned to Ireland to finish his career as player-manager of Cork Bohemians and hung up his boots in 1931 at the age of 42! He ventured into coaching and managed Ireland on several occasions whilst boss at Bohemians. He died on 30 May 1969.

## LAMBERT, Ray
*Defender*
**Born:** *1922 Bagillt, Flintshire, Wales* **Died:** 2009
**Playing career:** *Liverpool (1936-1956)*

Ray Lambert joined Liverpool as an amateur at the age of 13 in 1936 and became the youngest-ever player to join a League club at that time. Despite signing before World War II, he did not represent the club until after the conflict. He was 23 when the League resumed and he instantly justified his position in the Liverpool defence as a classy full-back. He was part of the 1947 League Championship winning side and helped Liverpool get to their first Wembley cup final but lost to Arsenal. Unfortunately, despite Lambert improving his performances, Liverpool started to steadily decline during the latter half of his time with the club. He retired a few weeks prior to his 34th birthday having only played for Liverpool. He then ran a newsagents in Flintshire before passing away in 2009.

Rickie Lambert

However, he could not show his true potential with the club and only spent a year at Anfield. His goals in the Champions League did however mean he netted in all four of England's professional divisions, the prestigious European competition and at international level. His penalty taking record was seriously impressive, too. Whilst at Southampton he scored all 34 penalties that he took, but he missed his first for Liverpool! He was capped 11 times by England. He announced his retirement from playing football in October 2017. He now lives in Formby but he did tell the Bristol Post in December 2018 that he is happy taking time away from the game but he does have his coaching badges and that he would not rule out a return to the sport in the future.

## LATHAM, George
*Half-back*
**Born:** *1881 Newtown, Wales* **Died:** 1939
**Playing career:** *Newtown, Liverpool, Southport, Stoke, Cardiff City (1897-1921)*

Gorge Latham was captain in the 7th Royal Welsh Fusiliers during World War I and awarded the Military Cross for his bravery on the Turkish front in 1917. Prior to the 1901 Boer War, he had played football for his hometown club, Newton. Liverpool signed the defender after he had returned from the war but he had to wait two years for his chance in the senior team. He made an excellent start on his debut as his new club ran out as 8-1 winners against Burslem Port Vale. He was only called upon occasionally during his four years with the Reds and would only play in 18 league games. He became the oldest debutant for Cardiff City when he was selected at the age of 41! He was part of the coaching staff but after two players fell ill he had no option but to play the game. He later moved into management with the Welsh side and masterminded the club's finest victory when Cardiff beat Arsenal 1-0 in the 1927 FA Cup Final. Latham also coached Great Britain's football team that participated in the 1920 Summer Olympics. He continued to coach until 1936 when he was involved in a bad biking accident that forced him to leave the game for good. He died in Newton three years later, only 58 years old. His hometown club, Newton, later named their stadium, Latham Park, after the historical figure.

## LAMBERT, Rickie
*Striker*
**Born:** *1982 Kirkby*
**Playing career:** *Blackpool, Macclesfield Town, Stockport County, Rochdale, Bristol Rovers, Southampton, Liverpool, WBA (1992-2015)*

Rickie Lambert was released by Liverpool at 15. The club he supported as a youngster and had big dreams to represent - deemed him surplus to requirements. Lambert was forced to make his way to the top from the very bottom – which is exactly what he done. His career started to shape nicely when he was at Rochdale, before moving to Bristol Rovers and scoring 51 league goals in 128 appearances. Southampton came knocking in 2009 and Lambert introduced himself to the world of football. After five successful years on the south coast his dream was to be achieved when Liverpool tabled a £4 million bid plus add-ons to secure their former man.

## LAWLER, Chris
*Right-back*
**Born:** *1943 Liverpool*
**Playing career:** *Liverpool, Portsmouth, Miami Toros (loan), Stockport County, Bangor City, Raufoss IL, IK Grand Bodo (1960-1981)*

Considering Chris Lawler played as a full-back, his goal scoring record is simply astonishing. From the 549 games he played for Liverpool, he scored 61 times – an average of a goal every nine games. Bob Paisley once praised the right-back, claiming that he had a "brain of a striker". During his time at Anfield he won the League Championship twice, the FA Cup twice and the UEFA Cup once. He was nicknamed the 'Silent Knight' due to the simplistic way he would go about keeping any opposition out during the game. Despite approaching 30 during the 1972/73 season, Lawler played in every one of Liverpool's 66 competitive matches during that season. Sadly, an injury to his cartilage against Queens Park Rangers in 1973 seemed to have impacted his ability significantly and he never returned as the player he once was. He moved to Portsmouth in 1975 before finishing his professional career with Norwegian club IK Grand Bodo. Despite his heroics in a Liverpool shirt, he was only capped 4 times for his country.

Chris Lawler

He did eventually return to Liverpool as a coach but he was released from his post in 1986 to make way for Phil Thompson. Since then, he has done some scouting work for the club and he also works in Skelmersdale, coaching young children.

## LAWRENCE, Tommy
*Goalkeeper*
**Born:** *1940 Dailly, Scotland*
**Playing career:** *Liverpool, Tranmere Rovers. (1962-1973)*

Tommy Lawrence was a fearless goalkeeper who gave his all for Liverpool during the 1960s. He was nicknamed 'The Flying Pig' by the Kop who thought he was carrying a bit too much weight! Lawrence quit his job in the Rylands wire factory in Warrington to pursue a career in football and was signed by the area's club as an amateur before he signed professional papers with Liverpool on 30 October 1957, a few months after his seventeenth birthday. He was largely kept out of the senior side by Jim Furnell for the first five years of his career at Anfield, but when the stopper got injured early into the 1962/63 season, Lawrence was given his opportunity to shine. He would go on to become Liverpool's number one for the next eight years! When Ray Clemence signed for Liverpool, he had to wait two years to fully tussle the position off him. Lawrence only missed four league games in six seasons at the 'Pool as they won the League Championship twice plus the first FA Cup in the club's history. However, he did have one sour moment in red. Liverpool were beating Arsenal 1-0 with 20 minutes to go when Lawrence made a blunder to allow Arsenal to equalise as the ball went through his legs. After the match had finished he apologised to Bill Shankly about the error and said it should not have happened. The manager replied with: "it's not your fault. It's your f****** mother who should have never opened her legs"! Shankly was unwilling to break up the team that brought him so much success during the mid-60s but a humiliating knockout by Watford in the FA Cup quarter-finals proved to be the penultimate game that Lawrence would play for the club. Clemence came in to replace the veteran and he moved to neighbours Tranmere in the summer. He was also the first goalkeeper to play in a sweeper role.

Goalkeepers would also not get sent off for taking the last man down in those days, so if they did get past them he just tackled them to the floor! When he retired from the game, he returned to work at Rylands. He shot to fame in 2015 when a journalist asked him if he could remember the Everton v Liverpool cup tie in 1967 – to which he responded by stating he played in it! He died on January 10 2018, aged 77.

## LAWRENSON, Mark

*Defender*

**Born:** *1957 Penwortham, Lancashire*
**Playing career:** *Preston North End, Brighton & Hove Albion, Liverpool, Barnet, Tampa Bay Rowdies, Corby Town, Chesham United (1974-1992)*

Mark Lawrenson almost joined Liverpool four years prior. Whilst he was playing for his local side Preston, both Liverpool and Brighton were in a bidding war to secure the defender's services. Both clubs had bid £75,000, but it was the latter who were able to pay more and he moved to the Seagulls for £100,000. Four years later and Liverpool had finally got their man – for £900,000! When he signed for the Merseyside club he was the club's record transfer and also became the most expensive defender in Britain. The money was certainly worth it, as Lawrenson was a fantastic player.

He was a great tackler, read the game extremely well and had considerable speed and skill. He started his time off at Anfield by replacing Alan Kennedy at left-back for a while and during the 1981/82 season, he had played in 39 of Liverpool's 42 league matches. He was instrumental during the penultimate game of the season, where Liverpool beat Spurs 3-1 and won the League Championship – this was the first of three successive league titles for the club. In total, Lawrenson played 356 times for the Reds and won five League Championships, one FA Cup, three League Cups and one European Cup. He officially left Liverpool in March 1988 to manage Oxford but left after seven months after he was furious that the club had sold their best player. He threatened to quit and the next day he was sacked! He moved to Tampa Bay in 1989 and featured as a player-coach for a few months before he was appointed manager of Peterborough in 1989. Again, he only lasted 14 months before he resigned over a row with the Chairman regarding players' appearance money. He brought his boots back out to play non-league football before he made a short return as a as a defensive coach for Kevin Keegan's Newcastle. He then became a member of BBC's *Match of the Day* and remains in the role in 2019.

Tommy Lawrence

## Le TALLEC, Anthony

*Forward*
**Born:** *1984 Hennebont, France*
**Playing career:** *Liverpool, Le Mans, Auxerre, Auxerre B, Valenciennes, Valenciennes B, Atromitos, Astra Giurgiu, Orleans, Annecy (1999-2015)*

Anthony Le Tallec was an exciting prospect who had shone for France at junior level. He arrived at Anfield from Le Havre in 2003 and there was much excitement around the signing. He had several attributes that lured Liverpool to him – excellent vision, superb passing ability and a tireless work ethic. Unfortunately, Le Tallec did not live up to his promise and his frustration was ultimately his own undoing as he was angry with his lack of senior side appearances. He was loaned out during his final two years at the club and left Anfield permanently in 2008. He left for Le Mans and continues to play in France, for the amateur side Annecy.

## LEE, Sammy

*Midfielder*
**Born:** *1959 Liverpool*
**Playing career:** *Liverpool, QPR, Osasuna, Southampton (loan), Bolton Wanderers (1975-1991)*

Plenty of players on this list have come through the youth academy at Liverpool and failed to make it into the senior side. Sammy Lee is just one of only a few who carved out a successful career at Anfield. After his promotion, he spent ten years with the first XI and won a whole cabinet worth of trophies! Four League Championships, four League Cups and two European Cups. Small in height (5 ft. 4 in.), the Kop used to sing: "He's fat, he's round, he bounces on the ground. Sammy Lee, Sammy Lee". He moved to London to join Queen's Park Rangers before finishing his career with Bolton Wanderers. He was capped 14 times by England and scored two goals. When he retired from playing, he moved into management and linked back up with Liverpool in a coaching role. He was then asked to join the England set up working alongside Sven-Goran Eriksson. He then developed a good relationship with veteran manager Sam Allardyce and joined Bolton as an assistant and then full-time manager. He returned to Liverpool in 2008 to become assistant to Rafael Benitez before becoming the caretaker manager at the club in the same year. He went back to Bolton in 2012 as head of Academy Coaching and Development before being appointed assistant manager at Southampton under Ronald Koeman. He returned to the England fold again under Allardyce two years later before following him to Crystal Palace and Everton. When 'Big Sam' got the boot from Everton, Sammy followed him and he has not been involved in football since 16 May 2018.

Sammy Lee

## LEISHMAN, Tommy
*Wing-half*
**Born:** *1937 Stenhousemuir, Scotland*
**Playing career:** *St Mirren, Liverpool, Hibernian, Linfield, Stranraer (1953-1970)*

Tommy Leishman excelled for Liverpool in the Second Division, but it was ultimately their promotion that cost him his time at Anfield. He arrived at the club at the age of 22 from St. Mirren in November 1959. He figured in 15 of the last 19 league matches that season and became an important player for the next two years. He played in a defensive three that Bill Shankly orchestrated after a poor start to the 1960/61 season. Liverpool were finally promoted after an eight-year hiatus from the topflight and with that, Leishman proved inadequate for the side. He was replaced by Willie Stevenson before moving to Linfield to became player-manager. He finished his career back in Scotland playing for Stranraer.

## LEONHARDSEN, Oyvind
*Midfielder*
**Born:** *1970 Kristiansund, Norway*
**Playing career:** *Wimbledon, Liverpool, Tottenham Hotspur, Aston Villa, Lyn Oslo (1989-2007)*

Oyvind Leonhardsen was voted Player's Player of the Year in 1994 when he was at Rosenborg and he swiftly moved to Wimbledon to try his luck in England. He impressed during a two and a half year stay and was twice voted as the club's Player of the Year. Both Fiorentina and Newcastle were tracking the midfielder when he declined a new contract in London. Nevertheless, it was his boyhood club that would land the star and he signed for Liverpool for £3.5 million in 1997. Leaonhardsen was a fantastic creative player and had a keen eye for goal. However, he lost his starting position during his second year with the club and once Gerard Houllier had replaced Roy Evans, he wasn't given any opportunities until the latter half of the season. He failed to convince the Frenchman and was sold to Tottenham in 1999. He had three successful years at Spurs, scoring 11 goals in 72 games, before he was frozen out of the team by Glenn Hoddle. He moved to Aston Villa on a free before returning home to finish his career. He retired from playing in 2007 at the age of 37. He is now a youth coach at former team Lyn Oslo.

## LESTER, Hugh
*Defender*
**Born:** *1891 Lehigh, United States* **Died:** *1933*
**Playing career:** *Liverpool, Oldham Athletic, Reading (1911-1920)*

American-born Hugh Lester became the first player born outside of the British Isles to play for Liverpool. He was also a notable amateur sprinter and finished the 100-yard sprint in only 10.5 seconds! However, he wasn't successful with Liverpool and only represented the side on two occasions. He moved to Oldham but the outbreak of World War I meant that the Football League would temporarily halt. After the conflict he returned to play for Reading and later turned out for several amateur sides including Weston-Super-Mare. He was killed in a motorcycle accident on 5 August 1933, along with his passenger, as the bike collided with a car in Abergele, north Wales.

## LEWIS, Kevin
*Winger*
**Born:** *1940 Ellesmere Port*
**Playing career:** *Sheffield United, Liverpool, Huddersfield Town, Wigan Athletic (1957-1967)*

Kevin Lewis can reflect on his career at Anfield and come to the conclusion that he was awfully unlucky. He was a talented winger, had a fantastic eye for goal and was an all-round brilliant player. Unfortunately, he was present in the side at the same time as Ian Callaghan. Born in Ellesmore Port, he returned to the north-west to play for Liverpool after he had shone with Sheffield United. He was one of Bill Shankly's earlier signings in June 1960. Originally, he kept Callaghan out of the side and even scored three more than Roger Hunt. He was soon replaced by Callaghan but did score both goals in a win against Southampton that would secure promotion to the First Division in 1962. Lewis found his way back into the side in the 1962/63 season before leaving for Huddersfield the following summer. The winger scored 44 goals in only 82 games at Liverpool and if he would have been part of any other Liverpool side, he surely would have been used much more frequently. He departed the Football League at only 24 to play football in South Africa but his playing career finished when he was 28 after a knee injury. He is now a pub landlord in the Staffordshire Moorlands.

## LIDDELL, Billy
*Winger*
**Born:** *1922 Townhill, Scotland* **Died:** 2001
**Playing career:** *Liverpool, (1946-1960).*
Sir Matt Busby was instrumental in Liverpool's capture of Billy Liddell. Busby discovered that representatives from Manchester City had gone to visit Liddell's parents to enquire about signing the youngster. However, the move fell through and Liverpool's former captain rang then Liverpool manager, George Kay, to suggest that he may be a prospect – and how right he was. He came to Liverpool in July 1938 and signed a professional contract nine months later. Prior to joining the club, he was hired as an accountant at Simon Jude & West. His parents had it written into his contract that he was still allowed to study just in case he didn't make it at Liverpool… how wrong they were! He trained full-time during pre-season but only two days a week during the season. He was the only Liverpool player who held two concurrent jobs. World War II broke out only a couple of months after his signing and he was forced to wait six years for his formal debut. He enlisted in the RAF and was sent to a training camp in Cambridge and later in Canada. He was present for Liverpool during wartime but made his debut for the club in the FA Cup against Chester at Anfield on 5 January 1946, scoring once. The domestic season started in the autumn but he had to miss pre-season as he was still with the RAF. He made his league debut against Chelsea and scored twice – including directly from a corner – as

Liverpool ran out 7-4 winners. As the years went by, there was plenty of interest in Liddell but he felt at home in Liverpool and never played for another team throughout his entire career! He won the 1947 League Championship with the club but that would be the only silverware he would receive. He played in 534 matches and scored 228 goals for Liverpool. On 21 August 1960, he made his final appearance for he club in a 1-0 defeat to Southampton in the Second Division. When he retired, no other player had more appearances for the club – Elisha Scott was second with 468. He was given a testimonial match and received £6,000 which helped him buy a new house. He continued with a career in accounting after he retired from the game and he later went on to become a bursar at Liverpool University. He suffered from Parkinson's disease and died in a nursing home on 3 July 2001.

## LINDSAY, Alec
*Full-back*
**Born:** *1948 Bury*
**Playing career:** *Bury, Liverpool, Stoke City, Oakland Stompers, Toronto Blizzard (1965-1979)*
Alec Lindsay was signed by Liverpool from his local club Bury in March 1969 when he was only 21 years old. He was given his first taste of action by Bill Shankly when

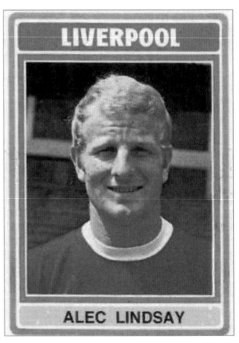

Liverpool thrashed Dundalk 10-0 in the Fairs Cup. He was kept away for the senior side after that match until he came on as a substitute to score the equaliser against Ipswich. However, this was only one of six league matches he would participate in during his full debut season with the club. After Shankly had told him he wanted to emulate his silky moves and finishing from when he was at Bury, Lindsay informed him that he had the wrong player! "Jesus Chris, Bob," said Shankly to Bob Paisley. "We've signed the wrong bloody player". After this incident, the half-back put in a transfer request that was accepted. However, perhaps miraculously, his fortunes would change forever. Shankly moved him to play at left-back and although he lacked pace, this decision launched his Liverpool career. He would cement the position for many years to come and was an instrumental figure to help Liverpool win the League Championship, FA Cup, European Cup and UEFA Cup over the following years. He played 248 times for the club and scored 18 goals. He lost his place to Phil Neal midway through the 1974/75 season but remained with the club until August 1977 when he was transferred to Stoke. However, the Potters had three managers in a short period of time and Lindsay moved to north America where he was voted MVP for new team Toronto Blizzard. He returned to England in 1979 and played for non-league team, Newton, before finishing his career and becoming a publican at Foundry Arms in Leigh.

## LITMANEN, Jari

*Attacking midfielder /Second Striker*
**Born:** *1971 Lahti, Finland*
**Playing career:** *Reipas, HJK, MyPa, Ajax, Barcelona, Liverpool, Ajax, Lahti, Hansa Rostock, Malmo FF, Fulham, Lahti, HJK (1977-2011)*

Jari Litmanen was labelled the next big thing in European football when he thrived playing with Ajax in Amsterdam. He had played for five years in his native Finland prior to joining the Dutch club in 1992. In his second season with Ajax, he scored 26 goals in only 30 league matches and helped Ajax win the title. He was also voted Player of the Year. He was rewarded with a chance to play for Spanish giants Barcelona but after Louis Van Gaal was sacked, he was left out of the team.

Jari Litmanen

Gerard Houllier came to his rescue and gave him a chance to join his boyhood club. Whilst at Ajax, his teammates would complain that he would not stop talking about Liverpool and when he left the Dutch club, he had 'You'll Never Walk Alone' playing on the speakers as he said his final goodbyes. Liverpool had tried to sign the player twice before but did not have the necessary funds available. When he joined the club there was doubt over a niggling ankle injury that he had whilst at Barcelona, and these doubts proved true when he missed all three of Liverpool's 2001 finals. He left the club in 2003 after being severely underused by his manager. Twice he scored in successive games only to be placed on the bench for the third! He returned to Ajax but failed to emulate earlier success and returned to Finland. He was capped 137 times by Finland and scored 32 goals. When he retired he was the first Finnish team sport player to be honoured with a statue. He moved into coaching before he established himself as a pundit in the media industry.

### "DID YOU KNOW?"

*"Liverpool have won more European Cups than any other English team - six in total (so far!)."*

## LIVERMORE, Doug
*Midfielder*
**Born:** *1948 Prescot*
**Playing career:** *Bolton Wanderers, Liverpool, Norwich City, Bournemouth (loan), Cardiff City, Chester (1965-1980)*

Doug Livermore was a hardworking player who later became assistant to Roy Evans whilst he was manager of Liverpool. He signed professional forms with the club in 1965 but would only appear 18 times over the next five years. After only making one appearance into the 1970/71 season, he moved to Cardiff before finishing his playing career with Chester in 1980. Despite having a fairly average career as a player, he was successful in coaching and managerial roles. He returned to Cardiff as a coach before filling a similar role under John Toshack at Swansea. He was also assistant to Mike England when he was manging Wales. He had three managerial positions with Tottenham twice and Swansea once all in caretaking roles. His final involvement in football came with Leicester when he was appointed assistant caretaker manager and despite saving the club from relegation, he was not further rewarded and left his post.

Doug Livermore

## LIVINGSTONE, George
*Inside-forward/or Wing-half*
**Born:** *1877 Dumbarton, Scotland* **Died:** 1950
**Playing career:** *Sinclair Swifts, Artizan Thistle , Parkhead, Dumbarton, Heart of Midlothian, Sunderland, Celtic, Liverpool, Manchester City, Rangers, Manchester United (1895-1915)*

Not only did George Livingstone play for Liverpool, Manchester United and Manchester City, he also represented Celtic and Rangers! He made his international debut against England on 5 April 1902 at Ibrox after the newly-built West Tribune stand collapsed where 26 spectators lost their lives. The game was deemed unofficial so caps did not count and he made his official debut for his country four years later. He joined Liverpool in 1902 and scored on his debut in a 5-2 against Blackburn Rovers on the opening day of the 1902/03 season. He played in 31 league matches that season but left the following year. Despite not making too much of a name for himself whilst in Merseyside, he was well respected by him teammates and he was a bit of a joker in the dressing room. He is the only player to date to play for and score for both Manchester and Old Firm sides. When he retired from the game, he set up a plumbing and gas-fitting business but continued to be associated with the sport. He also served for the King's Own African Rifles in East Africa. After the war, he became manager of Dumbarton but only lasted a sole season before becoming a coach at Rangers and Bradford. He died on 15 January 1950 at the age of 73.

## LLOYD, Larry
*Defender*
**Born:** *1949 Bristol*
**Playing career:** *Bristol Rovers, Liverpool, Coventry City, Notts Forest, Wigan Athletic. (1968-1982).*

Larry Lloyd had already won four England amateur international caps by the age of 17, but he had only played one season with Bristol Rovers when Billy Shankly pinpointed him as the long-term replacement to Ron Yeats. He came to the club's attention when he starred in a FA Cup match against Everton only two months before his signing for Liverpool. Although he lacked pace and skill, he was dominant in tackling and was superior in the air to many opposition attackers.

**Mark Crossley**
@bignorms

Me and me old mate the legendry Larry Lloyd, golfing at cala nova today, great day not so big fella anymore

Larry Lloyd

He signed for £50,000 in 1969 and was introduced into the team the following season, where he held down the left-back position for many years. He featured in the team that lost to Arsenal in the FA Cup. The following year a controversial disallowed goal snatched the Championship away from Liverpool as Lloyd certainly had to go through the heartbreak before the ecstasy. Liverpool captured the League Championship and the UEFA Cup in 1973 and Lloyd featured in all of Liverpool's 66 competitive matches that season – he also headed in the final goal of the European final. A thigh injury kept him out for 12 months and when he returned, his style of football was not how Shanks envisioned Liverpool going forward.

At the age of 25 and still very much in his prime, he moved to Coventry in August 1974 after a fee of £240,000. He failed to settle with the Sky Blues and transferred to Nottingham Forest where he would return to haunt Liverpool as his team pipped the 'Pool to the 1978 League Championship and knocked them out of the European Cup as Forest went on to win the tournament. He left the club in March 1981 to become player-manager at Wigan before a stint with Notts County. He fell on hard times in 2001 and was forced to sell his winning medals as he was out of work. "Selling my European medals in the greatest regret of my life," Lloyd said. "I feel sick when I think about it. But needs must when the devil drives and the devil was certainly at the wheel then". After leaving football entirely, he worked as an outspoken pundit on GEM AM and Century 106 radio stations, covering Forest. He now lives in Spain working in PR for a property company.

## LOW, Norman
*Aberdeen/Scotland*
**Born:** *1914 Aberdeen, Scotland*
**Died:** 1994
**Playing career:** *Rosehill Villa, Liverpool, Newport County, Norwich City (1931-1950)*

When Norman Low ventured into professional football, his father was a certified legend at Newcastle and he had rather large boots to fill. He was never on the Magpies' books but he did sign for Liverpool from Rosehill Villa in 1933 when he was just 19 years old. Tom Bradshaw momentarily lost his place to the youngster for the first 11 games of the 1934/35 season but he later regained his place from Low. He played just two more times for Liverpool and his final game for the club came on 26 September 1936 in a 2-0 away loss to Leeds. He left for Newport before finishing his career at Norwich in 1950. He moved into management and spent five years at the helm with final club Norwich before five more years with Port Vale - where he won the Fourth Division Championship in 1958/59. He was also chief scout at Liverpool for a while before he emigrated to North America in 1968 and became the coach of American side Cleveland Stokers.

## LOWRY, Tommy
*Defender*
**Born:** *1945 Liverpool* **Died:** 2015
**Playing career:** *Liverpool, Crewe A (1964-1977)*

Tommy Lowry was one of many reserve team players who were used on the final league match of the 1964/65 season away to Wolves as Liverpool had a FA Cup final game only five days later. This was the only opportunity Lowry got with the senior side whilst at the club. He did, however, move to Crewe and became a fantastic servant for the club – spending 11 years there and setting the appearances record of 475. When he retired from the game he worked at Rolls-Royce for over 25 years.

## MACDONALD, Kevin
*Midfielder*
**Born:** *1960 Inverness, Scotland*
**Playing career:** *Leicester City, Liverpool, Leicester City (loan), Rangers (loan), Coventry City, Cardiff City (loan), Walsall (1976-1993)*

Kevin MacDonald was brought to Anfield to fill the huge void that was left by Graeme Souness when he departed for Italy. The replacement managed to get an extended run in the side midway through the 1985/86 season – where Liverpool won the league and cup double – but a broken arm kept him out of the team for some time. He was back in time to make the starting XI that played in the FA Cup and he was the unsung hero of the day. He continued to be an important player for the club but disaster struck on 20 September 1986 when MacDonald suffered a double leg fracture after coming on from the bench. He returned to football 15 months later when he was loaned out to Leicester. He came back to Anfield and played in a couple of games but was loaned back out to Rangers. He never truly recovered from his awful injury and he left for Coventry City before finishing his career with Walsall. When he retired from playing he joined Leicester's coaching staff and was even caretaker manager for four games in 1994. He juggled coaching roles with both Aston Villa and Ireland in 2007 before he left the national fold. He was named Swindon manager in 2013 and took them to the play-offs, although they did not go up. He returned to Villa but on the 20th August 2019 he left the club following an investigation into physical and verbal bullying by him.

## MACDOUGALL, Ted
*Forward*
**Born:** *1947 Inverness, Scotland*
**Playing career:** *Liverpool, York City, Bournemouth, Manchester United, West Ham United, Norwich City, Southampton, Bournemouth, Blackpool (1966-1980).*

Ted Macdougall joined Liverpool as a trainee in 1964 and on the day of his 19th birthday, he was offered a professional contract by Bill Shankly. He was restricted to just one first team appearance when he was used as a substitute in a UEFA Cup match. The likes of Roger Hunt and Tony Hateley kept the youngster away from the senior side. When he arrived at Bournemouth in 1969, few predicted he would firmly establish himself as a legend of the club. In 146 league appearances he scored 103 goals! His fine ability to find the net did not go unnoticed, and Manchester United picked the Scotsman up. He failed to emulate his fine form on the south coast and left Old Trafford the following season. He retired from football in 1980 after returning to Bournemouth and adding a further 16 goals. He joined Portsmouth in 1998 as a reserve team coach but was sacked the following year. He also spent time in America where he was Youth Director of Coaching with the Atlanta Silverbacks. Whilst playing for Bournemouth, he started his own business – a sports shop in Boscombe called 'Ted MacDougall Sports'. Another branch opened in Poole and Geoff Hurst was at the grand opening. He was also the landlord of the Mill Arms in Hampshire after retiring from the game. In July 2013, Bournemouth's redeveloped south stand was named after MacDougall in recognition of his service to the club.

## MAGILTON, Jim
*Midfielder*
**Born:** *1969 Belfast, Northern Ireland*
**Playing career:** *Liverpool, Oxford United, Southampton, Sheffield Wednesday, Ipswich Town (1988-2006)*

Jim Magilton spent two years in Liverpool's youth academy before being awarded a professional contract in 1988. He failed to force his way into the side though and after two years he left without appearing for the senior side once. However, he did find success with various other English clubs and appeared in over 500 Football

League fixtures. He was also capped by his country 52 times. His final club Ipswich Town – whom he spent the final seven years of his playing career with – gave him his first action in management. He had intended to look for a coaching role with a different club, but he approached the board to fill the vacancy after Joe Royle departed in the summer. He spent three years with the Town before being sacked after failing to make the play-offs. He moved to Queen's Park Rangers and spent two years as manager there between 2009 and 2011 before leaving for Shamrock Rovers. Whilst manager at QPR it was rumoured that Magilton headbutted midfielder Akos Buzsaky after a bust up in the changing rooms! In 2012, he moved to Australia to take charge of Melbourne Victory and he went into the record book as the manager with the worst winning percentage – just 16.67%. His most recent role was manager of the Northern Ireland U-21 team but he was released in 2016. He has recently stated that he is looking to return to football in the near future.

Mike Marsh

## MARSH, Mike
*Midfielder*
**Born:** *1970 Liverpool*
**Playing career:** *Liverpool, West Ham United, Coventry City, Galatasaray, Southend United, Southport, Barrow, Kidderminster Harriers, Boston United, Accrington Stanley (1987-2003)*

Mike Marsh was a fantastic trainer whilst at Liverpool – he just failed to emulate those performances on the actual playing field! Although he was never globally known, he did possess enough skill to make people wonder what could have been. In 1987 Marsh was playing for Kirkby Town when Phil Thompson was advised to watch the youngster play. After he had been to see him, Liverpool swiftly signed the midfielder. He was a reserve at the club for four years, himself admitting that he was not quite at the level to represent the senior side. He was given his first break in the 1991/92 season when he was frequently used and he took his fine form with him to the following campaign. His most memorable moment came in the UEFA Cup against Auxerre on 6 November 1991 at Anfield. Liverpool had lost the opening leg 2-0 but Marsh scored their second goal in the final leg to help secure a 3-2 aggregate victory. He was later shipped to West Ham in a swap deal that brought Julian Dicks to Anfield in September 1993. He later reconnected with Graeme Souness at Galatasaray in 1995 for a few months. Unfortunately, a knee injury finished his professional career when he was just 28 and he accepted an insurance pay-out that stated he could not play in the Football League again. This proved tricky as he won the Conference with both Kidderminster and Boston but was unable to go up with the teams because of the contract he signed! Marsh joined the Liverpool academy in July 2009 and coached the U-16s and U-18s. In August 2012 he was promoted to the senior side by Brendan Rodgers. He left Melwood in the summer of 2015 to join the England coaching set up, working with the U-17s and U-18s.

### "DID YOU KNOW?"

*"An 8-0 victory at Stoke City in November 2000 ranks as the club's record away win."*

Javier Mascherano

## MASCHERANO, Javier

*Defensive midfielder/Centre-back*
**Born:** *1984 San Lorenzo, Argentina*
**Playing career:** *West Ham United, Liverpool, Barcelona, Hebei China Fortune (2003-2010)*

Javier Mascherano was a starlet in his native Argentina and shot to global recognition after his displays in the 2003 FIFA World Youth Championship when he was on the books of River Plate. He joined Brazilian team Corinthians for £7.5 million but there was confusion as to who actually owned the player. The team had signed a controversial deal with London-based investors, Media Sports Investments (MSI). They helped provide the money for the player but in return, they would have a say on which club signed him and they would receive financial benefits! The relationship between Corinthians and MSI became strained and he left the club for West Ham in 2006. He only played seven times for the Hammers in a largely controversial time with the club before Rafael Benitez saw the opportunity to bring a world-class player to Anfield. He flew to London and met the Argentine in Canary Wharf, explaining to him the role he wants him to play for Liverpool by using stones! After several legal setbacks, Liverpool initially paid West Ham £1.6 million to loan the midfielder with a view to make him a permanent player in January 2008.

In only his eleventh game for Liverpool, he was one of the stars as AC Milan finally got revenge in the 2007 Champions League final. On 29 February 2008, he signed a permanent contract with Liverpool for a fee of £17 million. He would stay with the club for three years and play in over 130 games before he moved to Barcelona in 2010. He had copious amounts of success with the Spanish side and won every honour available to him whilst at the Nou Camp. He spent a year playing football in China during the 2018/19 season before returning home to feature for Estudiantes de La Plata. He is still contracted with the club in 2019.

## MASON, Stuart

*Full-back*
**Born:** *1949 Whitchurch, Shropshire*
**Died:** 2007
**Playing career:** *Wrexham, Liverpool, Chester-City, Rochdale, Crewe Alexandra. (1965-1977)*

Stuart Mason started his career with non-league side Whitchurch Alport before joining Wrexham as a 16-year-old in November 1964. He spent two years playing in the reserves before he was finally given a chance with the Welsh side. That same year, having impressed dramatically for Wrexham, he moved to Liverpool. Unfortunately, he was unable to break into the first team with the club and he eventually returned to Wrexham. He moved to Chester in 1973 before finishing his career playing in Wales. He was the former captain of Shropshire County Cricket Club during his younger years too. When he retired from playing football he owned his own sports shop in Wrexham. He also had a spell as assistant commercial manager at Wrexham before coaching at Chester's Centre of Excellence.

## MASSIE, Jason

*Midfielder*
**Born:** *1984 Liverpool*
**Playing career:** *Liverpool, Rio Grande Red Storm, Prescot Cables, Cape Cod Crusaders, Harrisburg City Islanders, Marine, Prescot Cables (loan), GPS Portland Phoenix, Catarqui Clippers (1996-2014)*

Jason Massie spent eight years in Liverpool's youth academy before being released. He had been part of the team since U-12s and made it all the way up to play for the reserves, failing at the final hurdle.

Once he departed the 'Pool he had a short stint playing for Prescot Cables before he moved to America to chase his dream of becoming a professional footballer. He finally made it in 2009 when he played for Harrisburg City Islanders. He returned to England for a brief spell with non-league club Marine before he headed to the States once again. He is currently contracted with the Cataraqui Clippers of League1 Ontario.

## MATTEO, Dominic
*Defender/Midfielder*
**Born:** *1974 Dumfries, Scotland*
**Playing career:** *Liverpool, Sunderland, Leeds United, Blackburn Rovers, Stoke City (1992-2009)*

Dominic Matteo was brought to Liverpool at only 11 years old after he caught Kenny Dalglish's eye whilst watching his son play for Birkdale United. However, it was Graeme Souness who gave the player his chance with the senior side in October 1993. During his debut he loudly sang 'You're Never Walk Alone' before he finally realised that he was no longer a fan but a servant to the club! Matteo was breaking into the side the same time as Robbie Fowler and he had plenty of opportunities under Souness.

However, when the Scotsman left, he had to settle for sporadic appearances. He was informed by Gerard Houllier that he will no longer be starting and he moved to Leeds in the summer of 2000. He was made club captain when Rio Ferdinand moved to Manchester United in the summer of 2002. He reconnected with Souness at Blackburn before finishing his career with Stoke in 2009. After he retired he ran up heavy gambling debts and was forced to declare bankruptcy in 2015. He has been studying with UEFA for his coaching badges and regularly appears as a pundit for LFC TV. In November 2019 he required an emergency surgery after suffering a brain tumour.

## MATTHEWS, Billy
*Centre-half*
**Born:** *1897 Denbighshire, Wales* **Died:** 1987
**Playing career:** *Liverpool Bristol City, Wrexham, Barrow, Bradford Park Avenue, Stockport County, Chester, Northwich Victoria (1920-)*

Billy Matthews made 13 wartime appearances and scored eight goals for Liverpool. In the 1919/20 season he made his official debut for the club as they ran out 3-0 winners over Derby County on 3 April 1920. He played as centre-half during his first game but played as a forward for his other eight – "Liverpool think I will make a centre-half, but I know I never shall. It is not in my bones to play there!". He was a large man who possessed incredible amounts of strength. Matthews scored three goals in two games at the start of the 1921/22 season but only netted once in the following five matches. He was never given another opportunity to prove himself at the club after that as Liverpool went on to win the League Championship that season and the next. In March 1922 he left for Bristol City but the club were relegated the following year. However, they bounced back up before he wanted to move closer to his childhood home and joined Wrexham. He finished his career with Bradford Park Avenue. The Welshman was a fitness fanatic and was a keen cyclist well into his seventies! He later became a coach and had a spell as manager of Llangollen. He then moved into scouting and he was the man responsible for discovering Blackpool legend Glyn James. He died on 18 December 1987.

## MAXWELL, Leyton

*Midfielder*
**Born:** *1979 St Asaph, Wales*
**Playing career:** *Liverpool, Stockport County (loan), Cardiff City, Barry Town (loan), Swansea City, Carmarthen Town, Mansfield Town, Rhyl, Bangor City, Caernarfon Town, Aberaman Athletic, Barry Town, Avtex Athletic (1997-2010)*

Leyton Maxwell was born in the same town as Ian Rush and dreamt of a fantastic Liverpool career. He scored a brilliant goal on his debut for the club in the League Cup against Hull. However, this would be the one and only appearance that Maxwell would make for the club. "I scored and you really think you've made it when that happens". After a year without first team action he was loaned out to Stockport County. When he returned, he fell further down the pecking order and he eventually moved to Cardiff City but failed to impress there too. He had a trial with rivals Swansea where he was once again unsuccessful. However, the damage was done and he was continuously teased by Cardiff fans! He had a brief spell with Mansfield before dropping into the non-leagues. He has since trained as a telecommunications engineer and is currently working for Vodafone in Cardiff.

Gary McAllister

## McALLISTER, Gary

*Midfielder*
**Born:** *1964 Motherwell, Scotland*
**Playing career:** *Motherwell, Leicester City, Leeds United, Coventry City, Liverpool, Tadcaster Albion (1981-2010)*

Gary McAllister joined Leeds in 1990 whilst being linked to a move to Liverpool. He was part of the Championship winning side of 1991/92 that possessed several brilliant players. Whilst negotiating with Leeds for a better contract, he had a more luxurious deal with Coventry and joined the Sky Blues at the age of 31. The fee of £3 million was considered as a lot for someone of his age, but he was soon made captain of the side and demonstrated exactly why he went for that sum. When McAllister was 35 Liverpool signed the Scotsman, which came as a surprise to everyone following English football! He wasn't a regular with the side until the latter half of his debut season when he absolutely led from example and became an important player for Gerard Houllier. His finest moment in a Liverpool shirt came when he scored a free-kick from 44 yards out to ensure Liverpool would be picking up all three points at Goodison Park. He was part of the treble winning team of 2001 and after just two seasons with the 'Pool, he returned to finish his career off with Coventry as player-manager. He moved full-time into management after his playing days and managed both Leeds and Aston Villa. He is currently assistant manager to Steven Gerrard at Rangers. (Photo taken at Jamie Carragher Testimonial)

## McATEER, Jason

*Midfielder*
**Born:** *1971 Tranmere, Birkenhead*
**Playing career:** *Bolton W, Liverpool, Blackburn Rovers, Sunderland, Tranmere Rovers (1991-2007)*

Jason McAteer was a life-long Liverpool fan and finally achieved his dream when he signed for the club instead of Premier League champions Blackburn in 1995. The dominant team of the 1980s certainly helped Liverpool sign future stars. He joined non-league team, Marine, in 1991 after he was spotted playing Sunday league football. He signed for Bolton and helped the team gain Premiership status in addition to featuring for the Republic of Ireland in the 1994 World Cup.

Liverpool captured their man at the start of the 1995/96 season but they previously broken his heart five months earlier as they prevented his Bolton side from reaching the League Cup final. He made an impact with Liverpool playing as a right-wing back. He was always dangerous going forward with his pinpoint accuracy, but he left much to be desired from a defensive perspective. He was a regular of the team from 1995-1997 but momentarily lost it during the start of the 1997/98 campaign. However, his determination proved vital as he regained his position back. When Gerard Houllier fully took over from Roy Evans it was obvious that McAteer would not be at Liverpool for much longer and he moved to Blackburn for £4 million. He finished his career back in Merseyside with Tranmere in 2007. One year after he retired he became John Barnes' assistant manager at the club but they were both sacked only three months into the new season. Throughout his career he was known as not being the brightest, and when he met snooker legend Jimmy White, he shouted: "hey Jimmy… One hundred and eighty!". However, he has done heroic work organising the 'Tsunami Soccer Aid' charity-match that over 38,000 people attended at Anfield on Easter Sunday 2005. This match raised £412,000 for survivors of tsunamis. He now works as a television pundit for Asia-based ESPN Star Sports. (Photo: Sony Xperia - Champions League)

## McAULEY, Hugh

*Winger*
**Born:** *1953 Bootle*
**Playing career:** *Liverpool, Tranmere Rovers (loan), Plymouth Argyle, Charlton Athletic, Tranmere Rovers, Carlisle United, Formby (1970-1981)*

Hugh McAuley started his career with Liverpool's youth setup and was even rewarded with a professional contract in 1970. Despite staying with the club for four years, he was never selected to play for the senior side. He was given his first chance of professional football when he was loaned out to neighbours Tranmere in 1973. He left Anfield for £12,000 in 1974 and won promotion to the Second Division in his first year at Plymouth. He moved to Charlton in 1976 for two years before returning to Tranmere. He hung up his boots in 1981 whilst at Formby. He later returned to Liverpool as a coach and was instrumental in their youth development from then on. He nurtured players such as: Michael Owen, Steven Gerrard, Jamie Carragher and Robbie Fowler.

### "DID YOU KNOW?"

*"Liverpool are the first English club to win the international treble of Club World Cup, Champions League and UEFA Super Cup."*

Jason McAteer

## McAULEY, Hugh
*Midfielder*
**Born:** *1976 Plymouth*
**Playing career:** *Liverpool, Northwich Victoria, Conwy United, Southport, Leigh RMI (1995-2006)*

Another Hugh McAuley, another player who never represented Liverpool's senior side! This time though, he was never offered a professional contract and was released from the academy. He did, however, make 104 Football League appearances for Cheltenham Town and Kidderminster Harriers. Away from that, he remained in the non-leagues of England for the remainder of his career. He has since become the director of The Innovation Group, who are a customised luxury car sourcing company. His company currently sponsor Doncaster Rovers Belles who play in the Women's Super League.

## McBAIN, Neil
*Half-back*
**Born:** *1895 Campbeltown, Scotland* **Died:** 1974
**Playing career:** *Campbeltown Academicals, Hamilton Academical, Ayr United, Manchester United, Everton, St Johnstone, Liverpool, Watford (1914-1947)*

Prior to joining Liverpool in 1928, Neil McBain had served both Manchester United and Everton. The Reds signed the defender from St Johnstone for £1,000. Whilst at Liverpool, he replaced long-serving full-back Tommy Lucas for the final games of the 1927/28 season when he played in 10 of the final 11 matches that campaign. However, he would only go on to record two more appearances from the bench before leaving for Watford. He moved into management and had 33 years in that role. He started with Watford and remained with the club for eight years. He then moved to Ayr United before returning to manage in England. He also had a two-year spell with Estudiantes de La Plata in Argentina before heading back to Ayr to finish his involvement with football.

### "DID YOU KNOW?"

*"Liverpool's first ever game was a 7-1 win against Rotherham Town. Malcom McVean had the honour of becoming scorer of the first goal."*

## McBRIDE, James
*Left-half*
**Born:** *1874 Renton, Scotland* **Died:** 1900
**Playing career:** *Renton Wanderers, Renton, Liverpool, Manchester City, Ashton North End*

James McBride was a regular member of the Liverpool team that won the Lancashire League in the club's first-ever season. He was also present for the club's inaugural season as Football League members, winning the Second Division and being promoted to the First Division. He moved to Manchester City in the following summer and he finished second to… Liverpool! Tragically, McBride died suddenly in his home in Manchester on 25 May 1899, he was only 25 years of age.

## McCARTNEY, John
*Half-back*
**Born:** *1870 Ayrshire, Scotland* **Died:** 1942
**Playing career:** *Newmilns F.C., St Mirren, New Brighton Tower,Liverpool (1892-1896)*

John McCartney was a hard-Scottish man who was strong in tackling. He was a member of the team that won the Lancashire League and the Second Division title with Liverpool during the club's first two seasons. He was known for his strong challenges that would often end in injury for someone! However, he got a taste of his own medicine on 21 November 1896 when Alf Milward kicked him deliberately in the Merseyside derby – being sent off in the process. He died in 1942.

## McCLURE, Billy
*Midfielder*
**Born:** *1958 Liverpool*
**Playing career:** *Liverpool Reserves, Persepolis, Mount Wellington, Papatoetoe (1974-1997)*

Billy McClure started his career off with Liverpool, signing for them in 1974. He largely spent his three years playing in the reserves, although he was called up to the senior side on eight occasions. In 1977, he became the first foreign player to play in the Iranian football league. He returned to England briefly before he moved and settled in New Zealand. He played for Mount Wellington and Papatoetoe before retiring in 1997. He was also part of the New Zealand squad that made it to the 1982 FIFA World Cup.

## McCONNELL, John

*midfielder*

**Born:** *1885 Motherwell, Scotland* **Died:** 1947
**Playing career:** *Glasgow Ashfield, Motherwell, Liverpool, Airdrie, Aberdeen (1902-1915)*

John McConnell was completely tearing up the Scottish League before he moved to Liverpool in 1909. A versatile half-back, he could play on either the right or left side. He made 13 appearances during his debut season when Liverpool finished second behind Villa. He was used more frequently the following season before completely falling out of favour at Anfield. He returned to Scotland in May 1912 by joining Aberdeen. When he retired as a player he became a painter and decorator, working for a firm in Motherwell.

## McCOWIE, Andrew

*Striker*

**Born:** *1875 Cambuslang, Scotland* **Died:** 1957
**Playing career:** *Liverpool, Woolwich Arsenal, Middlesbrough, Chesterfield Town (1897-1902)*

Andrew McCowie demonstrated his ability whilst playing in Scotland for Glasgow amateurs Cambuslang Hibernian. He signed for Liverpool in 1896. McCowie helped Liverpool establish themselves as a First Division side and scored five league goals when they finished runners-up behind Aston Villa in 1898. He finished his career with Chesterfield but a bad injury forced him to retire in 1902. He died in Cambuslang, Lanarkshire, in 1957, aged 81.

## McDERMOTT, Terry

*Midfielder*

**Born:** *1951 Liverpool*
**Playing career:** *Bury, Newcastle United, Liverpool, Cork City, APOEL (1969-1987)*

Terry McDermott was a fantastic midfielder that helped Liverpool to success during the 1970s. He needed two years to settle in the side, but when he did, he absolutely flourished. If he wasn't scoring goals he was creating them. If the team were out of possession he'd be the one to win it back. He supported Liverpool as a boy but made his debut in professional football for Bury. He later moved to Newcastle United in February 1973. He played 56 times for the Magpies and even played Liverpool in the 1974 FA Cup final before moving to Anfield later in the year. He was finally given a run in the side during the memorable 1976/77 season and he became an instrumental figure for many years. He was also voted as the FWA Footballer of the Year in 1980. He returned to Newcastle in September 1982 and helped the club win promotion to the First Division in 1984. He finished his playing career in Cyprus playing for APOEL. When he hung up his boots in 1987, he went into management. He has had two spells at St. James' Park, a stint with Huddersfield, Birmingham and is the current assistant at Blackpool. (Photo from an interview on the Anfield Wrap – see: https://www.youtube.com/watch?v=JgTDICBDbec)

Terry McDermott

## McDONALD, Ian
*Midfielder*
**Born:** *1953 Barrow-in-Furness*
**Playing career:** *Barrow, Workington Town, Liverpool, Colchester United, Mansfield Town, York City, Aldershot, (1970-1988).*

Ian Macdonald began his football career with his hometown club Barrow before he joined Workington in 1973. Liverpool came knocking only a year later but he never represented the side at senior level. He had two loan spells with Colchester United and Mansfield Town – he helped Town win the Third Division title in 1977. He then moved to York City and settled with the club for four years before joining his final club, Aldershot. He made 340 league appearances for the Hampshire club and even captained the side to promotion to the Third Division in 1987. He later moved into management and had a sole season with the Shots as caretaker manager in 1991. He then ventured back into management a whole 22 years later to manage the club he first played for 40 years ago, Workington.

## McDONNELL, PETER
*Goalkeeper*
**Born:** *1953 Kendal*
**Playing career:** *Netherfield AFC, Bury, Liverpool, Oldham Athletic, Dallas Tornado (loan), Hong Kong Rangers, Barrow, Morecambe, Barrow (1971-1992)*

Peter McDonnell may be the greatest decorated goalkeeper for a club without playing a single game for them! He earned two European gold medals as he on the bench against both Club Brugge in 1976 and Borussia Monchengladbach in 1977. He left Liverpool in August 1978 and moved to Oldham Athletic, where he made 137 appearances in four years of service. The Cumbrian then headed east to play in Hong Kong before returning to England in 1983 as player-manager of Barrow in the Northern Premier League. He was widely acknowledged as the best goalkeeper in the Conference, where he won the FA Trophy with Barrow in 1990. He is currently a referee in the North Lancashire and District Football League.

## McDOUGALL, Jimmy

*Forward/half-back*

**Born:** *1904 Inverclyde, Scotland* **Died:** 1984
**Playing career:** *Port Glasgow Athletic, Partick Thistle, George Patterson, Liverpool, Aston Villa, Villa Park, Chelsea, Charlton Athletic, The Valley, South Liverpool (1928-1931)*

Jimmy McDougall is a member of Liverpool Football Club's official Hall of Fame - and rightly so too. The Scotsman spent ten years at Anfield and was an instrumental figure for the club. He made his name with Partick Thistle by scoring 21 goals in 36 matches that season. Originally an inside-left, he was moved to half-back whilst at Anfield and he remained in that position for the rest of his time in Merseyside. He was a well-tempered player who oozed calmness and assurance when on the ball. He made his debut against Bury on 25 August 1928 and remained involved with the senior team until 1938! It is unfortunate that such a talent was part of a Liverpool team who were rarely above average. The furthest Liverpool got in the FA Cup during McDougall's stay was the quarter-finals and he won no silverware whilst at Anfield. He was also made captain of Scotland whilst he was playing for the 'Pool. Rather remarkably, he scored eight goals after his first 25 league games but could only manage another four in his next 313! However, as aforementioned, he was moved to play in the centre of defence. Once he left the club he stayed in the area and played for non-league side South Liverpool as well as coaching their youth team. He died at his home in Allerton on 3 July 1984.

## McGARVEY, Frank

*Forward*

**Born:** *1956 Glasgow, Scotland*
**Playing career:** *St Mirren, Liverpool, Celtic, St Mirren, Queen of the South, Clyde (1974-1993)*

When Frank McGarvey arrived at Liverpool there was a lot of hope for the youngster. He had scored 52 goals in 132 league matches for St Mirren and Liverpool supporters were praying he could emulate that with the club. Unfortunately, he never played a single game! He had a year with the Reds but could never break into the senior side and moved to Celtic where he became a bit of a legend. He was sold to the Scottish team for £270,000 and he became Scotland's most expensive footballer for a short time.

He scored 78 times for Celtic before heading back to St Mirren. He finished his career playing in the non-leagues of Scottish football and hung up his boots in 1996. McGarvey was quite unlucky. He finished his playing career only a few years before footballer's wages were massively inflated. He now works as a joiner in Scotland and revealed in his autobiography that he had to overcome a long-time gambling addiction. In 2016, he was still playing five-a-side football when an opponent's elbow struck his face and he lost four teeth! He has since stated that incident influenced him to give the game up altogether.

## McGREGOR, John

*Defender*

**Born:** *1963 Airdrie, Scotland*
**Playing career:** *Queen's Park, Liverpool, St Mirren, Leeds United, Rangers (1979-1992)*

John McGregor was on the verge of joining Rangers when it looked like a move to Anfield was on. However, Queen's Park Rangers rejected the bid and he finally moved to Liverpool in 1982. He stayed with the club for five years but failed to make a single senior side before eventually leaving for Rangers. Whilst he was with the Scottish club, he won the 1988 League Cup after beating Aberdeen in the final. When he retired as a player he moved into coaching and found employment with his final club as reserve manager, a role he held from 1992-2003, before being replaced by John Brown.

## McGUIGAN, Andy

*Forward*

**Born:** *1878 Newton Stewart, Scotland* **Died:** 1948
**Playing career:** *Hibernian, Liverpool, Middlesbrough, Southport Central, Accrington Stanley, Burslem Port Vale, Bristol City, Barrow, Exeter City (1898-1907)*

Andy McGuigan was a quality attacking player. His tricky forward play, with his superior eye for goal, gave Liverpool many options going forward. He was the first Liverpool player to score five goals in a league game – a number of Stoke's players were suffering from food poisoning at the time, however! They had to take it turns to leave the pitch to throw up and at one time, seven players left. He made his debut for the club on 6 October 1900 away to Derby and scored five times in 14 league matches he was selected in that season.

He did, however, help the club to win their first League Championship in 1901. He left the 'Pool after the following season and played for several English clubs before finishing his career with Exeter City. When he retired as a player he returned to Liverpool and became a director with the club. He was serving in that role when Liverpool won the League Championship in two successive years from 1922-1923.

## McInnes, Jimmy
*Defender*
**Born:** *1912 Ayr, Scotland* **Died:** 1965
**Playing career:** *Liverpool F.C., Third Lanark A.C, Second World War, Anfield, Spion Kop (1937-1940)*
Jimmy McInnes moved to Liverpool just in time to play in the final 11 league fixtures of the 1937/38 season. McInnes made his debut in a 3-1 win against Brentford on 19 March 1938 - which included the only goal he officially scored for Liverpool. He did score again on the opening day of the 1939/40 season but as the Football League was postponed only three games into the campaign, goals and appearances were expunged from the record books. After the conflict, McInnes joined Liverpool's administrative staff when he retired in 1946. He was Liverpool's secretary from 1955 until he took his own life on 5 May 1965, the day after Liverpool beat Inter Milan 3-1 in the semi-finals of the European Cup. Supposedly, he was overwhelmed with his job responsibilities and there was so much to be done, he had to resort to sleeping in a camp bed in his office. As Liverpool grew more successful, McInnes's job became harder, which ultimately led to his suicide.

## McKINLAY, Donald
*Defender*
**Born:** *1891 Glasgow, Scotland* **Died:** 1959
**Playing career:** *Nottm Forest , Anfield, Racecourse Ground, Wrexham, Merseyside, Liverpool (1910-1929)*
Donald McKinlay was a real tough man who wore the Liverpool captain's band with pride from 1922-1928. He spent 19 years with the club and when he was asked about his time in Merseyside, he said: "if I had 20 years to go again, I would go back to them". McKinlay absolutely bled red. He made his debut for the club when he was 19 years old on 20 April 1910 when his team beat Nottingham Forest 7-3.

He was used sporadically during his first two seasons with the 'Pool before he found a regular starting place that he held for many, many years. During World War I he appeared regularly for the club in wartime. However, once the Football league resumed in 1919/20, he became an integral player for the club and arguably formed the best full-back pairing in Liverpool's history with him on the left and Ephraim Longworth on the right. He led his men to two successive League Championships in 1922 and 1923. After 19 years of loyal service to the club, he was given a fourth benefit match from Liverpool which raised £468. He is a member of Liverpool Football Club's Hall of Fame. When he left Anfield he stayed in the local area and played non-league football for a while with Prescot Cables. He became a publican in the city of Liverpool when he retired from playing. He died on 16 September 1959.

## McMAHON, Steve
*Midfielder*
**Born:** *1961 Halewood, Liverpool*
**Playing career:** *Everton, Aston Villa, Liverpool, Manchester City, Swindon Town, (1979-1998).*
Steve McMahon was an influential figure for Liverpool's success in the late 1980s. He started off as a ball boy at Everton and eventually signed for his boyhood club. He was a regular player for the side for three years and was voted supporters' player of the year during his inaugural season as a professional.

Steve McMahon

Steve McManaman

He felt it was time to move on and he chose Aston Villa instead of Liverpool in 1983. However, Liverpool would finally get their man two years later, parting with £350,000 for the midfielder. In only his third game for the club, he scored a thumping effort that snatched a win away to former club Everton. His strong tackling set an example of how Liverpool would move forward in future years. He was injured late into his debut season and had to miss the FA Cup final against Everton, although the Reds triumphed. He won two League Championships and two FA Cups whilst at Anfield. He played 277 times and scored 50 goals. After six years with Liverpool, he moved to Manchester City before finishing his career in the west-country with Swindon. He moved into management and got his first taste with Blackpool, where he stayed for four years. He then went over to Australia to take charge of Perth Glory but he left his post within 12 months. He has since worked as a pundit for ESPN Star Sports and served on the board of the Profitable Group.

## McMANAMAN, Steve

*Winger*
**Born:** *1972 Kirkdale, Merseyside*
**Playing career:** *Liverpool, Real Madrid, Manchester City (1989-2005)*
Steve McManaman grew up as an Everton supporter but joined Liverpool at 14 years old. He was awarded a professional contract with the club and was given his first taste of action when he was 18 and came on against Sheffield United in 1990. He was used sporadically and only as a substitute for the remainder of his debut season. However, he was awarded with a starting position on the opening day of the following season and he showcased what the Kop could expect for the remainder of the campaign. He played in 51 games and scored 10 goals. His fitness levels were incredible as he'd always be the last one to stop running. He ran the show against Sunderland in the 1992 FA Cup final as Liverpool romped home with a 2-0 win. He picked up a few niggles over the next few seasons as Graeme Souness lost his job after several questionable performances. However, it was playing under Roy Evans where McManaman truly shone, performing with freedom and finding the net more frequently.

In total, he won two trophies with Liverpool and represented the club 364 times, scoring 66 goals. He swapped rainy England for sunny Spain in 1999 and had four good years with Real Madrid before returning to England to finish his career with Manchester City. When he retired from the game he undertook extensive media work that also saw him as the ambassador for the 2010 Champions League final that was held at the Bernabeu. He has also worked for ESPN Star based in Singapore. He co-owns several racehorses with former teammate, Robbie Fowler, and has stated his intentions to move into football management in the future.

## McNULTY, Steve

*Defender*
**Born:** *1983 Liverpool*
**Playing career:** *Liverpool, Burscough, Vauxhall Motors, Barrow, Fleetwood Town, Luton Town, Tranmere Rovers (loan), Tranmere Rovers (1990-2016)*
Steve McNulty spent 13 years in Liverpool's youth academy before he was released in 2003. He has since embarked on a career mainly in non-league football but has had success. He has achieved promotion with Luton and Tranmere – helping the latter to two successive promotions both via the play-offs. He left Merseyside in 2019 to play for York, who he is still contracted to.

## McOWEN, Billy

*Goalkeeper*
**Born:** *1871 Blackburn* **Died:** 1950
**Playing career:** *Cherry Tree, Blackburn Olympic, Blackburn Rovers, Darwen, Liverpool, Blackpool, Nelson (1888-1888)*
Billy McOwen transferred to Liverpool in 1892 but was not a regular until the following season. Sidney Ross stood in goal and remained in the starting position until he was forced to retire through injury. McOwen did, however, have the honour of becoming Liverpool's first-ever goalkeeper in a Football League match, away to Middlesbrough Ironopolis on 2 September 1893. He played in 23 of the 28 league games that season, conceding only nine – Liverpool also went the whole season unbeaten! Goalkeepers had significantly less protection during the early origins of the Football League, so it was important that they were strong and brave.

Billy McOwen

McOwen once tried to lower the bar so the ball didn't go into the net! He left the club when Liverpool were promoted to the First Division as he could make more money in his job as a dentist. Throughout his career he faced 13 penalties and saved 12 of them!

# McPHERSON, Archie

*Inside-left/Wing-half*
**Born:** *1909 Buchanan, Stirling, Scotland*
**Died:** 1969
**Playing career:** *Bathgate, angers, Liverpool, Sheffield United, Falkirk (1926-1938)*

Archie McPherson was a tricky winger who found the net on a regular occasion. He missed only two matches from his debut on 23 November 1929 to the end of the season and scored five times. Only him and Tommy Lucas were ever-present members of the squad the following year as Liverpool were unaware of who consisted of their best XI. As he spent longer at Anfield, his playing time decreased as he was gradually falling out of favour with the club. He played his final game for Liverpool in a home match against Leicester City on 17 November 1934 before moving to Sheffield United.
He finished his career in Scotland with Falkirk in 1938.

He also played cricket and was quite the batsman for Clackmannan County who participated in the Scottish Counties Championship. He returned to football 21 years after his retirement to manage Alloa Athletic for a decade. He died in his native Scotland in 1969.

# McPHERSON, Bill

*Striker*
**Born:** *1884 Ayrshire, Scotland* **Died:** 1969
**Playing career:** *Beith, St Mirren, Liverpool, Rangers, Heart of Midlothian (1906-1908)*

When Bill McPherson joined Liverpool in 1906, the club had just won its second League Championship and were looking good. Unfortunately, the team failed to reproduce the successes of the previous season and despite the Scotsman scoring on his debut, Liverpool eventually lost to Woolwich Arsenal. Although the team's performances were inconsistent, McPherson did contribute with 11 goals from 32 games. He settled with the club midway through the following season and brought his overall appearance tally to 55 before moving to back to Scotland to join Rangers in 1908. He scored in three consecutive rounds before setting up a cup final against Celtic. The tie was drawn twice and when it was revealed that a third match would have to be played, fans from both clubs rioted and set fire to the facilities! The plans for an additional replay were abandoned and the trophy was withheld that year.

## McQUEEN, Matt

*Various*

**Born:** *1863 Harthill, Scotland* **Died:** *1944*
**Playing career:** *West Benhar, Leith Athletic, Heart of Midlothian, Leith Athletic, Liverpool (1885-1899)*

Matt McQueen arrived at Anfield along with his brother only two months into the club's first season. He had eight siblings and his family lived in north Lanarkshire, a small village of only a couple of hundred that primarily made a living working in the local coalmines. He was already capped by Scotland by the time he arrived in England and he and his brother both made their debut against Newton that finished 9-0 to Liverpool! He was a versatile player and certainly the only player to win Championship medals as both an outfield player and goalkeeper! When he retired from playing he became a qualified referee. He was chosen to represent Liverpool's Board of Directors on 16 December 1919 and then four years later he was given the opportunity to manage the club. He took over the position and successfully defended the title. A car accident then changed his life forever as he was forced to have a limb amputated. He retired from the injury but continued to attend Liverpool matches up to his death on 29 September 1944.

## McVEAN, Malcolm

*Winger*

**Born:** *1871 Jamestown, Scotland* **Died:** *1907*
**Playing career:** *Third Lanark, Liverpool, Burnley, Dundee, Bedminster (1892-1897)*

Malcolm McVean will always be remembered for being the goal scorer of Liverpool's first official goal in the Football League against Middlesbrough Ironopolis on 2 September 1893. Liverpool were promoted in their inaugural season but found life difficult in the First Division as the standard of play rose significantly. They were subsequently relegated back down to the second tier of English football. He remained at Anfield and won another winners medal for the 1995/96 promotion to the First Division. He left for Burnley but also experienced relegation with his new team. Prior to signing for the 'Pool he had begun an apprenticeship working as a shipyard boilermaker, a career he returned to after he hung up his boots. He died in Bonhill in June 1907, only 36 years old.

M·McVEAN

M'VEAN, LIVERPOOL.

## MEIJER, Erik

*Striker*

**Born:** *1969 Meerssen, Netherlands*
**Playing career:** *SV Meerssen, MVV Maastricht, Fortuna Sittard, Royal Antwerp, Eindhoven, Fortuna Sittard, MVV, PSV, KFC Uerdingen, Bayer Leverkusen, Liverpool, Preston North End (loan), Hamburger SV, Alemannia Aachen (1984-2006)*

In the summer of 1999, Liverpool were in the market for a tall striker, and Gerard Houllier believed that Erik Meijer would be the man to help strengthen the team. He only lasted a season and a half at Liverpool, with 10 starts and 17 substitute appearances. Although he only found the net twice during his stay at Anfield, his attitude and willingness on the pitch did not go unnoticed by fans of the club. When Liverpool were in the 2001 UEFA Cup final he attended the match and partied with Liverpool fans. After his playing days had come to a close, he became assistant coach of Alemannia Aachen and then Director of Sport until 2011. He continues to be a patron for A.F.C Liverpool, a club run by the fans of Liverpool's professional team.

## MEIRELES, Raul

*Midfielder*

**Born:** *1983 Porto, Portugal*
**Playing career:** *Boavista, Aves (loan), Porto, Liverpool, Chelsea, Fenerbahce (1990-2012)*

Prior to moving to England in 2010, Raul Meireles had played football in his homeland for the entirety of his career. He started with Boavista before impressing during his debut campaign and signing for his hometown club Porto. However, he had to wait a couple of years before cementing his name into the first XI but remained an integral member of their squad when he did. As his reputation grew, so did his global recognition. He starred for Portugal in the 2008 European Championship and the 2010 World Cup – where he scored the opening goal as his country thrashed North Korea 7-0. Meireles only spent a year at Anfield and his time could be viewed as a success. He only missed five Premier League matches and played in eight cup fixtures. He was originally played out of position by Roy Hodgson but when he moved to a more central role he flourished. His sensational volley away to Wolves was voted Liverpool's Goal of the Season.

Raul Meireles

Unfortunately for Liverpool fans, he moved to Stamford Bridge in the summer of 2011 and played regularly during his debut season in London. He was brought on for the final 15 minutes against Liverpool in the FA Cup final where he won his first English silverware. He was, however, suspended from the Champions League final against Bayern Munich as he had been cautioned in the previous game against Barcelona. He left Chelsea after just a year and moved to Turkish club Fenerbahçe. He retired in 2016. He and his wife opened up a clothing store whilst he was playing that was still in business in 2019.

## MELIA, Jimmy

*Midfielder*

**Born:** *1937 Liverpool*
**Playing career:** *Liverpool, Wolves, Southampton, Aldershot, Crewe Alexandra (1952-1972)*

Jimmy Melia was a local lad who came through the youth academy. He would turn out for the senior side over 300 times and spend ten years in total with Liverpool. A great midfielder with a keen eye for goal, his 79 goals were crucial as he won two honours with the club. The Second Division title in 1961/62 and the First Division title only two years later. Melia was one of 11 siblings but he was the only one to carve a career out of professional football. In total, he made 571 league appearances for five different clubs. When he called time on his playing career he coached in the United Arab Emirates, Kuwait and America before being appointed Brighton's chief scout. When they were relegated, Melia moved to Portugal to manage Belenenses. He then returned to America and served as Technical Director to Liverpool's academy in Texas before joining Cleveland Cobras in 1979. He continues to coach at academies in America, but explains the goal is not to help these youngsters become pro footballers, but to help them go to college for free on a soccer scholarship.

### "DID YOU KNOW?"

*"Alex Raisbeck was the first Liverpool captain to lift the Football League first division championship trophy (in 1901)."*

Neil Mellor

## MELLOR, Neil

*Striker*
**Born:** *1982 Sheffield*
**Playing career:** *Liverpool, West Ham United (loan), Preston North End (1999-2011)*

Neil Mellor's father, Ian, made his name with Manchester City and his son was part of their academy until he was released. He dreamt of playing in light blue but when Liverpool offered to take him into their youth setup, he could not refuse. He started off well in the academy and was the team's top scorer during the FA youth cup run in the 2000/01 season. The following campaign he was in even finer form, scoring 27 goals for the U-18s and 18 goals in 18 games for the reserves. He was awarded with a new contract in 2003 after making his senior side debut and starting the next three games. He was loaned out to West Ham in August 2003 but a lack of playing opportunities and fitness brought him back to Liverpool quicker than expected. He continued his scoring form in the reserves and after 44 matches, he had netted 45 times. His best spell with the club came in 2004 and included a dramatic winner against Arsenal in front of the Kop. Injuries continued to hamper Mellor's career and he moved on to Preston in 2006. He scored 38 league goals in four years for his new side before calling it quits in 2012. Since retiring from the game he has gone into the media sector and has worked extensively with both Sky Sports and LFC TV. (Neil's Twitter profile has over 95,000 followers - https://twitter.com/neilmellor33)

## MERCER, Billy

*Goalkeeper*
**Born:** *1969 Liverpool*
**Playing career:** *Liverpool, Rotherham United, Sheffield United, Nottingham Forest (loan), Chesterfield, Bristol City (1987-2003)*

Billy Mercer was born in Cantril Farm and joined Liverpool as a trainee before turning professional at the age of 18 in 1987. He remained with the club for the next 18 months but never represented the senior side. He signed for Rotherham on 16 February 1989 and stayed in Yorkshire for five years, playing in over 100 league matches. Shortly after his departure from Anfield, Mercer travelled to Hillsborough as a supporter for Liverpool's FA Cup semi-final against Nottingham Forest. He was situated in the upper tier of the Leppings Lane end, directly above where the tragic incident took place. He moved to Sheffield United in 1994 but was largely left out of the side at Bramall Lane during his 12-month stay. He was loaned out to Chesterfield and made such a good impression with the club that they tabled a £100,000 bid the moment his loan had expired. He remained at the Saltergate for four years before he moved to Bristol City in 1999, retiring in 2003. When he hung up his boots, he moved into coaching with Bristol City before having similar roles with both Sheffield Wednesday and Burnley.

## METCALF, Arthur

*Forward*
**Born:** *1889 Sunderland*    **Died:** *1936*
**Playing career:** *Newcastle United, Liverpool, Stockport County, Swindon Town, Accrington Stanley, Aberdare Athletic, Norwich City (1907-1926)*

When Arthur Metcalf arrived at Anfield in 1912, he had only played 12 games for Newcastle, finding the net twice. He was an intelligent forward who had much more to his game than sheer pace. He left Liverpool with a fantastic goals-per-game ratio (2.25) and was the club's top scorer in his debut 1912/13 season with 18 goals. He also bagged a hat-trick that season, as Liverpool beat Arsenal 4-1 in a second-round victory. Metcalf got injured the following campaign and was left out of action for the next five months, although he did recover in time to participate in the 'Pool's FA Cup run that stretched all the way to the final.

His final season in red was in 1914/15 and he added seven more goals to his name before he moved to Stockport County after World War I. He finished his career in 1926 whilst playing for Norwich City. When he retired he worked at Anfield as a gateman but took ill and passed away whilst on duty on 9 February 1936, at the age of 46.

## MILES, John
*Forward*
**Born:** *1981 Bootle*
**Playing career:** *Liverpool, Stoke City, Crewe Alexandra, Macclesfield Town, Accrington Stanley, Milton Keynes Dons (loan), Fleetwood Town, Droylsden (loan), Stockport County, Altrincham, Warrington Town, Cammell Laird (1999-2014)*
John Miles started his career in the youth department at Liverpool and was awarded a professional contract in 2001. He managed to turn out for the reserves a couple of times before he was told he had no future at the club. He moved to Stoke in March 2002 but only made one substitute appearance before he was on his way out. He failed to settle again with third club Crewe and was loaned out to Macclesfield. The loan was made permanent and he spent four years with the club. He had three years with Accrington Stanley before moving to Fleetwood and then dropping into the non-leagues of football. In total, Miles played for 13 clubs throughout his 12-year career!

## MILNE, Arthur
*Centre-forward*
**Born:** *1914 Brechin, Scotland*
**Died:** *1997*
**Playing career:** *Brechin Vics, Dundee United, Liverpool, Hibernian, St Mirren, Coleraine, Cowdenbeath (1934-1953)*
Arthur Milne signed for Dundee United when he was 20 years old and rather remarkably, scored four times on his senior debut – no other player has been able to match that in the club's history! He scored 77 goals in 73 league appearances which is another record, as no other player has been able to match the goal-per-game ratio. His performances in Scotland would have certainly influenced Liverpool to sign the forward. He was given a trial with the English club but there was mass confusion with what followed. As he was trialling at another club, he was deemed as a free agent.

Instead of joining Liverpool, he joined Scottish team Hibernian! He scored a whole heap of goals for his new club, but he was unable to emulate the sensational form he was in for Dundee. World War II disrupted his career but he did feature for both Dundee and Aberdeen during wartime - which was acceptable as long as the contracted club gave their permission. After the conflict, he continued to play in Scotland with St Mirren before finishing his career with Cowdenbeath. He also served in the war and after his playing career had concluded he moved into a coaching role with Coleraine. He died in 1997.

## MILNE, Gordon
*Midfielder*
**Born:** *1937 Preston*
**Playing career:** *Preston Amateurs, Morecambe, Preston North End, Liverpool, Blackpool, Wigan Athletic (1956-1972)*
Bill Shankly had been well aware of Gordon Milne's talent prior to his signing for Liverpool as he used to play for Preston with his father, Jimmy Milne. The midfielder was selfless, often creating goals for teammates to steal the spotlight. Liverpool were promoted to the First Division after the 1961/62 season and Milne had transitioned into a topflight player effortlessly. He became an important competitor for the club and only missed a couple of league fixtures over the next three years. He won the League Championship with the club in 1964 but he missed the 1965 FA Cup final through injury – his father missed Preston's 1938 cup win through injury too. Liverpool won the domestic title again in 1966 but Milne was out injured for two months during the latter half of the season, ultimately missing out on selection for the victorious 1966 World Cup. He was sold to Blackpool in May 1967 when he was 30 years old and he spent three years with the club before hanging up his boots with Wigan as player-manager in 1972.
He clearly enjoyed his role at Wigan as he moved into management, having stints with England U-18s, Coventry, Leicester, Besiktas and Trabzonspor to name a few. He also became the Chief Executive of the League Managers Association as well as serving as Director of Football at Newcastle United.

Jan Molby

## MINSHULL, Ray

*Goalkeeper*
**Born:** *1920 Bolton* **Died:** 2005
**Playing career:** *Liverpool, Southport, Bradford, Wigan Rovers (1939-1960)*

Despite spending four years with Liverpool, Minshull only made 31 appearances and was forced to leave Anfield for more playing opportunities. He signed for Southport in 1951 and made 217 appearances for the club before moving to Wigan Rovers' as player-manager. When he finished playing entirely, he coached in Gibraltar and Austria. He also became a successful youth coach at Everton during the 70s and 80s, unearthing talents such as Gary Stevens and Kevin Ratcliffe. He died in February 2005, at the age of 84.

## MOLBY, Jan

*Central midfielder/Central defender (Ajax)*
**Born:** *1963 Kolding, Denmark*
**Playing career:** *Kolding, Ajax, Liverpool, Barnsley (loan), Norwich City (loan), Swansea City (1981-1998)*

Jan Molby entered the record books as one of the most talented players to ever pull on a Liverpool jersey. Although he was slightly overweight, he compensated for that with his vision, incredible skill, superb passing and lethal shooting ability.

John Molyneux

When Graeme Souness left Liverpool, the Dane was invited to a ten-day trial with the club – he ended up staying for 12 years! He impressed so much during his first game for the club on trial, that Joe Fagan had signed him only two days later. Molby was undoubtedly one of the 'Pool's best players during the double season of 1985/86 and when Kenny Dalglish took over, he could not believe he was in the reserves. Whilst playing under the Scotsman, Molby had unending freedom and demonstrated his versatility by either playing in a deep-lying role or directly behind the striker. He won two League Championships and two FA Cups whilst at Liverpool, recording 292 appearances and scoring 61 goals. He left for Swansea in 1996 before hanging up his boots after two years with the Welsh club. He spent the final year with the club as player-manager before moving into management full-time after his retirement. He has managed at Kidderminster Harriers twice and Hull. He has worked for BBC radio and has also played in several high-profile poker events.

## MOLYNEUX, John

*Right-back*
**Born:** *1931 Warrington, Lancashire*
**Died:** 2018
**Playing career:** *Chester, Eric Sibley, Liverpool, Don Welsh, Ewood Park, Blackburn Rovers, Southend United, Tony Rowley (1949-1962)*

John Molyneux joined Liverpool in 1955 for £4,000 with £1,500 of this to be paid after he had played in 12 fixtures. He was a powerful right-back with a strong physique. Although he may not have been the slickest on the ball, his no-nonsense approach was certainly appreciated by the Kop after they had just watched their team be relegated from the First Division the season prior. Molyneux was a regular of the side for six of the eight years that the club were in the Second Division for. His final season saw Liverpool promoted but he was left out to accommodate for new arrival Ron Yeats. Upon Liverpool's promotion, the full-back moved to Chester City and played a couple more years before cartilage trouble ended his professional footballing journey. Molyneux was capped 249 times for Liverpool and scored 3 goals.

## MONEY, Richard

*Defender*
**Born:** *1955 Lowestoft*
**Playing career:** *Scunthorpe United, Fulham, Liverpool, Derby County, Luton Town, Portsmouth, Scunthorpe United. (1973-1989).*

By the time Richard Money was 24, he had already compiled 300 league fixtures for lower-league clubs Scunthorpe and Fulham. He signed for Liverpool for a fee of £50,000 but failed to make the first XI regularly, despite the team's erratic form that season. His highlight for Liverpool was his fantastic defensive display against Bayern Munich in the 1980/81 European Cup semi-final second leg against Bayern Munich. The 1-1 result on the night meant that Liverpool would progress to their third European Cup final in the space of only five years! He moved into management after his playing days and has managed six English clubs and even had stints in Sweden and Australia. His most recent role was with Hartlepool United where he was appointed manager on 11 December 2018, but he took on a more senior role with the club the following month. However, after just five days in his new role, he left his position after he was verbally abused in a fish and chip shop.

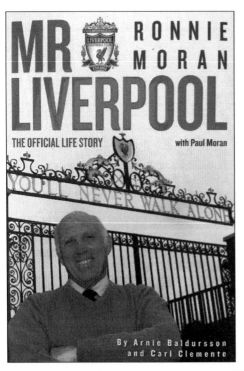

## MOORCROFT, Dave

*Centre-back*
**Born:** *1947 Liverpool*
**Playing career:** *Liverpool schoolboys, Everton, Preston North End, Skelmersdale United, Dallas Tornado, Tranmere Rovers (1961-1973)*

Dave Moorcroft came through Everton's youth setup after spending a year with Liverpool's schoolboys. He signed his first professional contract with Preston in 1967 but would drop into non-league football the following season. He ventured over to America in 1968 and spent two years playing for Dallas Tornado before returning to England to finish his career with Tranmere in 1973 at the age of 26 after an irreparable injury. When he finished his career he moved into retail and had a stint as a youth coach with his final club. He later carved a successful profession in the protective clothing business.

## MORAN, Ronnie

*Left-back*
**Born:** *1934 Liverpool*
**Playing career:** *Liverpool (1952-1964).*

Ronnie Moran joined Liverpool at 15 years old after he was recommended to the club by a postman who used to deliver to Liverpool's chairman! He started playing football with Crosby Boys before he won a scholarship to study at Bootle Technical College which offered advanced facilities and therefore an increased chance of development. A week after signing for the club, Everton had asked Moran to trials, but it was too late. Liverpool's chairman, Samuel Williams, and manager, George Kay, had visited the youngster at his home with the postman to finalise the deal. He signed professionally with the club in January 1952, a few days prior to his eighteenth birthday. He made his senior debut at left-back against Derby in November 1952 but largely found himself away from the team, playing only 13 times throughout the next 18 months. However, when Eddie Spicer broke his leg, it paved the way for Moran to be included in the first team and he would only miss six league matches over the next five years! When Bill Shankly arrived at the club in 1959, the full-back was captain. Unfortunately, he suffered an injury on 1 October 1960 and was out injured for the next 14 months.

He returned from his setback and helped steer Liverpool to the First Division title only two yeas after they had been promoted to the topflight of English football. He eventually lost his position to Chris Lawler during the 1964/65 season but he did make a return at the end of the campaign to feature in both legs against Inter Milan. In total, he represented the 'Pool 379 times and won the Second Division and the First Division as a player. When his playing days had concluded, Shankly offered him a role with the coaching staff, which he accepted. He later filled in as caretaker manager on two occasions, firstly after Kenny Dalglish's resignation in 1991 and after Graeme Souness was recovering from a triple by-pass heart operation in 1992. He retired indefinitely in 1998 after 49 years with Liverpool and he was awarded a testimonial match against Celtic on 16 May 2000.

## MORIENTES, Fernando

*Striker*
**Born:** *1976 Caceres, Spain*
**Playing career:** *Zaragoza, Real Madrid, Liverpool, Valencia, Marseille, Santa Ana (1993-2015)*
Fernando Morientes made his name with Albacete in 1993 before joining Real Zaragoza and scoring 36 goals in only two seasons for the club. This prompted Real Madrid to sign the striker and he was able to showcase his fine goalscoring ability on the biggest European stage. He won the Champions League three times with the club. He was loaned out to Monaco in 2004 and he scored nine goals in 12 Champions League games which resulted in him being named the European Striker of the Year. Madrid would have certainly regretted the loan move, as Morientes netted in both legs during the quarter-finals to eliminate the club that paid his wages! In total, the Spaniard scored 99 times for the Spanish giants before Ronaldo's move forced him to seek employment elsewhere. He arrived at Liverpool in 2005 but was cup-tied for the remainder of the Champions League campaign as he had played for Madrid earlier in the season. However, Liverpool conquered without the striker in Istanbul. He had to wait four games into his Anfield career before finding the net – which was followed up by another goal in the next match.

There was no doubt that Morientes was a skilful player, but he never truly established himself with Liverpool and had to settle for a place in the squad, other than the team. He returned to Spain after 18 months with Liverpool and signed for Valencia. He initially finished his career in 2010 with Marseille before briefly coming out of retirement to play three games for Spanish side Santa Ana. He moved into management when he finished his playing days and had a stint with Real Madrid's youth academy before taking his first senior role with Fuenlabrada. However, he was sacked in 2016 after the club had failed to progress during the eight months he was in charge.

## MORRIS, Fred

*Winger*
**Born:** *1929 Oswestry* **Died:** 1998
**Playing career:** *Walsall, Mansfield Town, Liverpool, Crewe Alexandra, Gillingham, Chester, Altrincham, Oswestry Town (1950-1962)*
Fred Morris played for his local club, Oswestry Town, as an amateur before he signed professional papers with Walsall – playing in 227 matches for the club and scoring 49 goals. He moved to Mansfield before finally signing for Liverpool in May 1958. He was nearing 29 years old when he arrived at Anfield but he was still able to demonstrate what he brought to the team. He was not selected for the first two matches of the 1958/59 season but he did play in the following 41 and scored 12 times, an impressive tally from his right-wing position. An injury kept him out of the team during the early stages of the following campaign, but he did return to score twice as Liverpool beat Leyton Orient 4-3 on 21 November 1959. However, only days later, Bill Shankly arrived at Liverpool and Morris was one of the first to leave the club. He was transferred to Crewe before moving to Gillingham and finishing his professional career with Chester in 1962. He later returned to Oswestry and became manager of the non-league team. When he retired from playing, he ran a building contractor's business and took over a garage in Oswestry. He died in 1998, aged 69.

## MORRISSEY, Johnny
*Outside-left*
**Born:** *1940 Liverpool*
**Playing career:** *Liverpool, Everton, Oldham Athletic. (1957-1972).*

Johnny Morrissey spent several years in the youth academy before signing professionally in May 1957, shortly after becoming 17 years old. Kevin Lewis kept him out of the team for the first three years but he eventually started to play regularly from 1960 onwards. When Roger Hunt picked up an injury, Alan O'Court was moved to play through the middle to allow Morrissey to play on the left-wing. He failed to truly establish himself amongst Liverpool's talented squad and when Ian Callaghan was brought into the senior team, Morrissey was sold for £10,000 in 1962. The transfer took place without Shankly's approval and the manager threatened to leave the club after the deal was made. He spent ten successful years with Everton and won the league in 1963 and the FA Cup three years later. He finished his career with Oldham in 1973 and became a successful businessman mainly with property interests.

## MUGGLETON, Carl
*Goalkeeper*
**Born:** *1968 Leicester*
**Playing career:** *Leicester City, Blackpool (loan), Hartlepool United (loan), Stockport County (loan), Liverpool (loan), Stoke City (loan), Celtic, Stoke City, Rotherham United (loan), Sheffield United (loan), Mansfield Town (loan), Cardiff City (loan), Cheltenham Town, Bradford City (loan), Chesterfield, Mansfield Town (1986-2008)*

Carl Muggleton had a peculiar career. He started his playing days with Leicester in 1986 but only made 46 appearances across eight years – he was loaned out on seven occasions. He signed for Celtic in 1994 but only spent a year in Scotland before transferring to Stoke the following season. He made 149 appearances for the Potters in seven years but was once again loaned out frequently. In total, Muggleton had 13 loan spells during his career! He was loaned to Liverpool whilst contracted with Leicester but he never featured for the club. When he retired in 2008, he moved into coaching and had spells with Notts County, Gillingham and Barnet. Muggleton is also a qualified driving instructor.

## MURDOCH, Bobby
*Striker*
**Born:** *1936 Garston, Liverpool*   **Died:** 2017
**Playing career:** *Liverpool, Bolton Wanderers, Barrow, Stockport County, Carlisle United (1952-1976)*

Bobby Murdoch was a clinical striker who averaged a goal every three games throughout his career in professional football. He was a local lad who signed professionally for Liverpool in May 1957 after having two years as an amateur. He played in 15 of the final 18 league matches of the 1957/58 season and found the net on five occasions. However, he was only called upon twice the following season before leaving Anfield two months prior to the arrival of Bill Shankly. Murdoch later became a player for South Liverpool in 1965 and was appointed as player-manager in 1971, remaining in the role until 1976. When he retired from football he ran a taxi-cab firm in Liverpool before retiring in Cheshire. He died on 12 February 2017, aged 81.

## MURPHY, Danny
*Midfielder*
**Born:** *1977 Chester*
**Playing career:** *Liverpool, Crewe Alexandra (loan), Charlton Athletic, Tottenham Hotspur, Fulham, Blackburn Rovers (1993-2013)*

Danny Murphy started his footballing journey in the Crewe academy before he signed professionally for the club in 1993. His excellent performances saw Liverpool come knocking in 1997 and he signed on 15 July for £1.5 million. He was greatly experienced for a 20-year-old, having played for Crewe in 132 Football League matches. Despite the excitement, he failed to settle at Liverpool for the first three years of his time at Anfield and a lack of opportunities paved the way for him to return to Crewe on loan in February 1999.

Danny Murphy

However, when he returned, he finally demonstrated what all the fuss was about and started to pop up with important goals. He was instrumental in the treble-winning 2000/01 season as Liverpool won the League Cup, FA Cup and the UEFA Cup. He would only miss four league games over the next two years and he was voted best player by Liverpool fans in 2002/03, where he found the net on 12 occasions. Liverpool's following season was a big disappointment and this eventually led to him moving to Charlton in the summer. He moved to Spurs before settling at Fulham and spending five years at Craven Cottage prior to finishing his career with Blackburn in 2013. When he retired as a player he moved into the media sector and has had a successful career working with the BBC and Talksport. He is also a qualified physiotherapist.

### "DID YOU KNOW?"

*"When Roy Evans took over from Graham Souness as manager, he had been on the club's payroll for almost 30 years."*

## MURPHY, Neil
*Defender*
**Born:** *1980 Liverpool*
**Playing career:** *Liverpool, Luton Town (loan), Blackpool, Altrincham, Marine, Kidsgrove Athletic, Kendal Town, Maghull (1999-2010)*

Neil Murphy was part of the same Liverpool youth team as Steven Gerrard, Michael Owen and Jamie Carragher – yet he had a very different career in football. He was awarded a professional contract in 1999 after his fine performances in the academy. However, after only a year with the club, he was released without playing a single game for the first team. Blackpool picked the defender up but he only made seven appearances across two seasons with the Seasiders. He subsequently dropped into the non-leagues of football and finally found a regular starting spot during a four-year stay at Marine. He is currently playing for West Cheshire League side Maghull and has been there since 2010. When he realised he was not going to make it as a professional player he trained as a fireman and is currently employed in that position as well as working part-time as a coach at the Youth Academy.

## NAVARRO, Alan

*Midfielder*

**Born:** *1981 Liverpool*

**Playing career:** *Liverpool, Crewe Alexandra (loan), Tranmere Rovers (loan), Tranmere Rovers, Chester-City (loan), Macclesfield Town (loan), Accrington Stanley, Macclesfield Town, Milton Keynes Dons, Brighton & Hove Albion, Swindon Town (2000-2014)*

There was a lot of promise after Alan Navarro signed professionally for Liverpool in 2000, having come through the youth academy. However, after being named on the bench only twice – and not being used – he moved to local team Tranmere Rovers after a successful loan spell with the club. He spent three years there before moving on to Accrington Stanley. He eventually had two elongated stints with MK Dons and Brighton before moving to Swindon to finish his career in 2014. He is now employed for an insurance company that provide injury cover for athletes and he is also taking his coaching badges.

## NEAL, Ashley

*Defender*

**Born:** *1974 Northampton*

**Playing career:** *Liverpool, Brighton & Hove Albion (loan), Huddersfield Town, Peterborough United (1990-1998)*

Ashley Neal came through the youth academy at Liverpool and was awarded a professional contract with the club in 1990. He spent six years contracted at Anfield but failed to make a single appearance for the senior team and was loaned out to Brighton in 1996. He only made four appearances and was largely disappointing for the team who played in the lowest professional league in England. He was signed by Huddersfield in the same year but once again failed to appear for the club. He finished his career with Peterborough in 1998 after playing only eight times. In total, Neal played in 12 league matches throughout his career – a stark contrast to his father, who racked up 650 appearances for Liverpool alone. However, away from football and Neal runs a successful driving school.

Phil Neal

## NEAL, Phil
*Full-back*
**Born:** *1951 Irchester, Northamptonshire*
**Playing career:** *Northampton Town, Liverpool, Bolton Wanderers. (1968-1988).*

His son may not have made it as a footballer, but Phil Neal was certainly the real deal. Prior to joining Liverpool in 1974, he had featured in over 200 league games for Northampton. He was Bob Paisley's first managerial signing – and arguably the best of the bunch! He made his debut for Liverpool in a Merseyside derby and looked at complete ease playing in the tense match. This started off a phenomenal run of consecutive games that Neal played for Liverpool – a total of 417 between 23 October 1976 and 24 September 1983. Needless to say, that is a Liverpool record! He then missed three games through injury before playing in 127 more matches in a row! Neal played 50 times for England and is widely acknowledged as one of the greatest English full-backs of all time. In total, he played 650 times for Liverpool and scored 59 times from his full-back position. He won every club honour available to him bar the FA Cup during his time at Anfield: eight League Championships, four League Cups, four European Cups, one UEFA Cup and one European Super Cup. After 11 fantastic years with the club he left for Bolton and was appointed player-manager in 1985, remaining in that role until he retired as a player in 1989. He continued to manage Bolton and eventually left his post in 1992. He managed Coventry and Cardiff before stepping in as caretaker manager at Manchester City in 1996. He was Graham Taylor's assistant manager when at England and was also appointed assistant manager of Peterborough during the 1997/98 season before coaching and playing in Liverpool's master's side. He has most recently worked in broadcast media roles as a football pundit for both radio and television.

### "DID YOU KNOW?"

*"Joe Fagan was appointed manager in 1984 and in his first season, the club won the League title, the League Cup and the European Cup."*

## NEIL, Robert
*Centre-half and at Wing-half.*
**Born:** *1875 Glasgow* **Died:** *1913*
**Playing career:** *Heart of Midlothian, Liverpool, Rangers, (1896-1900)*

Robert Neil had a brief loan spell with Liverpool before signing for the club in May 1896. Rather peculiarly, he was a fantastic central-defender despite being only 5 foot, 4 inches tall! Liverpool had just returned to the First Division when the Scotsman signed for the club. He found the net twice in the league and scored another against West Brom in the FA Cup. However, after one season in England, he returned to Scotland due to a family bereavement and had a successful career with Rangers where he won four League Championships and one Scottish Cup. When he retired from playing football he became a restaurateur up until his death in March 1913, aged only 37.

## NEWBY, Jon
*Striker*
**Born:** *1978 Warrington*
**Playing career:** *Liverpool, Carlisle United (loan), Crewe Alexandra (loan), Sheffield United (loan), Bury (loan), Bury, Huddersfield Town, York City (loan), Bury, Wrexham (1988-2013)*

Jon Newby was a rapid striker who came through the youth academy at Liverpool. He won the 1996 FA Youth Cup alongside Jamie Carragher and Michael Owen – but the latter two would have much different careers to Newby. After spending ten years in the youth sector at Anfield, he was awarded a professional contract in 1998 but he failed to make a significant impact. He featured for roughly 30 minutes in four substitute appearances in the 1999/00 season and he was loaned out on four occasions before moving to Bury in March 2001. He scored 17 goals in 100 league games for the club but he moved to Huddersfield before returning to Bury. He joined Morecambe in 2007 and despite being the club's joint top-scorer, he was released after a year. He eventually dropped into the lower league of amateur football and had a brief stint as player-manager for Colwyn Bay. He continues to play at the age of 41 as of 2020 and is currently playing for Little Lever. He has since returned to Liverpool and is working as a coach and a scout for the club's academy, where his journey first took place.

*'Stevie was a real one-off. He made a great contribution
to the success of Liverpool Football Club'* – *Kenny Dalglish*

# S T E V I E
# NICOL
## MY AUTOBIOGRAPHY

5 League titles and a Packet of crisps

FOREWORD BY
**ALAN HANSEN**

## NEWELL, Mike

*Striker*
**Born:** *1965 Liverpool*
**Playing career:** *Liverpool, Crewe Alexandra, Wigan Athletic, Luton Town, Leicester City, Everton, Blackburn Rovers, Birmingham City, West Ham United (loan), Bradford City (loan), Aberdeen, Crewe Alexandra, Doncaster Rovers, Blackpool (1982-2001)*

Mike Newell spent a sole year in Liverpool's academy before being released and signed by Crewe in 1982. In total, he played for 13 different teams throughout his professional playing career, playing in 528 league matches and scoring 119 goals. He hung up his boots with Blackpool in 2001 after a sole season with the Seasiders. Newell swiftly moved into management and had his first taste with Tranmere as reserve manager. He became the manager of Hartlepool in 2002 before moving to Luton a year later. Whilst at the Hatters, he criticised the way Luton was being ran and gave evidence in a corruption scandal – he was sacked after four years in charge. He moved to Grimsby before having a six-year hiatus away from football. His latest post was with Wrexham as assistant manager but he left the club by mutual consent on 7 February 2019.

## NICHOLAS, Andrew

*Defender*
**Born:** *1983 Liverpool*
**Playing career:** *Liverpool, Swindon Town, Chester-City (loan), Rotherham United, Mansfield Town (loan), Barrow, Vauxhall Motors, Marine (2002-2014)*

Andrew Nicholas started his career with Liverpool in 2002 but left the club after a year without making a single appearance. Whilst at Anfield, he was timed as being faster than Michael Owen! When he was released, Swindon signed the defender and he spent five years in the west country before moving to Yorkshire to feature for Rotherham. This would be his final professional club before he began to drop into non-league football. He is currently back at Liverpool working as a coach for the club's international academy and has been in the role since 2012.

## "DID YOU KNOW?"

*"Actors Liam Neeson and Brad Pitt are both Liverpool FC fans!"*

## NICHOLSON, John

*Centre-half*
**Born:** *1936 Liverpool* **Died:** 1966
**Playing career:** *Liverpool, Port Vale, Doncaster Rovers (1957-1966)*

John Nicholson made one appearance for Liverpool during the two years he had with the club. Unfortunately for Nicholson, Ron Yeats arrived which spelt the end for the centre-half. He left for Port Vale in August 1961 and made over 180 appearances for the club before moving again to Doncaster. He sadly passed away whilst contracted with Doncaster on 3 September 1966 after he was involved in a head on collision with a lorry. He never regained consciousness from the incident and died at the age of 30.

## NICOL, Steve

*Defender*
**Born:** *1961 Troon, Scotland*
**Playing career:** *Ayr United, Liverpool, Notts County, Sheffield Wednesday, West Bromwich Albion, Doncaster Rovers (1979-2001)*

Steve Nicol was brought to Anfield as a 19-year-old by Bob Paisley in October 1981. He was viewed as long-term cover for the ageing right-back Phil Neal. He was signed for £300,000 from Ayr United where he was a part-time player and a builder! He began to demonstrate his ability for Liverpool during the greatly successful 1983/84 season when the 'Pool won the League Championship, European Cup and the League Cup – although Nicol did not feature in enough games for a League Cup medal. Neal was still playing for the club at the time and Nicol slotted nicely into midfield. He started just under half of the club's games that season and he came second in the PFA's Most Promising Player of the year, just behind Luton's Paul Walsh. Nicol is one of the most versatile players. He could play anywhere across the midfield or defence. The Scotsman was a regular for Liverpool during his 11 years with the club and retired after 468 matches and 46 goals. When he left Liverpool he had brief spells with a few other English clubs before hanging up his boots with the Boston Bulldogs. He moved into management after his playing days and held the record for the longest-tenured head coach in the MLS after managing New England Revolution for nine years. He now works as a commentator for ESPN FC.

## NIELSEN, Jorgen

*Goalkeeper*
**Born:** *1971 Nykobing Falster, Denmark*
**Playing career:** *Nakskov Boldklub, Helsingor IF, Naestved, olstykke FC, Hvidovre IF, Liverpool, Ikast FS (loan), Wolverhampton Wanderers (loan), Farum BK, Hellerup, Frem, (1975-2008)*

Jorgen Nielsen signed for Liverpool in 1997 and spent five years at Anfield. He was named on the bench on over 50 occasions but failed to make a single appearance! Unfortunately for the Dane, Sander Westerveld was sent off during a Merseyside derby on 27 September 1999 but Liverpool had used all of their substitutions, resulting in Steve Staunton having to use his shirt and go into goal. He returned to Denmark in 2003 and momentarily retired from football so he could focus on his political science university degree. He returned a year later but would indefinitely retire at the end of the season. In April 2019 he returned to the game as a goalkeeping coach at Nordvest.

## NIEUWENHUYS, Berry

*Outside-right*
**Born:** *1911 Transvaal, South Africa* **Died:** 1984
**Playing career:** *Boksburg, Germiston Callies, Liverpool (1933-1947)*

Berry Nieuwenhuys grew up loving sport. After finishing his schooling he went to work in the mines in Transvaal and played sport as a hobby. His first love was rugby but when he discovered football – and he realised he was pretty good at it – it took priority. Whilst playing a minor club game in South Africa someone ran onto the pitch and asked him if he would like to play for Liverpool. Confused but excited, he accepted. Only a few weeks later, he was playing in front of 50,000 people on the other side of the world! Eight years prior to his arrival in 1933, Arthur Riley had left South Africa to play for Liverpool. It was Riley's dad who spotted Nieuwenhuys and Lance Carr and contacted Liverpool's management to inform them he found two bright youngsters. He was told to hire them and the club arranged travel to England! He made his debut against Tottenham on 23 September 1933 and after a difficult first half, he began to shine and assisted two goals. His very next game was none other than the Merseyside derby and he opened the scoring after 30 minutes.

Not only was the South African a tricky winger, but he played in nine different positions for Liverpool – and he played them well. When World War II broke out, he served as a PT instructor in the Royal Air Force and played for both West Ham and Arsenal during wartime. In total, he spent 14 years with Liverpool – including wartime – and made 257 appearances, scoring 79 times. Without a doubt, Nieuwenhuys is one of Liverpool's all-time greatest players! When he retired from football he returned to South Africa and spent the majority of his time playing golf. He passed away in Grahamstown in the Eastern Cape Province of South Africa on June 12 1984, aged 72.

## NUNEZ, Antonio

*Midfielder*
**Born:** *1979 Madrid, Spain*
**Playing career:** *San Federico, Las Rozas, Real Madrid B, Liverpool, Celta, Murcia, Apollon Limassol, Huesca, Deportivo La Coruna, Recreativo (1998-2018)*

Antonio Nunez made his name with Third Division Spanish side Las Rozas. He grew up a Real Madrid fan so when they came knocking it was an obvious choice to join his boyhood club. Unfortunately, Madrid had a team full of superstars at the time, which resulted in Nunez only appearing sporadically for the club. He did, however, find the net on his debut. Frustration began to grow for the midfielder and when Liverpool had shown interest in him, he was on his way to Anfield. He came as part of a package deal that took Michael Owen to Madrid. In his first day of training with his new club, he injured his knee which kept him out of the team for the next three months. When he returned to full fitness he was given opportunities but failed to take them. He spent a year at Liverpool and only found the net once. He returned to Spain in 2005 to join Celta Vigo but he did feature in enough games to win a Champions League winners medal. He called time on his playing career at the end of the 2017/18 season, at the age of 39.

### "DID YOU KNOW?"

*"'You'll Never Walk Alone' is a tune from the 1945 Rodgers and Hammerstein musical Carousel. "*

## OGRIZOVIC, Steve

*Goalkeeper*
**Born:** *1957 Mansfield*
**Playing career:** *Chesterfield, Liverpool, Shrewsbury Town, Coventry City. (1977-1997)*

Although Steve Ogrizovic only played five times for Liverpool, he was a big part of their team. He was primarily used as cover for the astounding Ray Clemence and was brought to Anfield after only 18 games for Chesterfield. The towering goalkeeper – who served in the police force prior to signing for Chesterfield – conceded four goals on his debut for the club against Derby on 8 March 1978. This was also the first game that Clemence had missed since 1972, recording 336 straight appearances! 'Oggy' put in a much better performance against Leeds only three days later and kept a clean sheet, but Clemence had returned to start the next match. He moved to Shrewsbury in 1982 before joining Coventry two years later where he spent 16 years! He played in over 500 league matches for the Sky Blues and recorded his 719th appearance in club football against Liverpool on 1 April 2000. He was also a keen cricketer, having taken the wickets of Viv Richards and Chris Board! When he retired from playing football he became the goalkeeping coach at Coventry. After 35 years of service to the club, he has announced that he will retire from his role at the end of the 2019/20 season.

Alberto Ortego

## ORTEGA, Albert

*Winger/Left-back*
**Born:** *1982 Manacor, Spain*
**Playing career:** *Mallorca, Bordeaux, Espanyol, Manchester City, Liverpool, Olympiacos, Galatasaray, Watford, Udinese, Koper, Zavrc (1999-2016)*

Albert Ortega signed for Liverpool on deadline day during the 2008/09 season, for a reported fee of £8 million. However, two years later and the Spaniard was suspended by the club after speaking to Spanish press about his lack of playing time with Liverpool. He was swiftly listed for a potential transfer and moved to Greek club Olympiacos. He was capped by Spain 16 times. When the full-back retired on 24 January 2018 he did so via a social media post of him literally hanging up his boots on a tree!

## OTSEMOBOR, Jon

*Right-back*
**Born:** *1983 Liverpool*
**Playing career:** *Liverpool, Hull City, Bolton Wanderers, Crewe Alexandra, Rotherham United, Crewe Alexandra, Norwich City, Southampton, Sheffield Wednesday, Milton Keynes Dons, Tranmere Rovers (2002-2014)*

Jon Ostemobor came through Liverpool's youth academy and he was awarded a professional contract in 2002 after his exploits for the junior teams. He was given his debut for the senior team by Gerard Houllier when the Reds hosted Southampton in the League Cup third round match in November 2002. He was shipped to Hull on loan for the remainder of the season. In October 2003 he was shot in the buttocks during a night out in Liverpool city centre. Only a few weeks later and his car was torched. Thankfully, he was able to make a come back and featured in five more games for Liverpool. When Rafael Benitez arrived at Anfield, Otsemobor was shipped to Crewe on loan. They showed interest in signing him permanently but he wanted to give it one last shot with his boyhood club. Unfortunately it did not work out and he moved to Division Two side Rotherham in 2005. He then joined several other English teams before settling with Norwich for three years. He hung up his boots whilst contracted with MK Dons in 2014. He now works in property management and development.

## OWEN, Michael
*Chester/England*
**Born:** *1979 Chester*
**Playing career:** *Liverpool, Real Madrid, Newcastle United, Manchester United, Stoke City (1991-2013)*

Michael Owen was a phenomenal football player but also quite a controversial character. It was clear he was destined to play football for a living when he scored 97 goals in a single season for the Deeside Area Primary School's U-11 team. This was rewarded with a place in the FA's School of Excellence at Lilleshall and he was soon playing for England's youth teams. He scored 28 goals in only 20 games. When Owen was 16 years old he was playing for Liverpool's youth teams, despite the average age being 18. When Liverpool won the FA Youth Cup for the first time in their history, Owen had netted 11 goals from only five games. He was awarded a professional contract on his seventeenth birthday and was immediately introduced into the senior team. He was given his first taste of action during the final few games of the 1996/97 season, scoring on his debut against Wimbledon and becoming the club's youngest scorer at 17 years and 143 days old. Roy Evans had originally planned to ease him into the team, but when Robbie Fowler picked up an injury, Owen was called upon. He did not disappoint. He scored in the opening game from the penalty spot and made his European debut against Celtic on 16 September 1997 and it only took him six minutes to grab the opening goal. On October 1, 1997 he signed an improved five-year contract with Liverpool which was worth £2.5 million - It was clear that Liverpool knew they had a future world-class player in their ranks. He was joint top-scorer during his first Premier League season alongside Chris Sutton and Dion Dublin with 18 goals and his goal against Argentina in the 1998 FIFA World Cup made him a national hero. Injuries started to become more frequent but whenever he was fit, there was no doubt that he was going to score. A personal highlight would have been his two late goals that turned the 2001 FA Cup final on its head, in Liverpool's favour. When Rafael Benitez was appointed manager it spelt the end for Owen, he wanted to try something new – he wanted Real Madrid.

He joined Madrid for £8 million – which was an absolute steal but Owen was into the final year of his contract – and spent a sole season in Spain. He notched 13 goals from 20 starts but was struggling to break the formidable partnership of Raul and Ronaldo. He pleaded with Liverpool to buy him back but after Newcastle had submitted a £17 million offer, he had no choice but to join the club. He did not struggle with the Magpies but he certainly didn't set the world alight, netting 26 times in 81 league matches across four seasons. Then in 2009 – and still desperate to return to Anfield – he made a decision that would forever taint his Liverpool status – he joined Manchester United. He only found the net five times in 31 league matches but the damage was done, he still receives stick about that transfer today! He finished his career with Stoke in 2013 and has since worked as a pundit for BT and breeds racehorses. Owen is arguably the most gifted striker that Liverpool, if not England, have ever seen. But his decisions off the pitch will forever leave a sour taste in Liverpool's most faithful.

## PAGNAM, Fredrick
*Forward*
**Born:** *1891 Poulton-le-Fylde, Lancashire*
**Playing career:** *Blackpool Wednesday, Huddersfield Town, Southport Central, Blackpool, Liverpool, Arsenal, Cardiff City, Watford (1909-1926)*

Fredrick Pagnam's father expressed his disappointment that his son would pursue a career in football and not banking, the profession that he was involved with. However – luckily for Liverpool – his son ignored his advice. Although Pagnam's tenure with Liverpool was brief, his performances were incredible. The robust forward scored 30 goals in 39 games! He famously gave evidence during the 1916 match-fixing scandal, where players from both clubs agreed to let Manchester United win the game 2-0. Although the striker was approached, he refused to take part in the scandal. Whilst playing for Watford he scored three hat-tricks in five games! Upon retiring as a player, he managed Watford for three seasons before coaching overseas. That came to a sudden halt when him and his Dutch wife were forced to escape the Nazis in 1940!

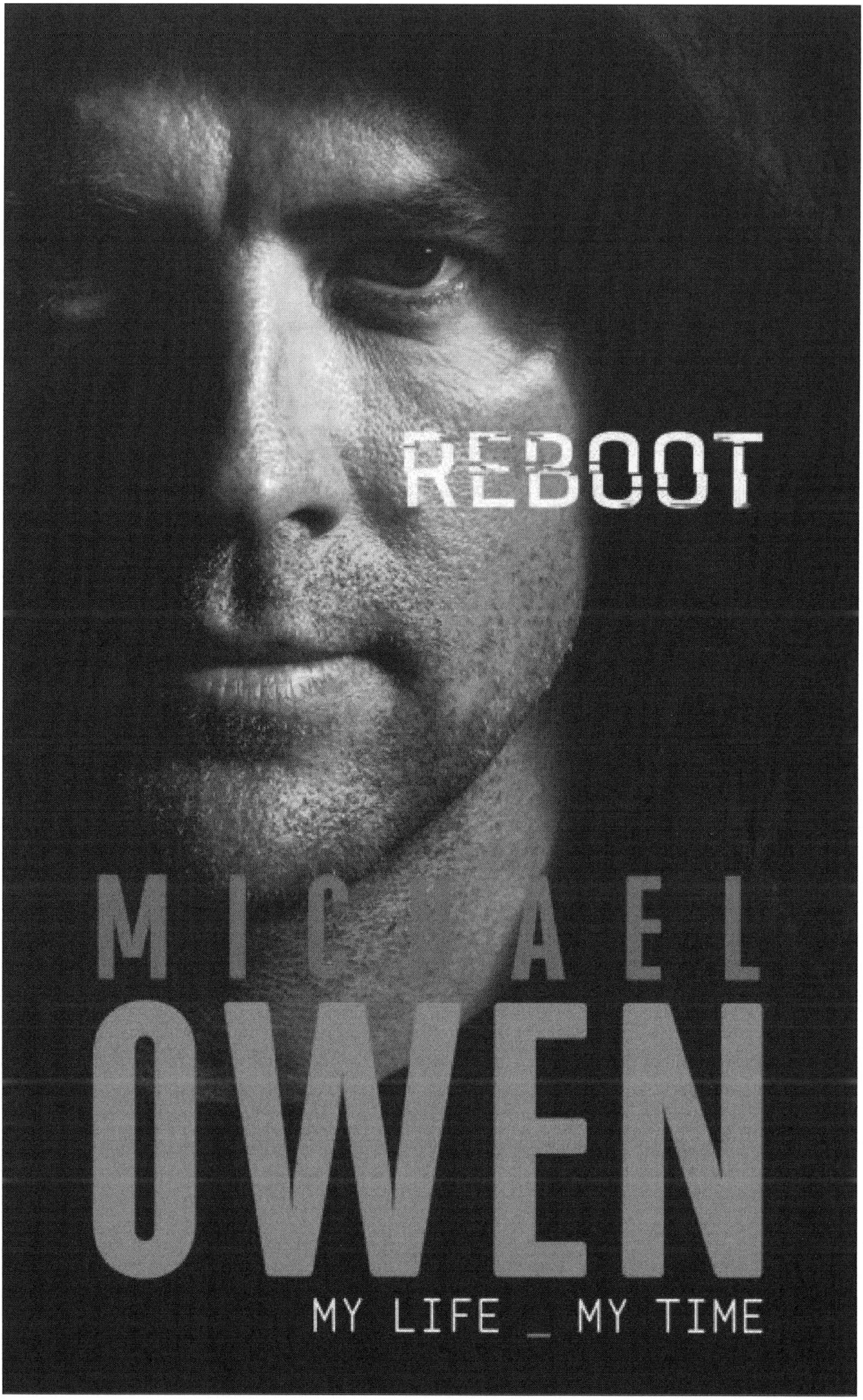

REBOOT

MICHAEL

OWEN

MY LIFE _ MY TIME

"This Club has been my life; I'd go out and sweep the street and be proud to do it for Liverpool FC if they asked me to."

**Bob Paisley**

## PAISLEY, Bob

*Left-half*
**Born:** *1919 Hetton-le-Hole* **Died:** 1996
**Playing career:** *Bishop A, Liverpool (1937-1954)*

Mr. Liverpool himself, Paisley spent a combined 50 years with the club as a player, manager and physiotherapist! When World War II broke out, he was just 19 years old and he was assigned to the Royal Artillery where he was a gunner in the 73rd Medium Regiment. He made his debut on the 5th of January 1946 in Liverpool's first post-war competitive match, beating Chester 2-0. He was famously dropped from the 1950 FA Cup final which he later insisted stood him in good stead for his managerial career as he could relate to players who he had to inform were missing out. The following season he became club captain. After retiring in 1954, he became the physiotherapist for the club and later became the reserve team manager in 1959 – the same season Bill Shankly arrived at Anfield. It didn't take long for Paisley to be instilled as the former's number two and Liverpool's era of dominance was imminent. After the 1974 FA Cup final, Shankly surprisingly announced his retirement from football and Paisley was employed as his successor. Although initially reluctant to take the role, he accepted and would become one of the greatest managers in football history.

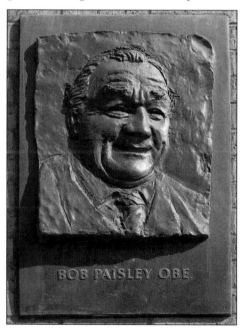

BOB PAISLEY O.B.E.

During his reign, he won six League Championships, three League Cups, one UEFA Cup, one UEFA Super Cup, six Charity Shields and perhaps most importantly, three European Cups. After retiring as manager, he continued his association with the club as director before being forced to retire due to ill health. He died in 1996 and Liverpool honoured their greatest ever servant by the opening of the Paisley gates at one entrance of Anfield.

## PARKINSON, Andy

*Attacking Midfielder*
**Born:** *1979 Liverpool*
**Playing career:** *Liverpool, Tranmere Rovers, Sheffield United, Notts County (loan), Grimsby Town, Notts County, Cambridge United, (1995-2015)*

Andy Parkinson was signed by Liverpool after one of his teammates put in a good word for him. First team opportunities were limited but he was grateful for his opportunity to play for Liverpool. After arriving home from Liverpool's summer tour to America he was summoned by Gordon Hughes and asked if he would sign for Tranmere. Despite wanting to stay with Liverpool, first team football was too difficult to turn down and he spent four years as Tranmere's skipper. After his career had finished he ventured into management and was appointed Tranmere's youth team manager in 2015, a role he still occupies in 2020.

## PARKINSON, Jack

*Forward*
**Born:** *1869 Blackpool* **Died:** 1911
**Playing career:** *Blackpool, Liverpool, Blackpool, Barrow (1896-1910)*

A Blackpool legend was voted into the club's Hall of Fame by supporters due to his goalscoring prowess which included being top scorer in their first ever season in the Football League. Played one game for Liverpool against Everton in 1900 before returning to his hometown club for a further ten years. Became manager of Barrow in 1910 and later took a job with the Corporation Baths. It was here that he met an untimely end whilst trying to rescue a work colleague from a tank of boiling water. Unfortunately, the plank that he was standing on collapsed and he also fell into the water and died. He was aged 42.

Jack Parkinson

## PARKINSON, Jack

*Striker*
**Born:** *1883 Bootle* **Died:** 1942
**Playing career:** *Liverpool, Bury (1903-1915)*

Jack Parkinson came from Bootle and worked as a railway clerk before signing amateur forms with Liverpool in 1910. Parkinson had all the attributes needed in a professional striker: he had pace, an incredible eye for goal and good hold up play. Away from football and he took part in sprinting competitions – winning a total of 20 titles across various competitions. He found the net 20 times in only 21 games as Liverpool were promoted back to the First Division. Annoyingly, Parkinson broke his wrist in the Reds' first game back in the topflight. Injuries were occurring more frequently, but when he was fit he was continuously finding the back of the net. He started the 1909/10 season in fine fashion, scoring 11 goals from only seven games. Over the next three seasons, he would net another 42 times and was awarded a national team call up. In total, Parkinson played 219 times for Liverpool and scored 128 goals, a goals-to-games ratio of only 1.71. He continued to live in Liverpool when he retired from playing and ran a newsagents in Commutation Row. He died on 13 January 1942.

## PARTRIDGE, Richie

*Midfielder*
**Born:** *1980 Dublin, Ireland*
**Playing career:** *Stella Maris, Liverpool, Sheffield Wednesday, Rotherham United, Chester-City, Milton Keynes Dons, (2000-2013)*

Richie Partridge signed for Liverpool in August 1996 having graduated from the Stella Maris academy. He was a quick-paced winger who could run rings around most defenders. He made his senior debut against Stoke in the League Cup on 29 November 2000, where Liverpool ran out as 8-0 winners. Partridge was very unfortunate in regard to injuries during his time at Liverpool. He damaged his left cruciate ligament in 1999 which prevented him from making his debut for many months. He had a successful loan spell with Coventry and was even voted fans' player of the season for the Sky Blues. He returned to make a couple of substitute appearances before he was released on 1 July 2005. He retired whilst playing for Airbus UK Broughton in 2013. In 2009, he studied a physiotherapy degree at the University of Salford and graduated with first-class honours. He then went back to Anfield and worked as a physiotherapist for the club's U-21 team before being promoted to the senior team in 2016, a role he still holds in 2020.

## PATERSON, Scott

*Defender*
**Born:** *1972 Aberdeen, Scotland*
**Playing career:** *Liverpool, Bristol City, Cardiff City (loan), Carlisle United, Cambridge United, Plymouth Argyle, Peterhead, Ross County, Greenock Morton, Partick Thistle, Dundee United, Partick Thistle (loan), St Johnstone, Gretna, Cove Rangers (1991-2008)*

Scott Paterson was a product of the Scottish Highland Football League and was so impressive that Graeme Souness submitted a £15,000 bid for the then 20-year-old. Unfortunately for the Scotsman, after two years at Anfield, he failed to appear in a single competitive match for Liverpool and moved to Bristol City. He finished his career where it all started with Cove Rangers in 2008. He moved into coaching after his playing days and was appointed youth team coach at Aberdeen before joining Livingston. In 2013, he was hired as interim manager at Partick Thistle and remained in that role until 2018.

## PAYNE, Jimmy

*Right-winger*

**Born:** *1926 Bootle, Lancashire* **Died:** 2013
**Playing career:** *Everton, Liverpool, Anfield, Bolton Wanderers, Burnden Park, Chelsea, Wembley, Maine Road, Manchester, Arsenal (1944-1956)*

Jimmy Payne may have grew up an Everton fan, but the moment he signed for the Reds his allegiances would have certainly swapped. Known as the 'Merseyside Matthews', Payne was a tricky winger who joined Liverpool in 1942 and made his debut against Bolton in 1948. Injuries would begin to plague Payne and even Liverpool's most faithful began to turn on the winger. In total, he played 243 times for Liverpool and scored 43 goals. He left the 'Pool for Everton in April 1956 but injuries were still occurring frequently which restricted him to minimal playing time – playing only six games and scoring twice. Prior to his thirtieth birthday, he retired from playing football and became a newsagent. He died on 22 January 2013, aged 86.

## PEARS, Stephen

*Goalkeeper*

**Born:** *1962 Brandon, County Durham*
**Playing career:** *Manchester United, Middlesbrough, Liverpool, Hartlepool United (1979-1998)*

Prior to joining Liverpool, Stephen Pears had spent ten years with Middlesbrough and racked up 327 league appearances for the club. He was called up to the England squad whilst at Boro but was forced to pull out after a collision with Dion Dublin fractured his cheekbone – he was never called up again and thus, never represented his nation. He was brought to Liverpool as cover for David James after reserve goalkeeper Michael Stensgaard had dislocated his shoulder whilst ironing! He never made an appearance for the Reds and moved to Hartlepool only six months later. After his playing days he returned to Middlesbrough and became the academy goalkeeping coach. He was promoted to the senior goalkeeping coach in 2007 but was released in 2013 after Aitor Karanka was appointed manager of the club. He had a short stint as assistant manager and goalkeeping coach at Hartlepool before moving to Gateshead as goalkeeping coach in 2015, a role he still occupies in 2020.

## PELLEGRINO, Mauricio

*Centre-back*

**Born:** *1971 Leones, Argentina*
**Playing career:** *CA Sarmiento, Velez Sarsfield, Barcelona, Valencia, Liverpool, Alaves (1982-2006)*

Mauricio Pellegrino perhaps suffered the worst nightmare a footballer can experience – missing the decisive penalty in the 2001 Champions League final. Rafael Benitez had previous experience working with the centre-back at Valencia and brought The Beatles fan with him when he joined Liverpool - he spent his first few days visiting every destination that was associated with his favourite band! His performances did not match his passion for the 'Fab Four' and he spent only five months with the club before playing for Deportivo for a sole season and hanging up his boots. He worked as a coach with Valencia after retiring and returned to Liverpool as assistant coach under Benítez in 2008 until the pair moved to Inter Milan in 2010. His first taste in management was with former club Valencia but he only lasted eight months before being giving the boot. In 2017 he was appointed manager of Southampton but was sacked after the club went on a 17-match winless streak! His most recent position was with CD Leganes but he was relieved of his duties in October 2019 after the club were bottom of La Liga after amassing just two points.

Mauricio Pellegrino

## PENNANT, Jermaine

*Winger*
**Born:** *1983 Nottingham*
**Playing career:** *Notts County, Arsenal, Watford, Leeds United, Birmingham City, Liverpool, Portsmouth, Real Zaragoza, Stoke City, Wolverhampton Wanderers, Pune City, Wigan Athletic, Billericay Town (1993-Still Playing)*

When Jermaine Pennant signed for Arsenal in 1999 he became the most expensive teenager in football history. Arsene Wenger was known for exposing talent in youth players, but this rebellious winger proved a bridge too far for the Frenchman. Whilst spending six and a half years at Arsenal, he only played 26 times. Liverpool came knocking in 2006 and signed the Englishman for £7 million with a potential to rise to £8 million with add-ons. Surprisingly, he hit the ground running. He started brightly in pre-season and even netted against Chelsea in the Premier League - a game Liverpool would win 2-0. The following season his performances started to drop off and was was loaned out to Portsmouth before being released all together. He moved to Spain before returning to England to turn out for Stoke. His last involvement with football was with Billericay Town, but he left the club on 28 December 2017. Although he has not officially retired from football, he has yet to be involved with the sport since then.

Pennant was constantly featuring in national newspapers for his destructive lifestyle. He has been caught drink-driving on multiple occasions and has most recently featured in E4's *Celebs Go Dating* where himself and his partner were consulting a dating expert for advice on their relationship. Once tipped to be the next big thing, fame and money stole the show for a very promising tricky winger.

## PEPLOW, Steve

*Right winger*
**Born:** *1949 Liverpool*
**Playing career:** *Liverpool, Swindon Town, Nottingham Forest, Mansfield Town (loan), Chicago Sting, Tranmere Rovers (1969-1981)*

Steve Peplow was an Anfield apprentice and waited patiently for a first team call up. He was given an opportunity against West Ham – which was also the first match to be televised in colour on Match of the Day. However, he moved on after only two more appearances. He established himself as a Tranmere player where he was converted into a right winger. On his wedding day in 1995, former Tranmere player and best man Barrie Mitchell – with the assistance of legendary commentator John Motson – managed to unearth the clip of Peplow's Liverpool debut which was titled 'love techniques for a beginner'! Thankfully, Peplow saw the funny side in the prank and was grateful to revisit his time playing for one of Europe's footballing giants.

## PIECHNIK, Torben

*Defender*
**Born:** *1963 Hellerup, Denmark*
**Playing career:** *Kjobenhavns BK, Ikast fS, B 1903, FC Copenhagen, Liverpool, AGF Aarhus (1980-1999)*

Torben Piechnik alerted almost every big club in Europe when his unlikely Denmark team won the 1992 European Championships. He was a brick wall during the tournament which undoubtedly influenced Liverpool to sign the defender. He was purchased for £500,000 in September 1992 and Graeme Souness must have thought he had signed a player perfectly capable of bringing Liverpool back to the summit of English football. Rather frustratingly, he was lacklustre. During his debut, former Liverpool player Dean Saunders, netted twice against his old team and questions were asked of Piechnik.

DANMARK

TORBEN
PIECHNIK

He only made one appearance the following season and was rather embarrassingly taken off at half-time after Newcastle had run the poor man ragged. Apparently, he refused to listen to advice in training and preferred to defend by allowing the attackers time on the ball, which opposed the way Liverpool played at the time, which was to press high. He returned to Denmark in 1994 and finished his career five years later. When he retired from the sport he worked as a real estate agent and a masseur.

## PILE, Chris
*Goalkeeper*
**Born:** *1967 Huyton, Liverpool*
**Playing career:** *Liverpool, Tranmere Rovers, Bury, Waterside Karori, Southport (1984-1992)*

When Chris Pile was selected to sit on the bench during Liverpool's 1985 European Cup triumph, the local lad must have believed that he had made it to the bigtime. He was not needed for the match and he never made an appearance for Liverpool. In fact, he never made a competitive appearance in professional football. He joined Tranmere as a non-contract player and then Bury. He did impress with the latter and he was offered a contract with the Shakers. Rather unfortunately, he broke his wrist on the day of the signing and the deal was scuppered! After this incident, in a desperate bid to play football, he moved to New Zealand and played for Waterside Karori. Around the same time Scottish giants Celtic, had shown interest in the 'keeper. However, he settled in so well in New Zealand that he ignored the proposal. Personal reasons saw him return to England in 1991 and he played a sole year for Southport before retiring after he had broken his hand for the third time in his career. He returned to New Zealand and remains there in 2020, working as a goalkeeping coach for the national team's youth sides. He has also had a brief spell working with Wellington Phoenix who compete in the Australian A-League.

## "DID YOU KNOW?"

*"Craig Johnston's 'Predator' football boot helped save Adidas from bankruptcy in the 1990's."*

## PLATT, Peter
*Goalkeeper*
**Born:** *1883 Rotherham*
**Died:** 1922
**Playing career:** *Liverpool, Blackburn Rovers, Ned Doig, Luton Town (1902-1909)*

When Peter Platt joined Liverpool, the club were forced to settle with Blackburn even though he was playing for Oswaldwistle Rovers as he was still contracted to the former. The 'keeper already had 15 appearances in a red shirt when he took over from Bill Perkins for the final seven games of the 1902/03 season. He started as Liverpool's number one the following season but lost his place to Charles Cotton midway through the campaign. He did make a comeback to feature in the final three matches of that season but those were the final games he would represent the club in. Whilst playing for the team, he was still working as a cotton weaver. He passed away at the age of 39 in Nuneaton after a mini-flu epidemic had hit the town in 1922.

## POTTER, Darren
*Midfielder*
**Born:** *1984 Liverpool*
**Playing career:** *Everton, Blackburn Rovers, Liverpool, Southampton, Wolverhampton Wanderers, Sheffield Wednesday, Milton Keynes Dons, Rotherham United (2003-Still playing)*

Darren Potter started his footballing journey in the youth academy of local rivals Everton. The Toffees released the midfielder when he was 15 years old, paving the way for Liverpool to snap the skilful youngster up. He was awarded a professional contract in 2003 but Liverpool's midfield was very strong and the youngster was just desperate to play for Liverpool in any capacity. "As far as I'm concerned, I'd give an arm and a leg just to get a shirt in any position". Indeed, Liverpool's talent proved too much for Potter to break into the team consistently, but he did feature in 17 matches for the Reds – only two of those came in the Premier League. He went on to play for Sheffield Wednesday in Yorkshire but was transferred to MK Dons in 2011, where he spent six years and played in over 200 Football League matches for the club. He is still playing at the age of 35 and is currently contracted with Tranmere.

Christian Poulsen

## Poulsen, Christian

*Defensive midfielder*
**Born:** *1980 Denmark*
**Playing career:** *Schalke, Sevilla, Juventus, Liverpool, Evian, Ajax, Copenhagen (1985-2015)*

A hot-tempered Dane who had quite the CV when he arrived at Anfield. Christian Poulsen was singled out as the best Spanish summer signing of 2005 and was a brilliant servant to Sevilla. He moved to Juventus where he was branded a coward by then AC Milan manager Carlo Ancelotti, for his cynical fouling. When he moved to Liverpool, there was a real buzz that he could bring some aggression that was absent from the midfield at the time. Unfortunately, that wasn't the case and he only featured in 12 league games which resulted in his move away. He retired in 2016 when he failed to find a club through three transfer windows. He was capped 92 times by Denmark during his playing days and on July 1 2019, he was appointed assistant manager at Ajax.

### "DID YOU KNOW?"

*"'South Africans Arthur Riley and Berry Nieuwenhuys were probably the club's first two foreign players. "*

## PRATT, David

*Defender/Outside-left*
**Born:** *1896 Lochore, Fife, Scotland* **Died:** 1967
**Playing career:** *Hill o'Beath, Celtic, Bradford City, Liverpool (1919-1927)*

David Pratt had started his career with Celtic before joining Bradford in 1921. Unfortunately for the Scotsman, his new team were relegated during his debut season and after one more year, he moved to Liverpool. Upon arrival at Anfield, he was making quite the name for himself through the sheer length of his throw-ins! In 1923, the Liverpool Echo reported: "Pratt was amazing the crowd with some of his throw-ins, I swear some reached the middle of the field". He had started his career as a winger but was developed as a centre-half by Bradford, with Liverpool transitioning him to play as a full-back. He played in the game that the Reds had secured the 1922/23 League Championship but failed to win a medal as he did not feature in enough games, having joined in the February of that season. Although he was a handy player for Liverpool, the most games he featured in a single season was 26. After five years with the club, he left for Bury in November 1927. Two years later and he joined Yeovil Town as a player-manager, a role he occupied for four years. He also managed Clapton Orient, Notts County, Heart of Midlothian and Bangor City - although they were all short spells. After the conflict had begun during World War II, he had enlisted into the Royal Air Force. After the war had concluded, he accepted the role to become Port Vale manager but had to vacate his post six months later – without taking charge of a single game – as the RAF refused to grant him release. He died in 1967, aged 71.

## PRITCHARD, Joe

*Midfielder*
**Born:** *1943 Birkenhead*
**Playing career:** *Liverpool, Tranmere Rovers, Ellesmere Port (1962-1970)*

Despite spending many years in Liverpool's youth academy, it was local club Tranmere that benefited from his training as a youngster. He was released by Liverpool and quickly snapped up by their neighbours, where he spent eight years and played in 178 league games. After retiring he worked as a joiner in Cammell Laird shipyard.

## PRUDOE, Mark
*Goalkeeper*
**Born:** *1963 Washington*
**Playing career:** *Sunderland, Hartlepool United, Birmingham City, Walsall, Doncaster Rovers, Grimsby Town, Sheffield Wednesday, Bristol City, Carlisle United, Darlington, Stoke City, Peterborough United, Liverpool, York City, Bradford City, Southend United, Macclesfield Town*

Mark Prudoe is another well-travelled player, having spent time with no less than 20 clubs including a brief stop at Anfield! He spent his younger years in the youth academy at Sunderland and retired whilst contracted with Macclesfield Town in 2004. After his playing days, he found employment with Grimsby Town, arranging stadium tours and events at Blundell Park. In 2005 he was appointed as goalkeeping coach at Hull, until he returned to Sunderland to coach in their academy in 2011, a role he still occupies in 2020.

## PURSELL, Bob
*Fullback*
**Born:** *1889 Campbeltown, Scotland* **Died:** 1974
**Playing career:** *Queen's Park, Liverpool, Port Vale (1911-1922)*

When Bob Pursell signed for Liverpool in 1911, the club were fined £250 as they were deemed to have tapped the player up. Indeed, it existed during the early origins of football too! For a full-back, Pursell was rather strong but still had pace to get up and down the field consistently. He was a regular for his debut season at Anfield but failed to cement a routine spot during the next two campaigns. Annoyingly for the Scotsman, he did not participate in any of Liverpool's eight FA Cup fixtures that season, where the club made it to their first final. Rather stupidly, Pursell agreed to throw a match on Good Friday 1915 against Manchester United. Intentionally, it was the full-back who conceded a penalty – only for Pat O'Connell to miss! He was issued a lifetime ban from football but after his service to his country during World War I, the sanction was lifted. He returned to Anfield but fractured his arm during a friendly game. He came back for two final games before he joined Port Vale. He played 113 times for the 'Pool but failed to find the net once. A broken leg whilst at Vale Park ended his career. He died 24 May 1974.

## RACE, Henry
*Forward*
**Born:** *1906 Liverpool*
**Died:** 1942
**Playing career:** *Liverpool, Manchester City, Nottingham Forest (1928-1936)*

Henry Race joined Liverpool in 1928 and he could not have asked for a better debut as his first goal for the club propelled a fine comeback against Derby after being 2-0 down. He netted again in the next away fixture at Arsenal but these would be the only two goals he would score during his first 11 games with Liverpool. He failed to cement a regular spot in the team during the next two seasons but when he was called upon, his pace and skilful play certainly helped Liverpool going forward. His fine sporadic performances influenced First Division team Manchester City, to sign the striker for £3,000 - a considerable fee during the time. Unfortunately, Race only featured in 11 games during three years at City and he moved to Nottingham Forest on 26 June 1933, where he was an important player for them. He served in World War II and was killed at El Alamein in Egypt whilst serving as a Corporal for Queen's Own Cameron Highlanders on 24 October 1942.

OGDEN'S CIGARETTES.

LIVERPOOL.

## Raisbeck, Alex

*Defender*
**Born:** *1878 Polmont, Scotland* **Died:** 1949
**Playing career:** *Hibernian, Stoke, Liverpool, Partick Thistle, Hamilton Academical (1896-1914)*

Alex Raisbeck was a fantastic servant and undoubtedly the first legend of the club. He was a natural leader and commanded the absolute best from his team, almost as if on the battlefield – which is unsurprising as he was one of seven brothers who either became soldiers or footballers! After only two seasons at Anfield, the defender was appointed captain of the club. Despite being under 6 foot, he was strong and versatile, which kept attackers at bay. He played 341 times for the 'Pool and scored 19 goals. After 11 years of service with the club he left to return to Scotland and finished his career with Partick Thistle in 1914. He moved into management the same year as his retirement as a player and managed Hamilton Academical, Bristol City, Halifax Town,

Chester City and Bath City. He returned to Liverpool to work as a scout after his managerial career up until his death on 12 March 1949, aged 70. He fathered 14 children and four of his sons served as World War II officers. Without a doubt, Raisbeck was the first player to demonstrate what it truly meant to play Liverpool and he has remained a legend of the club to this very day.

## RAMSDEN, Barney

*Defender*
**Born:** *1917 California* **Died:** 1990
**Playing career:** *Chelsea, Liverpool, Sunderland, Hartlepools United (1936-150)*

Barney Ramsden made his debut for Chelsea at the age of 19 and a string of impressive performances influenced Liverpool to bring the youngster to Anfield. His time with the club was split into two eras – pre and post-war. Prior to the Second World War he played occasionally but was primarily used as cover. After the war, he was regarded as the best full-back in the squad and started the first 18 games of the successful 1946/47 season. He eventually lost his place and moved on. After retiring from playing he became a representative for a ship's chandlers' firm in San Pedro.

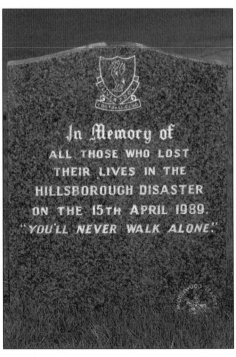

In Memory of
ALL THOSE WHO LOST
THEIR LIVES IN THE
HILLSBOROUGH DISASTER
ON THE 15TH APRIL 1989.
"YOU'LL NEVER WALK ALONE."

## RAWLINGS, Archibald
*Winger*
**Born:** *1891 Leicester*
**Died:** 1952
**Playing career:** *Shirebrook, Wombwell, Barnsley, Darfield United, Shirebrook, Northampton Town, Rochdale, Dundee, Preston North End, Liverpool, Walsall, Bradford Park Avenue, Southport, Burton Town (1920-1928)*

Prior to joining Liverpool in 1924, Archibald Rawlings had made his international debut for England with in a 2-0 win against Belgium in 1921. He was one of the stars in the Preston's 1922 FA Cup run that saw them reach the final but lose to Huddersfield 1-0. However, he shined in the semi-final after he scored one and created the other in the victory against Tottenham. Rawlings was viewed as the ideal replacement for Bill Lacey who was in his final season with the club when the former Preston winger was brought to Anfield. He made his debut in a goalless draw against Blackburn and this was the first of 11 consecutive games that he featured in. The following season and Rawlings only missed two matches and chipped in with seven crucial goals as Liverpool finished fourth. Midway through the following campaign he lost his place to Cyril Oxley and eventually left for Walsall before finishing his career with Burton Town in 1928. He died on 11 June 1952, aged 60.

Samuel Raybould

## RAYBOULD, Samuel
*Forward/Winger*
**Born:** *1875 Staveley, Derbyshire* **Died:** 1949
**Playing career:** *Derby County, Ilkeston Town, Bolsover Colliery, New Brighton Tower, Liverpool, Sunderland, Woolwich Arsenal, Chesterfield Town, Sutton Town, Barlborough United (1894-1909)*

Alex Raisbeck may have been the first certified legend of Liverpool Football Club, but Samuel Raybould was the club's first taste of an exceptional forward. He did not make a name for himself until he was 24 years old, when he scored ten goals in 13 games for New Brighton Tower. He signed for the 'Pool in 1900 and was the first player to score 100 goals for the club – it only took him 162 matches to achieve this feat. When Liverpool won their inaugural League Championship in 1901 he was the top scorer with 17 but he would almost double this tally two years later when he finished the season with 32 goals from only 34 games in the league and cup! Of course, as with the majority of the better players of the game, controversy plagued his time at Anfield. After becoming the first Liverpool player to notch 30 goals, he illegally agreed to sign for Portsmouth of the Southern League after the club had promised financial benefits. The approach was deemed unlawful and Raybould was banned from playing football for seven months. If that wasn't severe enough, he was also issued a lifetime ban from ever signing for Portsmouth. Liverpool were certainly the victims in this as their form slumped dramatically and they were subsequently relegated. He was moved to left wing when Liverpool started their quest to achieve topflight status again and he struggled. As the fans were so used to him scoring frequently, he copped most of the blame for their poor start to the season. Nevertheless, he improved and his 19 goals in the league helped his team win the Second Division. When Liverpool won their second League Championship, he assisted with 11 more goals. He spent one more season at Anfield before moving to Sunderland and then finishing his career in 1909. Despite his incredible eye for goal, he was never selected to play for England but he was called upon three times to represent the Football League against the Scottish League. He died on 17 December 1953, aged 78.

## REDKNAPP, Jamie
*Midfielder*
**Born:** *1973 Barton on Sea*
**Playing career:** *Bournemouth, Liverpool, Tottenham Hotspur, Southampton. (1989-2005)*

Jamie Redknapp started his career in Tottenham's youth academy - but it was Bournemouth who gave him his first opportunity. Prior to even playing a game for the club, Kenny Dalglish had visited the youngster but his father, Harry Redknapp, thought it was better for his son to stay at the Cherries for an extra year. When he was 17 years old he signed for Liverpool and became the most expensive signing for his age with a fee of £500,000. He never played under Dalglish but Graeme Souness came in and showed a lot of faith in the young midfielder. He made his full England debut against Colombia on 6 September 1995 when it was his shot that inspired the legendary scorpion-kick save! He did win one cup whilst at the club, the 1995 League Cup, but injuries hampered him showing his true potential. After 11 years he moved to Spurs before hanging up his boots in 2005. He briefly went into coaching but is now a regular face on television, working as a pundit for the BBC and Sky Sports . He is also one of the team captains on Sky One's *A League of Their Own.*

## REID, Thomas
*Striker*
**Born:** *1905 Motherwell, Lanarkshire* **Died:** 1972
**Playing career:** *Liverpool, Oldham Athletic, Manchester United, Barrow, Rhyl (1929-1935)*

Thomas Reid was not the agile, mobile or quick striker that is prominent in the contemporary game. Truth be told, he could not be further away from that! The best way to describe him would be a big lump up top – it just so happened to be he had a deadly eye for goal. He played in several positions for Liverpool but was mainly utilised as a striker. He made his debut for the Reds on the final day of the 1925/26 season, grabbing both goals as Liverpool drew 2-2 with Sheffield United. The following season, he scored braces on no less than five occasions. Reid was only used six times in his third and final season at Anfield which left him with 30 goals from only 55 games. He was 24 years old when he left Liverpool and he signed for Manchester United. United were soon relegated to the Second Division. He was loaned to Oldham whilst still contracted with the Red Devils and the fans were so impressed with his performances that they donated the £400 needed to keep him permanently! He finished his career in Wales playing for Rhyl Athletic in 1939. He died September 1972, aged 67.

# Reina, Pepe

*Goalkeeper*

**Born:** *1982 Madrid, Spain*
**Playing career:** *EF Madrid Oeste, Barcelona, Villarreal, Liverpool, Napoli (loan), Bayern Munich, Napoli (1988-2015)*

Pepe Reina was a product of Barcelona's La Masia. He played in 30 league games for Barca between 2000-2002 and participated in both of their games against Liverpool in the semi-finals of the UEFA Cup in the 2000/01 season. It was the arrival of Louis Van Gaal that influenced Reina's departure from Barcelona and he joined fellow Spanish team Villareal. He quickly settled in and established himself as their number one and was considered as the best 'keeper in La Liga during the 2004/05 season. Reina was 22 years old when he arrived at Anfield but for someone so young, he had bags of experience having featured in 175 senior team games. He was the hero in the 2006 FA Cup final after he saved three West Ham penalties to hand Liverpool the cup. He started his second season with the club poorly but as the season progressed he continued to grow stronger. He achieved 50 clean sheets in only 92 league matches, - which broke Ray Clemence's record by three games! In total, Reina played 394 times for Liverpool and won the European Super Cup, the FA Cup and the League Cup. The signing of Simon Mignolet spelt the end for Reina at Liverpool and he was shipped off to Napoli on loan before he left Anfield for good for Bayern Munich in 2014. He has since returned to Naples on a full-time basis and signed for AC Milan. He has most recently been loaned to Aston Villa and he will remain there until the conclusion of the 2019/20 season.

Pepe Reina

# REY, Josemi

*Defender*

**Born:** *1979 Torremolinos, Spain*
**Playing career:** *Torremolinos, Malaga B, Malaga, Malaga, Liverpool, Villarreal, Mallorca, Iraklis, Cartagena, Levadiakos, Skoda Xanthi (1997-2015)*

Josemi Rey was Rafael Benitez's first signing for Liverpool. He was a good player in Spain but he struggled to settle in England after he made a good start to his career at Anfield. Despite showing glimpses of the talent he possessed, injuries took over his first season at Anfield. Steve Finnan then made the position his and Rey was left out of the team almost exclusively. He did, however, win the Champions League and the European Super Cup whilst he was at Liverpool. He moved back to Spain to join Villarreal after only 18 months with the 'Pool and was on the move again after two years to join Mallorca. He finished his career in 2015 whilst playing for Indian side, Atletico Kolkata. He has since returned to Malaga and now works as a match delegate for the Spanish club.

### "DID YOU KNOW?"

*"Widely regarded as having some of the most loyal and passionate fans in world football."*

Karl Riedle

## RIEDLE, Karl

*Striker*
**Born:** *1965 Weiler im Allgau, West Germany*
**Playing career:** *TSV Ellhofen, SV Weiler, FC Augsburg, Blau-Weib Berlin, Werder Bremen, Lazio, Borussia Dortmund, Liverpool, Fulham (1983-2001)*

Karl Riedle made his name with Werder Bremen, where he won the Bundesliga in his first season with the German outfit. This was followed by a World Cup win with Germany in 1990 and following the conclusion of the tournament, he became one of the most expensive players in Europe when he moved to Lazio for £13 million. He joined Liverpool in 1997 and big things were expected from the ageing veteran. Prior to the summer, Liverpool's squad was fairly inexperienced and Roy Evans had hoped that the signings of Riedle, Paul Ince and Oyvind Leonardsen would add stability. However, the German was a massive disappointment for Liverpool as he failed to find his previous form. He left to become the caretaker manager at Fulham during the 1999/2000 season alongside Roy Evans. He finished his career at Craven Cottage in 2001 and announced his official retirement the following year. Since retiring he has set up a soccer camp in southern Germany.

## RIISE, John Arne

*Left-back*
**Born:** *1980 Molde, Norway*
**Playing career:** *Monaco, Liverpool, Roma, Fulham, APOEL, Delhi Dynamos, Aalesund, Chennaiyin, Rollon (1996-2016)*

John Arne Riise signed for Monaco for £700,000 in the summer of 1998 and spent three years with the French club building quite the reputation. When he decided he wanted a new challenge elsewhere he was frozen out of the team and was eagerly awaiting any potential bidders. When former Monaco manager, Jean Tigana, submitted a bid to bring the Norwegian to Fulham it looked to have been enough - until Liverpool improved their offer. He slotted nicely into the starting XI and helped Liverpool win the European Super Cup and Charity Shield during the first few months. He gained instant legendary status after his lengthy run saw him score the third and final goal for the 'Pool after they defeated Everton 3-1 in the Merseyside derby. A couple of months later he scored an absolute rocket against Manchester United that reached 70 mph! He was present on that famous night in Istanbul but was the only player to miss a penalty in the shoot-out. He did, however, provide the cross for Steven Gerrard to head home in the second half. He was in and out of the team during his final two years at Anfield and he eventually left for Roma. Riise played 348 times for Liverpool and scored 31 goals. During the twilight stages of his career he had stints in Cyprus and India before returning home to finish his career in 2017 with Rollon. He published his autobiography in 2018, titled: *Running Man* and on 4 January 2019 he had joined Maltese club Birkirkara as a sports director but was forced to resign only three months later due to personal reasons.

John Arne Riise

### RIZZO, Nick
*Left-winger*
**Born:** *1979 Sydney, New South Wales, Australia*
**Playing career:** *Sydney Olympic, Liverpool, Crystal Palace, Ternana, Ancona (loan), AC Prato, Milton Keynes Dons, Grimsby Town (loan), Chesterfield (loan), Perth Glory, Central Coast Mariners, APIA Leichhardt Tigers (1995-2013)*

Nick Rizzo was taught his trade in the youth academy of Sydney Olympic - but it was Liverpool that gave the winger his first professional contract. He made the bench six times during his two-year stay but failed to represent the Merseyside outfit once. Crystal Palace enquired about his services and he left for the London-based club. He wasn't a regular with Palace and moved to Italy to play for Ternana but injuries plighted his time with the Italian side. He eventually returned to England and spent three years contracted with MK Dons and after two loan spells with Grimsby and Chesterfield, he headed back home to turn out for Perth Glory. He remained in Australia for the rest of his career up until his retirement from the sport in 2013. Since retiring he has set up his own soccer school named 'Nick Rizzo International Football School'.

### ROBERTS, Gareth
*Defender*
**Born:** *1978 Wrexham, Wales*
**Playing career:** *Stockport County, Liverpool, Panionios, Tranmere Rovers (loan), Tranmere Rovers, Doncaster Rovers, Derby County, Bury, Notts County, Chester (1994-2015)*

Gareth Roberts was a trainee at Liverpool alongside Michael Owen and Jamie Carragher and was a member of the 1996 FA Youth Cup winning side. He was named on the bench for the final three league games of the 1997/98 season but he never represented the club. He had a brief spell in Greece after Liverpool but moved back to Merseyside and joined Tranmere. He spent seven years with the club and played in over 270 league matches for the team. He had a four-year stint with Doncaster after, before joining Derby and playing for several other English teams before retiring in 2017. However, he moved to Stalybridge Celtic and although he was primarily an assistant manager, he was still registered as a player by the club during the 2018/19 season.

### ROBERTS, Jack
*Forward*
**Born:** *1910 Anfield, Liverpool* **Died:** 1985
**Playing career:** *Marine, Orrell, Blundellsands, Northern Nomads, Southport, Liverpool, Wigan Athletic, Port Vale (1933-1940)*

Jack Roberts joined Liverpool in 1933 but made a sole league appearance. He transferred to Wigan and spent one season with the club before he finally found some stability and remained with Port Vale for five years prior to the outbreak of World War II. He retired as a professional player and enlisted into the Irish Guards. Roberts was captured by enemy forces in Tunisia on 25 March 1943 but managed to escape from an Italian prisoner-of-war camp and walked 400 miles to freedom with a broken neck! He died in June 1985, aged 75.

### ROBERTS, Trevor
*Goalkeeper*
**Born:** *1942 Caernarfon, Wales* **Died:** 1972
**Playing career:** *Liverpool, Southend United, Cambridge United. (1963-1971).*

Trevor Roberts was juggling football duties with his university studies as a youngster, as he was involved in Liverpool's youth academy whilst he was studying a geography degree at Liverpool University. He signed professionally in 1963 and despite spending two years at Anfield, he failed to make a single appearance for the club. He moved to Southend before joining Cambridge in 1970. In total, he made 207 Football League appearances and that would have surely been more if he had not tragically died at the age of 30. He had contracted a brain tumour and lost his battle with the illness in June 1972.

Liverpool University

## ROBERTSON, Thomas

*Full-back*

**Born:** *1875 Lanarkshire, Scotland* **Died:** 1923
**Playing career:** *Newton Mearns, St Bernard's,
Stoke, Hibernian, Millwall Athletic, Stoke, Liverpool,
Southampton, Brighton & Hove Albion (1894-1905)*

Thomas Robertson was was a strong full-
back who had a lot of power in his foot and
could tackle sublimely. He joined Liverpool
in 1900 and despite only being at Anfield
for two years, he did help the club win their
inaugural League Championship during the
1900/01 season. Glover moved south to join
Southampton in May 1902. This angered
Liverpool officials as the £400 fee they paid
Stoke was substantial at the time and they
were outraged that they only had two years
of service from the Scotsman! However,
Robertson enjoyed success with the Saints
and he won two successive Southern League
titles. He finished his career at Brighton and
retired in 1905. When he hung up his boots
he became a publican in Hove. He died on 8
December 1923, aged 48.

## ROBERTSON, Tommy

*Outside-left*

**Born:** *1876 Renton, Scotland* **Died:** 1941
**Playing career:** *East Benhar, Heatherbell, Motherwell,
Fauldhouse, Hearts, Liverpool, Hearts, Dundee,
Manchester United, Bathgate (1896-1905)*

Tommy Robertson made his name with
Hearts when he helped the team win the
Scottish Championship in 1897. He was
influential when they secured the title as
he scored four goals in a 5-0 victory against
Clyde! Only four days after playing his
only game for Scotland he had moved to
Liverpool. He scored on his debut against
Sheffield Wednesday and he was only absent
for one game over the next two seasons for
the Reds, assisting with 15 league goals
- an impressive feat from playing on the
wing. He was instrumental for Liverpool
when they clinched their first League
Championship in 1901 as he chipped in
with nine goals. However, his form began
to dip which led to his return Hearts. He
did come back to England for a brief spell
with no other than Manchester United but
his best days were certainly behind him and
he only featured in three league matches
for the club. Robertson played 141 times for
Liverpool and scored 35 goals during his
time at Anfield. He died on 13 August 1941.

Michael Robinson

## ROBINSON, Michael

*Striker*

**Born:** *1958 Leicester*
**Playing career:** *Preston. Manchester City, Brighton,
Liverpool, QPR. (1975-1986).*

Michael Robinson shot to fame when he
scored 13 goals for Preston at the age of 20.
He was brought to Manchester City off the
back of his performances for a considerable
fee of £750,000. Sadly for Robinson, he
failed to live up to the hype and he was
shipped to Brighton only one year later for
£400,000. He managed to revive his career
with the Seagulls and scored 43 goals in 133
appearances. Once Brighton were relegated
at the end of the 1982/83 season, there was
plenty of interest in the striker. Sevilla,
Manchester United and Newcastle were
all keen but once Liverpool came knocking
there was no doubt where the boyhood red
was heading. He failed to net in his first
nine games for Liverpool but he eventually
got the ball rolling after two goals in the
European Cup. Despite a topsy-turvy
career in red, he did win the 1984 League
Championship, League Cup and European
Cup – coming off the bench for the final in
Rome for the latter. He left after two seasons
with Liverpool to join QPR before spending
two years with Osasuna, bringing an end
to his career in 1989. He became a leading
pundit in Spain presenting El dia despuses
for 14 years. In addition to his duties there,
he worked for Canel+ and completed
extensive voice over work. However, in
2018, doctors discovered a malignant
melanoma and he died in his Madrid home
on 20th April 2020 at the age of 61.

### RODRIGUEZ, Maxi
*Winger/Attacking midfielder*
**Born:** *1981 Rosario, Argentina*
**Playing career:** *Newell's Old Boys, Espanyol, Atletico Madrid, Liverpool, Newell's Old Boys, Penarol, Newell's Old Boys (1999-)*

Maxi Rodriguez first shot to fame with Newell's Old Boys in his native Argentina. He remained with the club for three years before joining Real Oviedo on loan in the second tier of Spanish football. He also featured for Argentina in the 2001 World Youth Championship, scoring four goals including one in the final. He moved to Espanyol in time for the start of the 2002/03 season and his performances earned him a move to Atletico Madrid. He had a fantastic debut season but injuries restricted his playing time to just ten games the following season. During the 2008/09 Champions League group stages, Atletico and Liverpool were placed in the same group and Rodriguez scored in their 1-1 draw at Anfield. This certainly would have influenced Liverpool to make a move for the attacking player and he joined up with the squad in January 2010. He was used frequently by Rafael Benitez but Roy Hodgson utilised him sparingly, only featuring more regularly once Kenny Dalglish returned to the club. He left the club after 77 appearances to return to his boyhood club, Newell's Old Boys. When he departed from Anfield he wrote an open letter to fans of the club thanking them for their support and stating what an honour it was to play for a team of Liverpool's calibre. He left Old Boys in 2017 for Uruguayan team Penarol before returning a year later. He still remains contracted to the club where it all began in 2020.

### ROGERS, Fred
*defender*
**Born:** *1910 Frodsham* **Died:** *1967*
**Playing career:** *Liverpool (1934-1939)*

Fred Rogers was unlucky to play in the same Liverpool side that contained Robert Savage, Tom Morrison and Matt Busby. Despite restricted playing opportunities, he was able to represent the club on 75 occasions leading up to World War II. During his first two years at Anfield, he was only selected to play seven times in the league. However, just as he was starting to show his worth, the war took his best years away from him. He was stationed in Scotland and he guested for St Mirren and Celtic during wartime. After the conflict had concluded, he retired from football and became a painter for his local council in Frodsham. He died in 1967.

### ROSENTHAL, Abe
*Striker*
**Born:** *1921 Liverpool*
**Died:** *1986*
**Playing career:** *Liverpool, Tranmere Rovers, Bradford City, Tranmere Rovers, Bradford City (1938-1956)*

Abe Rosenthal was another product of Liverpool's academy who failed to make it to the first team. In fact, he was never offered a professional contract with the club and was subsequently released in 1938. Tranmere offered him his first taste of senior football but when he signed his contract in the same year as his release from Anfield, World War II was on the horizon. During the six years he first spent at Tranmere he was only able to play in 27 competitive fixtures - but he did manage to score eight goals. He moved to Bradford in 1946 before returning to Tranmere for a longer and more successful spell. He only played for two clubs in his professional career and had three spells with both clubs! He tragically died in February 1986, aged 64, having collapsed at his home in Woolton after he was chasing two intruders from his home.

### "DID YOU KNOW?"

*"There is no such thing as a Liver Bird. It is a mythical creature. The Liver Bird is an imaginary cross between an eagle and a cormorant."*

Ronny Rosenthal

## ROSENTHAL, Ronny

*Left winger/Striker*
**Born:** *1963 Haifa, Israel*
**Playing career:** *Macccabi Haifa, Club Brugge, Standard Liege, Udinese, Luton Town, Liverpool, Tottenham Hotspur, Watford (1979-1999)*

Ronny Rosenthal was on trial with Luton and scored two goals in three games for the club. Unfortunately for the Hatters, they could not negotiate a deal with parent club Sporting Liege, which allowed Liverpool to make a move for the man. He made his debut against Charlton and bagged a perfect hat-trick. However, the following campaign he was left out the team and he was forced to wait patiently as Liverpool recorded their then record of eight league victories in a row to start off the new campaign. He managed to net 19 goals in the reserves that year but first team opportunities were severely lacking although he did score a last-minute winner in front of the Kop in the Merseyside derby on 20 March 1993. He did play in enough games to receive a winner's medal for Liverpool's triumphant 1989/90 League Championship and he played in 97 games for the 'Pool, scoring 22 times. He moved to Tottenham in January 1994 after Spurs had paid £250,000 to secure his services.

He featured in 100 games for the north London outfit and scored 11 goals before he moved to Watford on a free transfer to help them win the Second Division. He retired as a player at the end of the 1998/99 campaign. He has continued to live in England and now works as a football consultant.

## ROSS, Ian

*Defender*
**Born:** *1947 Glasgow, Scotland* **Died:** 2019
**Playing career:** *Liverpool, Aston Villa, Notts County, Northampton Town, Peterborough United, Wolves, Hereford United (1966-1982).*

Ian Ross was a quality defender, perhaps best epitomised by his incredible performance against Bayern Munich in a European Fairs Cup game on 18 March 1971, where he man-marked Franz Beckenbauer and completely took him out of the game. The Scotsman signed for the 'Pool when he was 17 years old in August 1965 but was forced to wait two years for his debut. He was primarily used as a squad player but he did have a decent run in the team during the 1971/72 season – only to be sold in the following summer transfer window! Bill Shankly decided to drop Ross which angered the player, and he subsequently demanded to be sold. Aston Villa snapped him up for a club record fee of £70,000 and he went on to help the Midlands-based club win promotion to the First Division. He appeared 175 times in the league for Villa and finished his career with Hereford in 1983 before moving into coaching. He carved a successful career in Iceland and even came out of retirement to act as playing-manager for Valur. He returned to England to manage Huddersfield for a year before finishing his involvement with football in 1996 with Berwick Rangers. He died on 9 February 2019, aged 72.

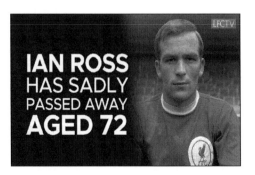

IAN ROSS HAS SADLY PASSED AWAY AGED 72

## ROSS, Sidney
*Goalkeeper*
**Born:** *1869 Edinburgh, Scotland* **Died:** 1924
**Playing career:** *Cambuslang, Liverpool, Cambuslang, Third Lanark, Clyde, Ayr Parkhouse (1890-1900)*

Sidney Ross was Liverpool's number one during their first and only season in the Lancashire League. They had a heavy presence of Scottish players in the team, with the majority of the regulars having the prefix 'Mc' in their surname. Thus, Liverpool were coined 'The team of Macs'! Unfortunately for the stopper, he picked up a nasty injury during the backend of the season and he never appeared for the club again. He moved to Scotland and spent eight years between five teams before retiring in 1900. He emigrated to Australia in 1910 and he died on 4 February 1924, at the age of 55, from Hodgkin's disease and heart failure.

## Rowley, Tony
*Centre-forward*
**Born:** *1929 Porthcawl, Wales* **Died:** 2006
**Playing career:** *Wellington Town, Birmingham City, Stourbridge, Liverpool, Tranmere Rovers (1951-1964)*

Tony Rowley was born in Wales to Italian parents and signed for Liverpool in October 1953. After having to settle for a place in the reserves, Rowley finally proved his worth on the opening day of the 1954/55 season by scoring a hat-trick. Rather harshly, he failed to net in his next two games and he was back in the reserves as both John Evans and Billy Liddell were scoring frequently. Rowley had a topsy-turvy career with Liverpool, he would come into the team and score plenty of goals but would miss much of the season through injuries or the occasional dip in form. He finally managed to stay in the side for 19 games during his final season at Anfield and he managed to reel off eight goals in six consecutive matches before once again injuries continued and he was sold to neighbours Tranmere. Whilst with Rovers he was selected to play his only game for Wales on 22 April 1959 against Northern Ireland. He finished his Liverpool career with 39 goals in 66 games, a goals-to-game ratio of only 1.62. He continued his fine scoring form for Tranmere, netting 47 times in only 100 league matches. When he retired from football he ran a printing business with former teammate Doug Rudham. He died on 28 April 2006, aged 76.

Neil Ruddock

## RUDDOCK, Neil
*Centre-back*
**Born:** *1968 Wandsworth, London*
**Playing career:** *Millwall, Tottenham Hotspur, Southampton, Liverpool, QPR, West Ham United, Crystal Palace, Swindon Town (1986-2003)*

Neil Ruddock was not short of offers when he decided to sign for Liverpool in 1993. Newcastle, Rangers, Blackburn and Chelsea were alongside the 'Pool fighting for his signature. He spent four years in total at Anfield but failed to pick up any silverware with the club. He had only made two appearances for the side when he was playing in a testimonial match. After only two minutes had passed, he broke Peter Beardsley's cheekbone in three places, which the victim claimed was intentional! He did state is his autobiography that "if anything the slight rearrangement of his face did Pete a favour..."! He eventually fell down the pecking order and went on to play for QPR, West Ham, and Swindon. After leaving Swindon, he featured on ITV's *I'm a Celebrity... Get Me Out of Here!* He was also involved in a TV programme that aimed to spot great potential in children who were unsigned to professional clubs. He appeared in Channel 4's *Celebrity Big Brother* in 2013 and in 2019 he made it to the final three of the BBC's *Celebrity MasterChef*.

Ian Rush

## RUDHAM, Doug

*Goalkeeper*

**Born:** *1926 Johannesburg, South Africa* **Died:** 1991
**Playing career:** *Johannesburg Rangers, Liverpool, Johannesburg Ramblers (1945-1967)*

Doug Rudham had previously turned down a professional contract with Chelsea when he was on tour to England with the South Africa national team. His performances attracted Liverpool's attention and he signed for the Reds when the club did not have an established regular goalkeeper. He eventually returned to South Africa just as Bill Shankly took over as Liverpool manager. He featured for Johannesburg Ramblers for three years before retiring from football. He died on 13 August 1991, aged 65, after a long battle with illness.

## Rush, Ian

*Striker*

**Born:** *1961 St Asaph, Wales*
**Playing career:** *Chester-City, Liverpool, Juventus, Leeds United, Newcastle United, Sheffield United, Wrexham, Sydney Olympic (1978-2000)*

Liverpool have had some fantastic strikers throughout their history: Roger Hunt, Gordon Hodgson, Michael Owen and Robbie Fowler to just name a few. However, there is one individual who rises above them all – Ian Rush. He is the club's record goal scorer with 346 goals, 61 clear of second-placed, Hunt. He was one of ten siblings growing up in a small town called Flint, in north-east Wales. He was 13 years old when he was scoring goals for fun for Deeside Primary schools, which alerted both Manchester United and Liverpool. Geoff Twentyman was Liverpool's scout when he realised the potential that Rush possessed and managed to convince Bob Paisley to splash £300,000 on the then 19-year-old – the highest fee ever paid for a youngster. The Welshman made his debut when he replaced Kenny Dalglish as Liverpool drew 1-1 with Ipswich on 13 December 1980. Surprisingly, Rush was actually quite a shy person and struggled to adapt to his new surroundings and the way that Dalglish would wind him up! Eventually, frustration became too much for the young man and he demanded to be selected for the first team or he would leave. Paisley notified him that he would happily allow him to depart the club.
Wound up, he decided to score as many

goals as possible in the reserves so other teams could be aware of his ability. He managed to find the net five times in only four games. Paisley's cunningness had worked, he had no intention to sell the striker but he needed to fire him up! He finally got his first goal for the club on 30 September 1981 against Oulu Palloseura in the European Cup. David Johnson picked up an injury not too long after the European match and Rush was brought into the team. It's fair to say that he was a man on a mission and bagged two goals against Exeter in the League cup before another brace against Leeds in the league. In all honesty, he just could not stop scoring and he finished the season with 30 goals. The 1983/84 campaign was probably Rush's best season in red. He scored a hat-trick against Aston Villa, four against Coventry and even managed to bag himself five against Luton! Prior to the game against the Hatters, he had soaked his boots in the bath. After that game, it became a ritual that he would repeat before every game! In total, Rush played 660 times for Liverpool, scoring 346 goals. His honours list is absolute ridiculous, too. Five League Championships, three FA Cups, five League Cups and one European Cup. He was voted PFA Young Player of the Year in 1983, which was followed by PFA Player of the Year in the following year. He also won the European Golden Boot in the same year. When he finally left Liverpool in 1987 he had a sole season with Juventus before returning to England to turn out for Leeds and Newcastle. He finished his career in 2000 with Sydney Olympic, bringing an end to a fantastic 22-year journey. Upon retirement, Rush worked as a media pundit and he had a short stint as Chester manager. He featured for Liverpool's Masters team and he released his autobiography titled: *Rush: The Autobiography*. It will take something very special to even come close to Rush's goal scoring record.

### "DID YOU KNOW?"

*"The origin of the name Liverpool, known as Lerpoole in the early 13th century, from the Old Norse "hlathr pollr" - the pool of the dirty water."*

169

## SATTERTHWAITE, Charlie

*Forward*

**Born:** *1877 Cockermouth, Cumberland*  **Died:** 1948
**Playing career:** *Black Diamond, Workington, Bury, Burton Swifts, Liverpool, New Brompton, Thames Ironworks, Woolwich Arsenal (1896-1910)*

Charlie Satterthwaite was an old-fashioned forward who used his sheer strength to shrug off opposition defenders. He scored a hat-trick in only his second game for the club and he was widely regarded as Liverpool's best ever signing at the time. During his second season, he played in 21 games and scored five goals – helping Liverpool to win their inaugural League Championship. He kept his place for the opening two games of the following campaign but was subsequently dropped thereafter. He would only play four more times for Liverpool's first team before he moved to New Brompton. He joined West Ham the following year and after a successful season, Woolwich Arsenal signed the striker – where he became the first player to score a First Division goal in the club's history. He was Arsenal's top scorer in two of his first three seasons with the club and he finished his time in north London after playing in 178 games and scoring 70 goals. He retired at the age of 33 in the summer of 1910, bringing an end to six years associated with the Gunners. His brother, Joe Satterthwaite, also played for Arsenal and they were the first pair of brothers to do so. He served as a corporal in the Royal Fusiliers during World War I. He died 25 May 1948, aged 71.

## SAUNDERS, Dean

*Striker*

**Born:** *1964 Swansea, Wales*
**Playing career:** *Swansea City, Cardiff City, Brighton , Oxford United, Derby County, Liverpool, Aston Villa, Galatasaray, Nottingham Forest, Sheffield United, Benfica, Bradford City (1982-2001)*

Dean Saunders was a classy player who had a lot of plaudits from English football fans. Ironically, he was on his way to Australia on a free transfer in 1985 before Brighton's manager had spotted him playing in a reserve game for Swansea. He netted 23 times during his debut season with the Seagulls, which influenced Oxford City to sign the striker. Mark Lawrenson had managed Saunders whilst at Oxford and after scoring 33 goals in 73 games he was on his way to Derby – much to the displeasure of Lawrenson. He was so infuriated by the move that he had handed in his resignation swiftly after! The Welshman continued his fine scoring form for the Rams, with 57 goals in 131 games for his new team. Liverpool made a move for the man in the summer of 1991 and he had signed for the club for a £2.9 million fee. Frustratingly, Saunders didn't quite cut it with Liverpool as he was reliant on his sheer pace – Derby's style of counter-attacking football was perfect for him. Although he wasn't prolific for the 'Pool in the league, he did manage to net nine goals in only five games in the UEFA Cup. He also chipped in with two goals during Liverpool's successful 1992 FA Cup run. In total, he played 61 times whilst contracted at Anfield and he scored 25 goals. He was sold to Aston Villa after only two years with Liverpool as the club were experiencing financial difficulties. Ironically, Saunders bagged a brace only nine days after departing Anfield as Villa ran out 4-2 victors against his old side! He did, however, link back up with Graeme Souness at Galatasaray and scored 15 goals in only 27 league games for the Turkish side. He returned to England to play for Nottingham Forest and Sheffield United before having a sole season in Portugal with Benfica.

Dean Saunders

He finished his career with two years at Bradford and retired in 2001. He remained with the club as a coach for a couple of years before taking up a similar role with both Blackburn and Newcastle. In 2007, Saunders enrolled in the Certificate in Football Management course at the University of Warwick Business School. In the same year, he became the assistant manager of the Welsh national team before going into management himself. He managed at Wrexham, Doncaster, Wolves, Crawley and Chesterfield. He has not been involved with football since 2015 and in 2019, he was arrested over a drink-drive incident.

## SAVAGE, Ted
*Wing-half*
**Born:** *1912 Louth, Lincolnshire* **Died:** 1964
**Playing career:** *Lincoln City, Liverpool, Manchester united, Wrexham(1928-1945)*

Ted Savage announced himself to the footballing world when he was playing for Lincoln in the Third Division at the age of 17. He played in 100 matches for the Imps between the years of 1928-1931. After the club had narrowly missed out on promotion to the second tier of English football, he was transferred to Liverpool in May 1931 for £2,750. Although he primarily played in a more defensive role for Lincoln, he was utilised as an inside-left on his debut for Liverpool and managed to grab a brace against Grimsby on 26 September 1931. He played in 104 more games for the club but he failed to score again! He did, however, play in the majority of games in his preferred role in the defence. He was never a regular at Anfield but he did play in 27 of a possible 42 games during 1934-1936. He made his final appearance against Wolves on 16 October 1937. He joined Manchester United in December 1937 but only featured five times for the Red Devils. He finished his professional career with Wrexham before the advent of World War II. He played for a fair few clubs during the wartime but never returned to football after the conflict. He found employment in the licenses trade after the war and managed the Primrose Hotel in Withens Lane, Wallasey. Savage suffered with heart problems through the duration of his life but when he died on 30 January 1964, aged 75, it was unexpected.

### John Scales
Football Consultant & Entrepreneur
London, United Kingdom · 500+ connections

## SCALES, John
*Defender*
**Born:** *1966 Harrogate*
**Playing career:** *Leeds United, Bristol Rovers, Wimbledon, Liverpool, Tottenham Hotspur, Ipswich Town (1984-2001)*

John Scales was only 19 when he left Leeds to join Bristol Rovers. He impressed greatly at Rovers, which earned him a transfer to Wimbledon. He topped off his fine debut season in London with an unlikely win in the FA Cup final – beating Liverpool in the process. After seven years with Wimbledon – and 240 league appearances later – he arrived at Anfield as an experienced defender looking to add more to his trophy cabinet. He was a sensible player who possessed lots of skill and a fantastic header of the ball – he won medals for high-jump competitions during his youth. Although he was a tidy player, he seemed to lack that little bit of extra quality to make it with a big club such as Liverpool. Scales only spent two years at Anfield before injuries finished his time with the club. He played 94 times for the 'Pool and scored 4 goals. He also won the 1995 League Cup with the team. His move to Tottenham caused some controversy after he had passed a medical to re-join boyhood club Leeds but opted against it and signed for the former instead. Sadly, injuries would continue to plague his career and he only played in 33 games during four seasons with Spurs. He moved to Ipswich for one last final season but he was forced to retire in 2001. After he hung up his boots, he became the England Beach Soccer coach before becoming the chairman of an events management company called Be Sport, who organise tournaments for schools.

## SCOTT, Alex

*Goalkeeper*

**Born:** *1913 Liverpool* **Died:** 1962
**Playing career:** *Liverpool, Burnley, Wolverhampton Wanderers, Crewe Alexandra (1930-1949)*

Alex Scott spent three years in the youth set-up before being released in 1933. He was later a part of the Wolves team that lost the FA Cup final to Portsmouth. Scott returned to Wolverhampton after his retirement in 1949 to run a general store and joined the police force before his death in 1962.

## SCOTT, Elisha

*Goalkeeper*

**Born:** *1893 Belfast, Ireland* **Died:** 1959
**Playing career:** *Linfield, Liverpool, Belfast United, Linfield, Belfast Celtic, Belfast Celtic (1909-1936)*

Elisha Scott is potentially the greatest goalkeeper in Liverpool's history – although Bruce Grobbelaar would like to debate that! He spent 22 years at Anfield from 1912 until 1934 and had World War I not taken place, he most certainly would have added to his 468 appearances. Scott wanted to emulate his older brother – who had just finished an eight-year career with Everton – and his sibling had arranged for him to have a trial.

Everton were not keen on the Irishman which was a huge bonus for Liverpool! Prior to moving to England, Scott actually started off as a striker. He became a goalkeeper because of an argument he had with a teammate. "What's the use of us scoring goals if you're letting them in? My granny could be a better goalie than you". The very next game, Scott's granny was named in goal! He signed for Liverpool on 1 September 1912 and made his debut exactly one year later against Newcastle. The Magpies were so impressed with his performance that they offered £1,000 for his services but, rather wisely, Liverpool declined the offer. He helped Liverpool win successive League Championships in 1922 and 1923 but he eventually lost his place to Arthur Riley. He left Anfield in 1934 and played for Belfast Celtic for two seasons before calling time on his playing days. He moved into management with Belfast Celtic and is still their most successful manager. In 1939, a survey was conducted by Liverpool fans to identify the most popular player in the club's history – Scott topped that list. He died on 16 May 1959, aged 65 and is buried in Belfast City Cemetery.

You can find an Elisha Scott Facebook tribute page at:
https://www.facebook.com/ELISHA-SCOTT-LIVERPOOL-GOALKEEPER-1912-34-85930541744/

## SEAGRAVES, Mark

*Defender*
**Born:** *1966 Bootle*
**Playing career:** *Liverpool, Norwich City (loan), Manchester City, Bolton Wanderers, Swindon Town, Barrow (1983-1999)*

Local boy, Mark Seagraves, never represented Liverpool in the league but was selected to play for the club once in the FA Cup and once in the League Cup during the 1985/86 season. He had a brief loan spell with Norwich but nothing fabricated from the move. He was, however, allowed to leave for Manchester City nine months later and spent three years with the club before moving to Bolton. It was his time with the Wanderers that he will most likely be fond of, spending five years with the club and playing in 157 league matches. During the latter stages of his time there he faced Liverpool in the 1995 League Cup final but lost 2-1 to his former side. He finished his career with Barrow in 1999 and was appointed coach at Wigan when he linked up with former teammate, Paul Jewell, in 2006. The following year he followed Jewell to Derby before finshing his relationship with the coach at Ipswich in 2011. In May 2013 he had began working in Delhi India, for a company called 'India On Track', which help to build a structure to allow children to play football in the country. The following year he started his own project, The Football Faktory, which was an academy for young Indian players.

## SEALEY, John

*Winger*
**Born:** *1945 Wallasey*
**Playing career:** *Warrington Town, Liverpool, Chester, Wigan Athletic (1961-1969)*

John Sealey started his career in the youth academy at Warrington Town and was signed by Liverpool in 1963. Despite spending three years at Anfield, he only featured in one game. He was selected to play in the final league game of the 1964/65 season as all of the regular starters were rested as Liverpool were present in the FA Cup final only days later. Sealey scored the second goal of a 3-1 win away to Wolves in front of 14,000 spectators, a dream come true for the local lad. In 1966, he moved to Chester on a free transfer alongside teammates John Bennett and Alan Hignett.

He transferred to Wigan two years later and had a sole season with Athletic before calling time on his professional career due to a serious knee injury that he failed to recover from. He remains an avid Liverpool fan and is a season ticket holder in the Main stand of Anfield.

## SHAFTO, John

*Forward*
**Born:** *1918 Humsbaugh*
**Died:** 1978
**Playing career:** *Hexham, Liverpool, Brighton & Hove Albion (1934-1939)*

John Shafto was supposed to join Everton. In fact, the club's minute books stated that it was decided what wage he was going to be offered and what donation would be given to his parent club, Hexham. Everton's scout had mentioned why he was staying in a hotel in preparation to sign the youngster. Unfortunately for the Blues, a Liverpool fan was present and upon hearing the news, he rang Anfield to notify the club about a potential signing. George Kay headed straight to sign the boy! He was one of 29 players used in his debut season as the club were going through a transitional period. He was first selected in the autumn of 1937 and made a fantastic start to his time at Anfield, scoring seven goals in 16 games – this included a brace against Everton in the final ten minutes to secure a 3-1 victory at Goodison Park! Unfortunately, Shafto was only picked on four more occasions as Liverpool's team began to gain stability. He moved to Brighton where he finished his professional career off the back of the outbreak of World War II. He did guest for Bradford during wartime. He died in 1978.

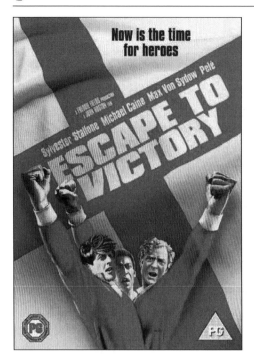

## SHANNON, Les

*Centre-forward/Inside-forward*
**Born:** *1926 Leighton Buzzard* **Died:** *2007*
**Playing career:** *Liverpool, Burnley. (1947-1958)*
Les Shannon started his footballing
journey with Liverpool and signed his first
professional contract with the club in 1944.
He was originally rejected by Everton as he
was small in height for a centre forward, 5
foot, 7 inches. He made his debut towards
the climax of the 1947/48 season when
he came off the bench to replace Albert
Stubbins against Manchester City. He
was selected for the first ten games of the
following season as Stubbins went on strike!
These would be the only 11 matches he
played for Liverpool but he did have the
honour of saying he scored for the club,
against Sheffield United in a 2-1 victory on
30 August 1948. He moved to Burnley and
became a bit of a legend having represented
the club 281 times. He retired in 1958 and
joined Everton as a youth coach, remaining
with the club for three years before being
appointed assistant manager at Arsenal.
He also had stints managing Bury and
Blackpool before he managed four clubs in
Greece and one in Norway. He returned to
England in 1985 and was part of Luton's
backroom staff for 15 years from 1986-2001.

His expansive knowledge of football helped
him land a role working alongside Pele,
co-ordinating the football sequences of the
1981 war movie *Escape to Victory* and he was
also employed as an advisor for Channel 4
series *The Manageress* in 1989. He died on 2
December 2007, aged 81, after a long battle
with Alzheimer's disease and 'You'll Never
Walk Alone' was played at his funeral.

## SHEEDY, Kevin

*Attacking midfielder*
**Born:** *1959 Builth Wells, Wales*
**Playing career:** *Hereford United, Liverpool, Everton,
Newcastle United, Blackpool (1975-1994)*
Kevin Sheedy was born in Wales but
qualified to play for Northern Ireland –
which he did on 46 occasions. He had made
his name with Hereford, playing for three
years whilst the club were in the Third
Division. He signed for Liverpool in July
1968 but had to wait almost three years for
his first team debut, coming on 14 February
1981 in a 2-2 draw with Birmingham. He
made two more league appearances for
the club the following season as well as
featuring in two League Cup ties, scoring
in both. It became apparent that if Sheedy
wanted to play more regularly he would
have to look for another club and that's
exactly what he done. Perhaps many may
have expected him to go anywhere bar
Everton! Despite the negative connotations
between the two clubs, he was a massive
success at Goodison Park, where he spent 10
years and played in over 270 league matches
for the Blues, scoring 67 times. He won two
League Championships with the club and a
European Cup Winners' Cup before moving
to Newcastle and finishing his career
with Blackpool in 1994. He moved into
management seven years later and he had
spells with Tranmere as caretaker manager
before joining Everton's youth coaching
team in 2006. He remained in the role until
2017 and he now coaches Al-Shabab's youth
team in Saudi Arabia.

## "DID YOU KNOW?"

*"The eternal flames on the club
badge are in remembrance of the
tragic loss of life at Hillsborough."*

## SHELDON, John 'Jackie'

*Winger*

**Born:** *1887 Clay Cross, Derbyshire*
**Died:** 1941
**Playing career:** *Manchester United, Liverpool, Tottenham Hotspur at Anfield, Villa Park, Aston Villa, Derby County (1913-1921)*

Jackie Sheldon had been playing for Manchester United when Liverpool signed the winger for £300. He could not break into the first team as superstar, Billy Meredith, had kept him out. Sheldon only missed three games during his debut season with the 'Pool after he was introduced at the backend of November – he also played in all eight FA Cup games that season as Liverpool lost the final to Burnley 1-0. During the last Football League season prior to World War I, he was an ever-present member of the squad with only Jimmy Nicholl making more appearances. Unfortunately, Sheldon's time at Liverpool will forever be tainted for his decision to not only agree to fix a match against Manchester United but for actually arranging for it to take place! He initially denied all involvement but he later confessed to a court that it was himself who persuaded other players to assist with the unlawful act. He was issued a life ban from playing football but after his service to his country during the Great War, the sanction was uplifted and he had two final good years with the club. He broke his leg whilst playing against Derby County and he never played for Liverpool again as he was forced to retire from the incident in 1921. He died on 19 March 1941, aged 53.

**JOHN SHELDON, Manchester United.**

Florent Siname Pongolle

## SINAMA PONGOLLE, Florent

*Forward*

**Born:** *1984 Saint-Pierre, Reunion*
**Playing career:** *Saint-Pierroise, Le Havre, Liverpool, Le Havre , Blackburn Rovers, Recreativo, Atletico Madrid, Sporting CP, Zaragoza (loan), Saint-etienne (loan), FC Rostov, Chicago Fire, Lausanne-Sport, Dundee United (1995-2015)*

Florent Sinama-Pongolle frustrated even the most forgiving Liverpool fans. One day he could be brilliant as he would beat man after man and score some good goals. The next he may well have not even showed up! He shone for France in the U-17 World Cup and he was the top-scorer with nine goals in addition to also being named the best player of the tournament. He was signed by Gerard Houllier in 2002 and immediately loaned back to Le Havre for a year. He arrived at Anfield in July 2003 and he was called upon 23 times after both Milan Baros and Michael Owen picked up consistent injuries throughout the campaign. When Houllier was sacked, Rafael Benitez admitted that he tried to sign the striker whilst he was manager of Sevilla. Despite putting in too many poor performances, Liverpool fans can be thankful for the Frenchman as his equaliser against Olympiacos paved the way for the 2005 Champions League. He did, however, miss the remainder of the season through a nasty injury not too long after the goal. He was loaned to Blackburn before moving to Recreativo in 2006. He played 66 times for Liverpool and scored 9 goals. Throughout his career he has played for 13 clubs! He is still classed as a professional footballer although he is a free agent as he has failed to find another club since leaving Saint-Pierroise in 2019.

## SKRTEL, Martin

*Centre-back*
**Born:** *1984 Handlova, Czechoslovakia*
**Playing career:** *Prievidza, Trencin, Zenit Saint Petersburg, Liverpool (2001-2008)*

Prior to joining Liverpool, Martin Skrtel was relatively unknown in European football. However, his fine displays for Liverpool, in a career that spanned 7 years with the club, made everyone aware of his capabilities. An old-fashioned defender, Skrtel was a tough tackler who refused to ever throw the towel in. He won the Russian Championship with Zenit St Petersburg in 2007 before moving to Anfield for £6.5 million in the following summer. His first two outings in red were worrying, however. He looked nervous when he came on as a substitute during the final 20 minutes of his debut against Aston Villa and then he was accredited with an own goal against non-league Havant & Waterlooville in the FA Cup defeat. Nevertheless, he played in the 18 of the final 23 games of the season and demonstrated why Liverpool had splashed the cash on the defender. He started the following season in the starting XI but an injury suffered at Manchester City kept him out of action for two months. He returned strong and slotted straight back into the team, playing in the majority of Liverpool's fixtures for the remainder of the season. As his time grew on at Anfield, Skrtel continued to improve and even won the 2012 League cup with the team. In total, he played 320 times for Liverpool and scored 18 goals. He left Merseyside for Fenerbahce in 2016 and remained with the club for three years. He has been capped 104 times by Slovakia and he is a tattoo artist in his spare time. He is currently contracted with Istanbul Basaksehir.

## SLATER, Bert

*Goalkeeper*
**Born:** *1936 Brechin, Scotland* **Died:** 2006
**Playing career:** *Falkirk, Liverpool, Dundee, Watford (1953-1969)*

Bert Slater may have been small in height for a goalkeeper, 5 foot and 8 inches, but he certainly knew how to play his position. He was 23 years old when he arrived at Anfield from Falkirk, with Tommy Younger heading the other way. When Bill Shankly arrived in December 1959 he took a likening to Slater and he became Liverpool's preferred number one. He played in 96 consecutive league matches before he was replaced by Jim Furnell after Liverpool were knocked out of the FA Cup by Preston in February 1962. He had only conceded once during three cup games against Preston but alas, he was made the scapegoat and he was told by Shankly that he was on his way to Dundee. Reluctant to leave, he told Shankly he wanted to stay and fight for his place. The manager then began to list six goalkeepers – all in order of importance – without mentioning Slater – he even named the U-12 'keeper ahead of him! Slater spent three years in Scotland before he moved to Watford and finishing his career in 1969 with the Hornets. He became a coach and then assistant manager before he finally left the club. Once he did, he worked for a company that designed golf courses and scouted for Dundee.

Martin Skrtel

## SLOAN, Don

*goalkeeper*

**Born:** *1883 Rankinston, Scotland* **Died:** 1917
**Playing career:** *Distillery, Everton, Liverpool, Distillery, Bathgate (1903-1910)*

Don Sloan had previously spent two years warming the bench at Everton before joining Liverpool for £300 in May 1908. Sam Hardy was the club's first choice 'keeper at the time which restricted Sloan to only six appearances in red. He failed to keep a single clean sheet and moved on after just over a year with the club. He returned to his former club, Distillery, and became player-manager of the Irish side. He died on New Year's Day 1917 whilst he was serving in The Black Watch, an infantry battalion of the Royal Highlanders of Scotland. He was killed on the frontline in France and three of his brothers were also victims of WW1.

## SMICER, Vladimir

*Attacking midfielder*

**Born:** *1973 Decin, Czechoslovakia*
**Playing career:** *Kovostroj Decin, Slavia Prague, Slavia Prague, Lens, Liverpool, Bordeaux, Slavia Prague (1985-2009)*

Vladimir Smicer grew to European prominence during his time with Slavia Prague. He was also a success playing in France for Lens. He was a fine player for Liverpool but unfortunately injuries took over and in the 184 matches he played, 74 of them had come from the bench. A personal highlight of his time at Anfield would have been when he scored a late goal against Chelsea on 24 March 2002 which sent Liverpool top of the table briefly.

Vladimir Smicer

It looked as if Smicer's time may have been up at Liverpool before Gerard Houllier left Anfield. When Rafael Benitez was announced as his replacement, the Czech had to undergo a knee operation that left him out of action for a large chunk of the Spaniards debut season at the helm of the club. He only made two starts from the 16 games he played in for Benitez but, in true fairy tale fashion, he signed off with the most memorable night in Istanbul. He scored Liverpool's second of the evening and he also slotted his penalty away to assist his team with the most unlikely of comebacks. After his contract had expired he returned to France to join Bordeaux but continued to struggle with injuries. He finally went back to where it all started with Prague and finished his career in 2009 there after two seasons. Only one day after his official retirement as a player he had become the sports manager of the Czech national team. In 2014 he stood for minor political party, VIZE, in the European Parliament Election; he stated that his priority was to reduce obesity amongst children.

## SMITH, Jimmy

*Striker*

**Born:** *1902 Old Kilpatrick, Scotland* **Died:** 1975
**Playing career:** *Dumbarton Harp, Clydebank, Rangers, Ayr United, Liverpool, Tunbridge Wells Rangers, Bristol Rovers, Newport County, Notts County, Dumbarton (1919-1946)*

Jimmy Smith was born to score goals, it's as simple as that. He made the Guinness Book of Records for holding the sensational record of 72 goals in a sole season whilst he was playing for Ayr! He Signed for Liverpool in September 1929 for £5,500 and made his debut against Manchester United which was followed by 38 consecutive games for the club, scoring on 23 occasions. He added 14 to his tally the following season but he remarkably lost his place midway through the campaign. He left Anfield having scored 38 goals in 62 games. Rather peculiarly, Smith's career spiralled downwards after his departure from Anfield and he finished his career back in Scotland for Dumbarton. He took over as the club's manager in 1939 and he was appointed director in 1941 as the Scottish side could no longer afford to employ a manager! He remained in this role until 1943. He died in 1975.

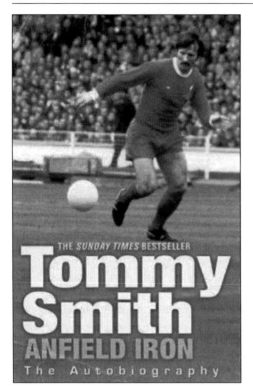

## SMITH, Tommy

*Defender*
**Born:** *1945 Liverpool*
**Died:** 2019
**Playing career:** *Liverpool, Tampa Bay Rowdies (loan), Los Angeles Aztecs, Swansea City (1962-1979)*

Is there a better story than a local boy representing his club for almost the entirety of his career? For Liverpool, Tommy Smith was that lad. "My grandfather and father supported Liverpool. There was no debate. No argument. I would also follow the Mersey Reds. Indeed it went a little deeper than that with me. I was a fanatic, brought up on a diet of football, football and more football". Smith virtually filled every role at one stage of his life serving Liverpool. He was a player, captain, coach and groundsman! His mother took him to Bill Shankly when he was 15 years old in May 1960 and that is how this story begins. When he started out in the reserves he played up front with Billy Liddell but he was later transitioned to play in the defence, a role he would shine in for his boyhood club. He first played as centre-back on 5 December 1964 as Liverpool thumped Burnley 5-1 in the league.

By the age of 20, he had become a regular member of the team but he continued to wear the shirt number 10, which confused opponents as they were expecting him to venture further upfield! He was present when Liverpool won the FA Cup for the first time and for the next ten years, he was the leader of Liverpool's great team. In total, he played in 638 games for the club and scored 48 goals, a fantastic effort for a defender. When it was time for him to leave Anfield he moved to America to play for Los Angeles Aztecs. After he had retired from playing football he returned for a brief spell coaching Liverpool's youth and even had a spell as manager of LA Aztecs when he was there. He wrote a column for 35 years for the Liverpool Echo up until 2014 and released his autobiography, *Anfield Iron* in March 2008. Smith was diagnosed with Alzheimer's disease in October 2014 and passed away from the illness on 12 April 2019, aged 74.

## SMYTH, Sammy

*Striker*
**Born:** *1925 Belfast, Northern Ireland* **Died:** 2016
**Playing career:** *Distillery, Linfield, Dundela, Wolverhampton Wanderers, Stoke City, Liverpool, Bangor (1942-1957)*

Sammy Smyth joined Liverpool at the age of 27 in December 1952 for a fee of £12,000. He was selected to go straight into the starting XI and made his debut against Stoke on 3 January 1953. His former side ran out as 3-1 victors to give Smyth a distasteful start to his Anfield career. Liverpool were in a relegation battle but Smyth finally came to life and his seven goals helped the club to survive the chop. Unfortunately, the following season did end in a drop down to the Second Division despite Smyth chipping in with 13 goals from 26 games – Liverpool were in the First Division for 50 years prior to being relegated that campaign. At the end of this season, the Irishman decided he wanted to return to his native land to focus on his business and Liverpool had to reluctantly let go of their star man. He also worked as a bookmaker when he returned to Belfast before establishing a sports distribution business. When his wife passed away he moved to the Caribbean to live with his daughter. He died in October 2016, aged 91. Prior to his death, he was the oldest person alive to represent Liverpool.

# SONG, Rigobert
*Defender*
**Born:** *1976 Nkenglicock, Cameroon*
**Playing career:** *Metz, Liverpool, West Ham United, Lens, Galatasaray, Trabzonspor (1994-2010)*

Rigobert Song holds the unwanted record of being the first player to be sent off in two successive World Cups. A bright star growing up who captained the Cameroon U-20 squad when he was only 16 years old – he would later captain the senior team too. He is the most capped Cameroon player with 137 appearances and featured in four World Cups. Six months after his exploits in the 1998 World Cup, he signed for Liverpool for a fee of £2.6 million. He was a comical character but from a footballing perspective, he failed to make any impact whatsoever whilst playing at Anfield. He made 38 appearances before he moved to West Ham in November 2000 but his erratic form followed him to London and he eventually moved to France on a permanent transfer to join Lens. Song finished his career in 2010 with Turkish club Trabzonspor. He is also the uncle of former Arsenal player, Alex Song. He is currently coaching with the Cameroon national team after having a short spell managing the senior team in a caretaker role in 2018. He was put into an induced coma for two days in 2016 but he has thankfully recovered well.

Rigobert Song

# SOUNESS, Graeme
*Midfielder*
**Born:** *1953 Edinburgh, Scotland*
**Playing career:** *Tottenham Hotspur, Middlesbrough, Liverpool. (1970-1983).*

Graeme Souness started his career with Tottenham but when he knocked on Bill Nicholson's door and demanded first team action, the gaffer's reluctance to play the youngster spelt the end of his Spurs' days. After six successful years with Middleborough he moved to Liverpool in 1978 and would go on to play over 350 times for the club. A midfield maestro with a keen eye for goal, Souness was the complete player. During his time with Liverpool he won the League Championship five times, the League Cup three times and the European Cup three times. His final game for Liverpool was to help them win the 1984 European Cup which meant that the Scotsman left the club on an absolute high. He spent two years in Italy turning out for Sampdoria before returning home to play for Rangers. It is with the latter that he gained his first experience of management. He was appointed player-manager of the Scottish team in April 1986 and managed to revitalise the team to reverse the dominance in Scotland from Celtic to Rangers. After Kenny Dalglish resigned as Liverpool manager in February 1991, Ronnie Moran was put in temporary charge but he stressed he did not want the job on a full-time basis. This paved the way for Souness to return to the club he was so successful at as a player. During the early stages of his inaugural season managing the club, Liverpool were looking like serious title contenders, but they eventually dropped off and finished sixth. They did, however, win the 1992 FA Cup after beating Sunderland 2-0 in the final. This would be the only silverware the club won with the Scotsman at the helm. He managed in Turkey, Italy and Portugal before a final stint at English club Newcastle capped the end of his direct involvement in professional football. In January 2007, he had made a formal bid of £20 million to buy Wolverhampton Wanderers but the bid was rejected as the then owners believed it was short of their expectation. Souness now works for Sky as a pundit but did have a previous role with RTÉ covering the 2010 FIFA World Cup.

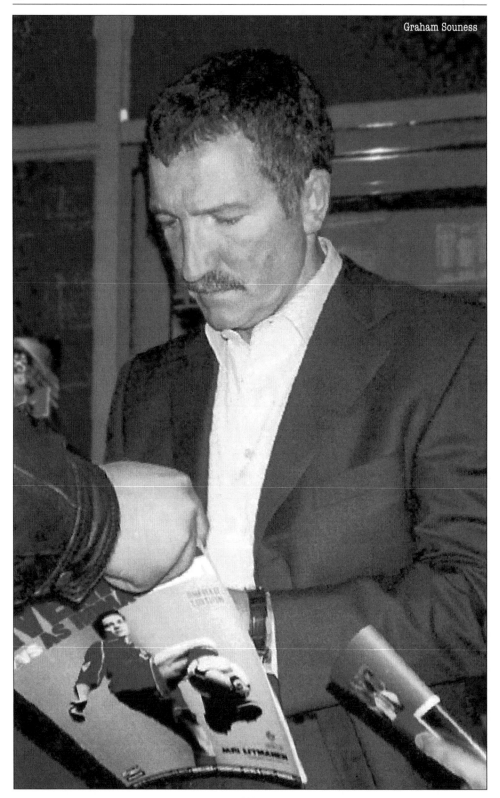

Graham Souness

## SPACKMAN, Nigel
*Midfielder*
**Born:** *1960 Romsey*
**Playing career:** *Bournemouth, Chelsea, Liverpool, QPR, Chelsea, Sheffield United. (1980-1996)*
Known for his sheer power and selfless play, Nigel Spackman made the good players around him look brilliant. A versatile player, Spackman spent only two years at Anfield but racked up over 60 appearances for Liverpool. When Ronnie Whelan injured himself, he stepped in to help Liverpool win the 1987/88 First Division title. After frustration grew from his lack of playing time, he moved to QPR before finishing his playing career with Sheffield United in 1996. He was appointed caretaker manager of the Blades in 1997 which resulted in his appointment on a full-time basis. A lack of investment in the squad – with addition to first team players leaving – led Spackman's decision to resign from the role in March 1998. He also had roles with Barnsley and Millwall but left mid-season again, which meant that he never saw out a full season with any of the three clubs that he managed initially. He briefly entered a media role with Sky Sports before joining Millwall as manager. He can now be seen working on Singapore's Football Channel, Seana Sport. He also continues to work on Al Jazeera's La Liga Coverage as well as LFC TV.

## SPEEDIE, David
*Striker*
**Born:** *1960 Glenrothes, Scotland*
**Playing career:** *Barnsley, Darlington, Chelsea, Coventry City, Liverpool, Blackburn Rovers, Southampton, Birmingham City (loan), West Bromwich Albion (loan), West Ham United (loan), Leicester City , Crawley Town (1978-2007)*
A surprise signing by Kenny Dalglish that also turned out to be his final one before he resigned in February 1991. Prior to joining Liverpool, David Speedie had established himself with long spells at Chelsea and Coventry City. A striker who scored goals for fun, his short time at Liverpool can be regarded as fairly successful. He played 14 times for the Anfield outfit and scored on six occasions. He scored very important goals too – a late equaliser against Manchester United and two early goals in the Merseyside derby. The Scotsman then made his way to Blackburn Rovers - where

Dalglish followed him only a few months later. In total, Speedie would make 519 league appearances and score 148 goals across various clubs during his career. After retirement, he lived in Dublin and commentated for Setanta Sports whilst playing for Francis AFC in Dublin's United Churches League. He returned to live in south Yorkshire to drive a taxi and play plenty of golf.

## SPICER, Eddie
*Defender*
**Born:** *1922 Liverpool* **Died:** 2004
**Playing career:** *Liverpool (1939-1953)*
Eddie Spicer was a sports fanatic growing up and excelled in both football and cricket. He signed professional forms with the club in 1939 but as World War II broke out, he was forced to wait to make his debut for the first team. He served during the conflict and joined the Royal Marines as a lieutenant when he had an interesting experience with an enemy solider. A German fighter had surrendered to him when he informed him that he was a professional footballer in Germany. His knowledge of the English game, in addition to players he had said he played against, allowed the two fighters to bond! Once the war had finished, Spicer made his league debut on the opening day of the 1946/47 season. He was still only 23 years old and was largely restricted to the fringes of the first team during his first few years with the club after the war, mainly filling in for Phil Taylor or Bob Paisley. Then, finally, he became a regular with the 'Pool during the 1949/50 season but an awful incident would finish his career. Dave Underwood was expected to collect the ball in the Liverpool goal but rather peculiarly he decided to hoof it instead, missing it and making contact with Spicer's leg! The unfortunate incident had fractured his leg in 19 places and he was in and out of hospital over the next 12 months. Thankfully he was able to walk again but his career in football had finished. He was granted a testimonial match by the club on 19 September 1955 - which helped the defender with £4,500 remuneration. When he retired he became a football correspondent in Wales for the Liverpool Daily Post and he ran a pub near Ruthin in north Wales. He died on Christmas Day 2004, aged 82.

Ian St John

## St John, Ian

*Centre-forward*
**Born:** *1938 Motherwell, Scotland*
**Playing career:** *Motherwell, Liverpool, Coventry City, Tranmere Rovers. (1956-1972)*

There aren't many more successful signings than Ian St John in Liverpool Football Club's history. He was a selfless striker who, despite small in stature, could out-jump even the tallest of defenders! Liverpool had spent six seasons in the Second Division when they turned their attention to St John. He was signed from Motherwell for £37,500 in May 1961 but Shankly had wanted the striker much earlier, with the club not being able to afford him. When the headlines read: "St John wants to go", Shankly was straight on the phone to finally land the long-term target. The money was immediately worth it as he netted a hat-trick on his debut in a 4-3 defeat to Everton in the Liverpool Senior Cup final at Goodison. Only two months later and fellow countryman, Ron Yeats, followed him to Merseyside. The Scotsmen helped Liverpool to the Second Division title, finishing eight points clear of second-placed Leyton Orient. St John only missed two league games during that campaign and managed to score 18 goals. In the second year of First Division football, the club had won the title for the first time in 27 years – with St John bagging another 21 goals.

He certified his legendary status when he scored the winner in the 1965 FA Cup final that saw Liverpool win it for the first time in their history. Throughout his time at Anfield, the Scotsman played in 425 games and scored 118 goals. He won The Second Division title, two League Championships and the aforementioned FA Cup. After ten years with the club he left for South Africa before returning to England to finish his career with Tranmere Rovers. He moved into management and had spells with both Motherwell and Portsmouth where he was relatively unsuccessful. He had stints as an assistant manager with Sheffield Wednesday before Coventry. He carved out a career in television too as he was half of the Saint & Greaves. He also had his own radio show on Radio City 96.7.

## STANIFORTH, Fred

*Outside-right*
**Born:** *1884 Kilnhurst*   **Died:** 1955
**Playing career:** *Bristol City, Grimsby Town, Liverpool (1906-1913)*

Fred Staniforth played amateur football until his signing with Bristol City in 1906. He spent four years in the west country and played in over 130 league games for the Robins. He made his first team debut on the right wing in a 2-0 defeat to Everton on 6 October 1906. He helped City finish in their highest league standing through their history when they finished runners-up at the end of that season – he was also present as the club lost 1-0 to Manchester United in the 1909 FA Cup final. He moved to Grimsby and spent two years with the club before Liverpool had signed the winger in May 1913. He made his debut for the 'Pool in a thumping 4-1 home defeat by Sheffield Wednesday on 4 October 1913. He was absent from the next five games before recording two final appearances for the club. He retired in 1913 after only one year at Anfield. When he retired from football he returned to Bristol and settled in the city until his death on 23 May 1955.

### "DID YOU KNOW?"

*"Ted Doig was 41 years old when he became the club's oldest player in March 1908"*

Steve Staunton

## STAUNTON, Steve

*Defender*

**Born:** *1969 Drogheda, Ireland*
**Playing career:** *Dundalk, Liverpool, Bradford City, Aston V, Crystal P, Coventry C, Walsall (1985-2005)*

Steve Staunton was an excellent servant to Liverpool and could play in several positions, demonstrating his versatility perfectly. Although he primarily played at left-back for the club, he did score a second-half hat-trick against Wigan after replacing Ian Rush! When Sander Westerveld was sent off after Liverpool had made all three substitutions he even went in goal during one Merseyside derby. He arrived from Dundalk in September 1986 and helped Liverpool win the 1989/90 League Championship after he had starred in the first 23 games of the season. He enjoyed playing under Kenny Dalglish and the Scotsman certainly rated the full-back. However, when Graeme Souness returned to the club as manager, he sold Staunton to Aston Villa in August 1991 – he would go on to become one of the best left-backs in the country! He did, however, return to the club in July 1998 but it was clear that his best days were long behind him. He spent two years at Anfield during his second spell before returning back to Villa and finishing his career with Walsall. He became an assistant manager with the latter before being appointed manager of the Republic or Ireland in 2006. He returned to league football to become Gary McAllister's assistant at Leeds and then manager with Darlington. Staunton was sacked by the club after they were relegated from the Football League in 2010. He was capped 102 times by Ireland as a player. His latest involvement with football was being appointed scout by Sunderland in August 2011 but he was relieved of his role in 2013.

## STEEL, Willie

*Full-back*

**Born:** *1908 Blantyre, Scotland*
**Died:** 1990
**Playing career:** *Bridgton Waverley, St Johnstone, Liverpool, Birmingham, Derby County, Dumbarton (wartime guest) (1926-1940)*

Willie Steel made his debut for Liverpool on 19 December 1931 in a 1-1 draw with Derby County. He would remain in the team for the duration of the season, only missing out on one occasion. He was a consistent figure in the Liverpool team for two more seasons before he lost his position to England international, Tommy Cooper. He was well respected by fans of the club, so when he decided to leave for Birmingham it felt like a kick in the teeth for the supporters. Steel had made 128 appearances during his time at Anfield. He finished his professional career with Derby but he did feature for Dumbarton during wartime 19 times. He returned to football in 1954 but as a manager. He firstly managed Airdrie for nine years before spending a sole season with Third Lanark. He died in 1990.

## STENSGAARD, Michael

*Goalkeeper*

**Born:** *1974 Copenhagen, Denmark*
**Playing career:** *Hvidovre, Liverpool, Copenhagen, Southampton, Copenhagen (1993-2001)*

Michael Stensgaard has gone into the Liverpool Football Club history books not for his performances – he never featured for the club – but for seriously injuring his shoulder when he was taking his ironing board out at home! When he finished as a player he finished his education and he was the first in Scandinavia to specialise in business conflict mediation. He is also a FIFA-licensed football player agent and acts as a mental coach for both athletes and businessmen.

Michael
Steensgaard
Negotiations & Conflict
Management

## STEVENSON, General
*Full-back*
**Born:** *1875 Padiham, Burnley* **Died:** 1961
**Playing career:** *Hapton, Padiham, Liverpool, Barnsley, Wellingborough, Millwall Athletic, Accrington Stanley (1893-1913)*

General Stevenson had a brother named Admiral, which could indicate that his dad may have been a military man! He was forced to wait a year to make his debut for the first team after he had signed in December 1897. He did, however, make the right-back spot his for 22 games during the backend of the 19th century. Stevenson was eventually replaced by Archie Goldie which paved the way for a move to Barnsley. He joined Millwall in 1903 and spent seven years with the club. He helped the Lions win the Western League in 1908 and 1909, captaining the team. He played 318 times for the club and scored nine goals before retiring in 1913. Millwall granted the full-back a benefit match that attracted a 10,000 audience. When he retired as a player he became a pub landlord and his son, Arthur Stevenson, was a professional rugby league player for Wigan and footballer for both Sheffield United and Middleborough.

## STEVENSON, Willie
**Born:** *1939 Leith, Scotland*
**Playing career:** *Rangers, Liverpool, Stoke City & Tranmere Rovers.*

Bill Shankly won a bidding war with Preston for the Scotsman's services in 1962. He signed for £20,000 and took over the left-half position from Tommy Leishman. Liverpool had settled well into the First Division and finished eighth before winning the League Championship the following season. Stevenson netted a penalty in the FA Cup semi-final to increase Liverpool's lead to 2-0, booking their ticket in the final in the process . Throughout his time in Merseyside, Stevenson was a classy midfielder who greatly assisted with the success that the club had at the time. When Liverpool lost to Borussia Dortmund in the final of the European Cup Winners' Cup, in anger, the Scotsman threw his runners-up medal out of the window, never to be seen again! In total, he played 241 times for the 'Pool and scored 18 goals. He moved to Stoke in 1967 before having spells in both Ireland and Canada. After he finished his career he became a publican and established his own cleaning company. He now lives in Macclesfield in well-deserved retirement.

## STEWART, Paul
*Defensive midfielder/Forward*
**Born:** *1964 Manchester*
**Playing career:** *Blackpool, Manchester City, Tottenham Hotspur, Liverpool, Wolves, Burnley, Sunderland, Stoke City, Workington (1981-2000)*

Paul Stewart was a fantastic servant for Blackpool, spending six years with the Seasiders and being entered into their Hall of Fame in the process. He joined Manchester City and Tottenham before Liverpool signed the midfielder in July 1992 for a fee of £2.3 million. During his four years with the club he was unambitious, lazy and frustrated the club's faithful. He is now a successful businessman in Blackpool and in 2016, he revealed that he was the victim of physical and sexual abuse by his junior team coach. He released his autobiography in 2017 titled: *Damaged*, which discuss the issues in further context. Whilst at Liverpool, he revealed that he struggled so much with the experience that he took cocaine and drank excessive amounts of alcohol to numb the trauma.

## STORER, Harry

*goalkeeper*

**Born:** *1870 Ripley, Derbyshire*
**Died:** 1908
**Playing career:** *Gainsborough Trinity, Loughborough, Woolwich Arsenal, Lincoln City, Liverpool's, William Barclay, Anfield, (1894-1901)*

Harry Storer made his name with Arsenal, where he spent 18 months in the Second Division before signing for Liverpool at the age of 25 years old in 1895. He replaced Matt McQueen in the Liverpool goal and the latter continued to play for the club in an outfield position! He played in the final 11 games of his debut season and helped the club make an immediate return to the First Division. He only missed out on seven of the following 87 domestic games as he was firmly established as the club's number one. He suffered an injury in December 1896 and once he regained fitness he was loaned to Hibernian as their goalkeeper was out injured. They had a cup game against Rangers coming up and it became apparent that Liverpool were doing the Scottish side a favour - Hibs' subsequently lost the game 3-0. Once he returned to Liverpool, William Perkins was installed as the club's main stopper and Storer was restricted to the rare appearance. He ran a pub alongside his career but it was frowned upon. However, the Chairman of Liverpool Licensing Sessions decided that he was only making another income for his family and would imminently make that his primary profession, so he was allowed to keep his property. Storer was also an excellent cricketer, playing in six first-class matches for Derbyshire during the 1985 season – his brother, Bill, played six Tests for England. Harry's son would also become a footballer and move into management after his playing career. Harry Storer died on 25 April 1908, aged only 37, through consumption.

## STORTON, Trevor

*Central Defender*

**Born:** *1949 Keighley*
**Died:** 2011
**Playing career:** *Tranmere Rovers, Liverpool, Chester-City, Oswestry Town, Telford United (1967-1989)*

Trevor Storton started his footballing journey with Tranmere in 1976. He spent five years with the club and made over 130 appearances.

Bill Shankly identified the defender as someone who could take Liverpool to the next level and he was subsequently signed for £25,000. Storton would win the UEFA Cup in his debut season but he was never a regular member of the team. He made his league debut away to Leeds in September 1972 but he would only record four more domestic outings for the club. He was shipped off to Chester where he became a legend with the club. He spent ten years there and played in 468 competitive fixtures. He became player-manager of Oswestry Town from 1984-86. He then spent three years playing for his brother at Telford United, winning the FA Trophy with the club in 1989. He devoted seven years as Bradford Park Avenue's manager and he was working as assistant manager of Halifax Town when he was diagnosed with cancer. He lost his battle with the illness on 23 March 2011, aged 61.

## STOTT, James

*Winger*

**Born:** *1871 Darlington*
**Died:** 1908
**Playing career:** *South Bank, Middlesbrough, Liverpool, Grimsby Town, Newcastle United, Middlesbrough (1887-1900)*

James Stott may have only spent one year with Liverpool but he was the club's top-scorer during that time. He scored 14 goals from only 17 games which gave him a goals-to-games ratio of 1.21! He started off well and played in 13 of the opening 14 fixtures before returning for three more during the latter half of the season. The highlight of his time with the club would have been his hat-trick against Middlesbrough as Liverpool thumped their opponents 6-0. Stott moved to Newcastle and was made captain from 1896-1898, helping the club gain promotion to the topflight at the end of that spell. He made 125 appearances for United which spanned across four years. He was once disciplined by the club's board as he was fouling too often – a stark contract to today's game! He tragically contracted a brain tumour and died in a mental institution on 9 October 1908, aged 37.

## STRONG, Geoff

*Inside-forward/Left-back*
**Born:** *1937 Kirkheaton* **Died:** 2013
**Playing career:** *Arsenal, Liverpool, Coventry City (1960-1971)*

When Geoff Strong arrived at Anfield in 1964 he had already been an experienced player, having played for Arsenal for seven years prior. He signed for Liverpool in November 1964 for a fee of £40,000 and he was brought in to replace Alf Arrowsmith. The versatility that Strong demonstrated greatly assisted Bill Shankly as he knew that the player could play in several positions. Despite this, he did not make the strongest starts to his Anfield career. He was in and out of the team during his first season with the club but he was present for the FA Cup final as Gordon Milne missed out on the finale through injury.

He was also called upon for both legs in the European semi-final against Italian giants Inter Milan. Nevertheless, he featured more frequently the following campaign as he settled into life at Liverpool. He continued to be a heavy presence of the team before being transferred to Coventry City after six years with the club. Strong represented Liverpool on 201 occasions, scoring 33 times. He won the FA Cup and the League Championship with the 'Pool. After he retired he lived in Birkdale and became a successful businessman, owning a thriving hotel furnishing company and co-owned a pub with former teammate, Ian Callaghan. He died at a care home in Southport on 17 June 2013, aged 75.

Albert Stubbins

## STUBBINS, Albert

*Centre-forward*

**Born:** *1919 Wallsend* **Died:** 2002
**Playing career:** *Newcastle United , Liverpool, Ashington (1937-1954)*

"A-L-B! E-R-T! Albert Stubbins is the man for me…" would often be sung around Anfield when the striker notched yet another goal for the club. He was one of the most respected players for Liverpool in the post-war era and it's easy to understand why the clinical striker was such a hit with the club's supporters. He notched a sensational 244 goals for Newcastle during wartime that included 23 hat-tricks. Both Merseyside clubs wanted to sign the striker but he chose Liverpool, departing the Magpies for £13,000 - which was only £1,000 less than the then transfer record. He found the net on his debut for the club and only missed two league games for the remainder of the season. He finished the campaign as the joint top-scorer at the club with both himself and Jack Balmer bagging 24 each. Stubbins was also planning for the future and wanted to become a journalist so it was included in his contract that he would be able to write a column for Football Echo once his contract had finished. He made his final appearance for the club on 3 January 1953 against Stoke. He played 178 times for Liverpool and scored 83 goals, winning the League Championship once. He did indeed enter the world of sports journalism after his retirement and coached New York Americans alongside his profession. He is the only footballer to appear of the cover of the Beatles' *Sgt. Pepper's Lonely Hearts Club* Band album and also featured as a minor character in Stephen Baxter's time-travelling novel, *The Time Ships*. He died on 28 December 2002, aged 83.

Daniel Sturridge

## STURRIDGE, Daniel

*Forward*

**Born:** *1989 Birmingham*
**Playing career:** *Manchester City, Chelsea, Bolton Wanderers (Loan), Liverpool, West Bromwich Albion, Trabzonspor (2006-)*

Birmingham-born striker, Daniel Sturridge, starred for Manchester City as a youngster where he became the first player to score in the FA Youth Cup and the FA Cup in the same season. Despite playing for England at every level, it is fair to say that his career has never reached the heights that his early promise had indicated. His time at Anfield began in 2013 with the club paying a £12 million fee for his services. Over the next six years he did clock up 50 goals and formed a deadly partnership with Luis Suarez, nicknamed the 'SAS'. Repeated injuries prevented a higher total and eventually prompted a loan move to West Bromwich Albion and his permanent departure in 2019. A subsequent stint at Turkish side Trabzonspor was brought to an abrupt end on the same day that he received a four month worldwide ban and £150,000 fine for breaching betting rules. He was found guilty of encouraging his brother to place a bet on a move to Sevilla.

Luis Suarez

## SUAREZ, Luis
*Forward*
**Born:** *1987 Salto, Uruguay*
**Playing career:** *Nacional, Gronigan, Ajax, Liverpool, Barcelona (2006-)*

Luis Suarez's career came to promise in the Netherlands, firstly with Gronigan and then, more noticeably, with Ajax of Amsterdam. It was here that he became the Dutch League's top scorer and Player of the Year. His status as one of the world's best strikers has sometimes been over-shadowed by controversy, not least his penchant for biting chunks out of his opponents. Rather ironically, it was such an incident that indirectly led to his move to Anfield. He was serving a ban for biting a PSV player when Ajax started to make enquiries to see if anyone would be keen to take him off their hands. Interest from the Liverpool board and almost £23 million answered that question. It also started a remakable run of goals in a red shirt which began on his debut in February 2011 until his departure just over three years later. By then, he had notched up a tally of 69 goals in only 110 games, won the Premier League Golden Boot, and had

been named both the PFA Player of the Year and Football Writers' Player of the Year. At this time, he was widely regarded to be the most influential player in Europe, which also made him top of the biggest clubs' wishlist. It took an offer of over £80m from Barcelona to prize him away from Merseysde in July 2014. Since that time, he has remained in the forefront of European football, as part of a formidable forward line that has included such greats as Lionel Messi and Neymar.

## TALLEC, Anthony
*Forward*
**Born:** *1984 Hennebont, France*
**Playing career:** *Liverpool, Le Havre (loan), Saint-etienne (loan), Sunderland (loan), Le Mans, Auxerre B, Valenciennes B, Atromitos (1999-2015)*

Anthony Tallec was tipped to be the next big thing. Unfortunately, he had nothing like the career he was speculated to have had. He joined the 'Pool from Le Havre alongside Florent Sinama-Pongolle but was immediately loaned straight back to the French club. Eventually, a lack of first team opportunities at Anfield got the better of him and he was eager for a move away from the club. He spent seven years at Anfield and played only 32 times – being sent out on loan on five occasions. Since leaving the club he has failed to make any impact in Europe's elite divisions and is currently contracted with Ligue 2 team Annecy.

## TANNER, Nick
*Defender*
**Born:** *1965 Kingswood, Bristol*
**Playing career:** *Bristol Rovers, Liverpool, Norwich City (loan), Swindon Town (loan) (1985-1990)*

Nick Tanner attracted the interest of Bristol Rovers when he was playing for amateur team Mangotsfield United. He was a good servant to the club and an important player, having made over 100 appearances for the Pirates. Liverpool made their move in 1988 and he was signed for £20,000. Tanner had to remain patient at the club as they had just won their seventeenth League Championship. He made his debut against Manchester City during the Christmas period of 1989 but would only feature in three more domestic fixtures that season. Liverpool won the title during his second season but the Bristolian had failed to make enough appearances to earn a medal.

He was forced to retire from a consistent back problem after four years with the club. Since retiring he has worked in the insurance industry and runs an event company whilst also undertaking work for BBC Radio Merseyside, reporting on Liverpool. In October 2019, Tanner was the number one manager in the Fantasy Premier League!

## TENNANT, Jack
*Defender*
**Born:** *1907 Newcastle upon Tyne* **Died:** 1978
**Playing career:** *Newcastle United, Washington Colliery, Stoke City, Torquay United, Liverpool, Bolton Wanderers, Stoke City (1925-1939)*
Having started out as centre-forward for amateur side Washington Colliery, Jack Tennant was transformed into a full-back when Torquay bought him from Stoke. He was brought to Liverpool in 1933 and made his debut for the club in the autumn of the same year. He made seven successive appearances before he missed out on the next 16 games of the campaign. He did make a comeback during the backend of the season but had to wait a whole year before he would be a regular in the team again. He left for Bolton and helped the club achieve promotion to the First Division in 1936. In total, he made 105 appearances for Wanderers prior to the advent of World War II. During wartime, he returned to guest for Liverpool. He died in 1978.

Michael Thomas

## THOMAS, Michael
*Midfielder*
**Born:** *1967 Lambeth, London*
**Playing career:** *Arsenal, Portsmouth, Liverpool, Middlesbrough, Benfica, Wimbledon (1984-2001)*
When Michael Thomas signed for Liverpool in May 1991 he had a lot to apologise for – his last minute goal for Arsenal in 1989 snatched a dramatic title that went all the way down to the wire. Luckily for the midfielder, his seven years at Merseyside were relatively successful. He won the 1992 FA Cup and the 1995 League Cup whilst at Anfield. He scored a fantastic goal in the FA Cup final win which helped his side beat Sunderland 2-0. Unfortunately, a nasty injury to his Achilles kept him out of action for 18 months. When he regained fitness his form returned with him and he played the holding midfielder role exceptionally well under new manager Roy Evans. Thomas played 163 times for the 'Pool and scored 12 goals. He left Liverpool to link back up again with Souness at Benfica before finishing his career with Wimbledon. When he retired from the game he set up his own security service and he also plays for the Liverpool Legends team. He currently resides in Liverpool.

## THOMPSON, David
*Midfielder*
**Born:** *1977 Birkenhead*
**Playing career:** *Liverpool, Swindon Town, Coventry City, Blackburn Rovers, Wigan Athletic, Portsmouth, Bolton Wanderers (1996-2007)*
Having graduated from the Liverpool academy, local boy, David Thompson, was awarded with professional papers in 1994. He was among the favourites from the fans as his fierce attitude did not go unnoticed. He was loaned out to Swindon during the early stages of his professional career with the club and his fine form in the west country awarded him with opportunities back at his boyhood club. He scored 5 league goals in 48 appearances before moving on to Coventry. He eventually finished his career with Bolton in 2007 due to a chronic cartilage problem in his knee. Despite featuring for the England U-21 team, he never made a senior cap for his country. He now works for BBC Radio Merseyside as a football pundit.

## THOMPSON, Peter

*Outside-left*
**Born:** *1942 Carlisle, Cumberland*
**Died:** 2018
**Playing career:** *Preston North End, Liverpool, Bolton Wanderers (1957-1978)*

Peter Thompson was a fantastic schoolboy who was virtually pursued by every top club in England! He chose Preston and broke into the first team at just 17 years old, making his debut against Arsenal in August 1960. After three years with Preston, the club's relegation paved a way to Liverpool. A vast crowd gathered to watch the young boy arrive. When Thompson sat down with Shankly, ready to sign the papers, he asked the manager for a signing-on fee. Shankly, in true Shankly fashion, was not too happy with the request. "You what? I am giving you the chance to play in the greatest city, in the greatest team that is going to be in the world and you want illegal money? Get out!" Luckily, the winger quickly signed the papers but it certainly did not get his career at Anfield off to the best start! Thankfully, he wasn't just good at football, he was fantastic. He primarily played on the left wing and would cut in to shoot with his preferred right foot. The pairing of Thompson and Ian Callaghan struck fear in opponents across all of Europe! After ten years of service he left for Bolton to finish his career, which he did in 1978. Shankly was once famously quoted about Thompson's ability: "If he had scored goals as well as well as everything else he did, he would have been in the same category as Jesus Christ!" When he retired from the game he ran a caravan park in Knott End-on-Sea and then hotels in the Lake District and Harrogate. He died on 30 December 2019, aged 76.

Phil Thompson

## THOMPSON, Phil

*Centre-back*
**Born:** *1954 Kirkby, Lancashire*
**Playing career:** *Liverpool*

Phil Thompson signed for his boyhood club professionally in January 1971 and made his debut at Old Trafford on Easter Monday the following year. He was originally utilised by Bill Shankly in midfield and he had qualified for enough games to win his first League Championship in 1973. The following season was to be Shankly's last and he had transitioned the local lad to play in the heart of the defence. He was calm and collected on the ball and opted to distribute the ball from the back instead of lump it up the field. During the 1974/75 campaign, Liverpool failed to win any silverware after they were beaten by Derby in the League Cup final. Astonishingly, this would be the last time Thompson would not win any trophy with Liverpool for the rest of his time with the club! The defender played 477 times and won seven League Championships, one FA Cup, two League Cups, two European Cups, two UEFA Cups and the 1977 European Super Cup. He eventually left Anfield in March 1985 for Sheffield United, before he called quits on his fine career. Thompson returned to Anfield to coach the reserves before his infamous sacking by Graeme Souness in 1993. He did, however, return once more as assistant manager in 1998 - he even managed the club for a little while whilst Gerard Houllier was recovering from a heart operation. When the Frenchman left the club, Thompson followed him. He has since become a pundit for Sky Sports and he features weekly on Soccer Saturday.

## TOMLEY, Fred

*Defender*

**Born:** *1931 Liverpool* **Died:** 1981
**Playing career:** *Liverpool, Chester (1953-1956)*

Local boy, Fred Tomley, had his dream come true when he signed for Liverpool in September 1953. Unfortunately, his stay at Anfield was brief and he only participated in two successive games for the club – against Bury and Lincoln in March 1955. He was sold to Chester in July of the same year but he failed to break into their team, making just one appearance. He was then shipped to Witton Albion and finished his career in the amateur leagues of England. He ventured into the pub trade after his career in professional football and ran the Harvester in Cantril Farm. He was also a popular figure in his local area as he had completed extensive charity work and helped organise a local junior football league. He died suddenly on 13 February 1981, aged 49.

## TORPEY, Stephen

*Forward*

**Born:** *1981 Kirkby*
**Playing career:** *Liverpool, Port Vale (1995-2011)*

Stephen Torpey was part of Liverpool's youth academy when he was a youngster but the club failed to offer him a professional contract. Port Vale signed him when he was released by the 'Pool in 2001 but he only featured in one league game for the Vale. He subsequently dropped into the non-leagues of football and remained there for the duration of his career. When he retired in 2011 he worked as a foundation coach with Liverpool's youth teams before Manchester City poached the trainer in 2014. He remains in his role with City in 2020.

## TORRES, Fernando

*Striker*

**Born:** *1984 Fuenlabrada, Spain*
**Playing career:** *Atletico Madrid, Atletico Madrid, Liverpool, Chelsea, Milan (loan), Milan, Atletico Madrid (loan) (1995-2015)*

Fernando Torres could possibly be the most clinical goal scorer that Liverpool have seen since the turn of the millennium. He started his career with Atletico Madrid and was awarded with a professional contract with the Spanish team. After six years with Atletico – and 82 goals in 214 league games – it was time for a change.

Fernando Torres

Prior to joining Liverpool in 2007, he had been capped by Spain and it did not take long to understand why Liverpool parted with a club record £20.2 million for his services. Pressure was piled on Torres whilst he was at his former club but when he arrived at Liverpool he was able to just play his natural game. He announced himself to the English game with fantastic goals against Chelsea, Marseille and Tottenham . During his debut season, Torres was involved in 33 of the 38 league matches but played less frequently in the cup games – although he did score a magnificent hat-trick against Reading in the League Cup. When he left Liverpool on very controversial terms for Chelsea in the first month of 2011, he had played in 142 matches for the 'Pool and scored 81 goals. He never truly settled with the Blues and failed to emulate the success he had at Anfield. Despite this, he scored a historic goal that guaranteed Chelsea's presence in the 2012 Champions League at the expense of Barcelona. He spent four years at Stamford Bridge and won the FA Cup, Champions League and Europa League before heading to AC Milan. He returned to Atletico for a couple of seasons before going to Japan for a sole year to finish his career. He announced his retirement on 21 June 2019 and football had lost a prominent player of the last couple of decades. He released his autobiography in 2009, titled: *Torres: El Nino: My Story* and also made a cameo appearance in the 2005 comedy film *Torrente 3: El protector*.

## TOSHACK, John

*Striker*
**Born:** *1949 Cardiff, Wales*
**Playing career:** *Cardiff City, Liverpool, Swansea City (1965-1980)*

When John Toshack arrived at Liverpool, he was second choice behind Frank Worthington who had failed a medical. The striker had spent the first five years of his senior career with his hometown club Cardiff. He arrived at Anfield for a club record fee of £110,000 and gained immense popularity with the supporters after he had headed the equaliser in a Merseyside derby in only his second game. He only scored seven times in 33 games during his debut season but his aerial dominance would become an important feature for Liverpool going forward. When Kevin Keegan arrived at Anfield it appeared to have sparked Toshack into life as the two formed quite the partnership up top. The club had been trophy-less for six years but came close in the FA Cup and the league during the 1971/72 season. Fortune would change drastically in the upcoming years, starting with the 1973 League Championship. Despite being an excellent servant to the club, the Welshman was unlucky with injuries during his time with Liverpool. This was best demonstrated by the fact he only ever played in 30 or more games once during his time in Merseyside. Nevertheless, Toshack notched up 247 appearances and scored 96 goals.

He left for Swansea in 1978 and became player-manager for the club for five years. Since officially retiring as a player in 1984, he has been involved with clubs from England, Wales – including national manager – Spain, France, Morocco and his latest post was with Iranian team, Tractor, in 2018. He also had a two-year period managing the Macedonian national team.

## TOURE, Kolo

*Centre-back*
**Born:** *1981 Bouake, Ivory Coast*
**Playing career:** *ASEC Mimosas, Arsenal, Manchester City, Liverpool, Celtic (1999-2017)*

There aren't many players who can say they represented Arsenal, Manchester City and Liverpool – but Kolo Toure certainly can. When Jamie Carragher had retired during the summer, the club were in desperate need of someone to replace him which paved the way for Toure. In fact, Liverpool were in a little bit of a defensive crisis at the time with both Daniel Agger and Martin Skrtel injured. Toure understood that he was never going to be first choice and finally did leave to join Celtic for a season, hanging up his boots in 2016. He represented Ivory Coast on 120 occasions, the second most capped player in the country's history. In 2017 he was appointed as a new member of the Ivorian Football Federation coaching staff and he joined Celtic as a technical assistant under Brendan Rodgers. When Rodgers left for Leicester in 2019, Toure followed him.

John Toshack

**T**

## TRAORE, Djimi
*Defender*
**Born:** *1980 Saint-Ouen, Seine-Saint-Denis, France*
**Playing career:** *Laval, Liverpool, Lens, Charlton Athletic, Portsmouth, Rennes, Birmingham City, Monaco, Marseille, Seattle Sounders FC (1996-2014)*

When Liverpool captured the signature of Djimi Traore, there were plenty of clubs after the young man. Paris Saint Germain, AC Milan, Parma and Lazio were interested, but he failed to make an immediate impact and was loaned out to French side Lens. Whilst Rafael Benitez was at the helm, Traore seemed like a different player and played frequently under the Spaniard. He played against AC Milan in Istanbul and his goal line clearance to deny Andriy Shevchenko proved to be decisive. The following season, first team opportunities began to dry up and he was sold to Charlton Athletic for £2 million in August 2006. He represented Liverpool on 141 occasions, scoring once. He featured for Mali on the international stage and was capped six times. He finished his playing career with Seattle Sounders and is now employed by the club as assistant manager, making his way up from their reserve side.

## TWENTYMAN, Geoff
*Central defender*
**Born:** *1930 Carlisle, Cumberland* **Died:** 2002
**Playing career:** *Carlisle United, Liverpool, Ballymena United, Carlisle United (1947-1964)*

Geoff Twentyman was an experienced defender prior to joining Liverpool, having spent six years with Carlisle and featuring in 149 league games. When he made his debut for his local team he was, at the time, the youngest ever player to play for the club at 17 years and four months. Bill Shankly actually managed the youngster at Carlisle and he developed the player into a central-defender. When he reached the National Service age he had no choice but to attend. However, Shankly got in contact with the War Office, pleading with them to allow Twentyman to play for Carlisle as he believed the club could win the Third Division with their starlet. Thus, he was given permission and featured in 32 matches that season but United narrowly missed out after finishing third. Although the defender would only feature occasionally for his team during his service, he did keep fit by representing an army team. Unfortunately for the club, after a fire in one of their stands, they were forced to sell their prized asset to Liverpool to recuperate the funds to remedy the issue. Shankly actually wrote Twentyman a letter informing him that he was at a fantastic club and he wished him well with Liverpool – if only they both knew the future! Unfortunately for the former United player, his time with the club coincided with a rugged time in their history. He left Anfield without any silverware but he did make 184 appearances and scored 19 goals. He left to become player-manager at Ballymena in 1959 – the year Shankly joined – and the manager pleaded with him to stay with Liverpool but his mind was made up and he departed the club. He returned to finish his career with Carlisle before moving into management. He managed both Morecambe and Hartlepool for short spells before being appointed as a scout at Liverpool and Rangers. He died in Southport on 16 February 2004, aged 74.

## UNDERWOOD, David

*Goalkeeper*
**Born:** *1928 London*
**Died:** 1989
**Playing career:** *QPR, Watford, Liverpool, Watford, Fulham, Dunstable Town, Hastings United, Barnet (1949-1968)*

David Underwood joined Liverpool after transferring from Watford in December 1953 but he was one of three 'keepers who were all vying for that number one spot. Following his arrival, he slotted straight into the team but he had a nightmare of a debut. Eddie Spicer was shielding the ball for Underwood to collect but instead of picking the ball up he opted to kick it, shattering Spicer's leg and finishing the defender's career off! He shared duties with the other three goalkeepers – Charlie Ashcroft and Russell Crossley – during his time at Anfield and only made 50 appearances for the club before returning to Watford. Throughout his career he had three different spells with the Hornets and finished his playing career with Barnet in 1968. He did, however, have his first taste of management when he was appointed player-manager of Hastings United in 1966. When he hung up his boots he managed Wealdstone and became the chairman of Barnet, where he helped England superstar, Jimmy Greaves, overcome his addiction to alcohol. He also ran a haulage business before his death on 25 January 1989, aged 60.

## UREN, Harold

*midfielder*
**Born:** *1885 Barton Regis, Bristol* **Died:** 1955
**Playing career:** *Liverpool, Wrexham (loan) Everton, Wrexham (1903-1913)*

Harold Uren played his first game for Liverpool's reserves in April 1906, the same month he signed for the club as an amateur. He finished the season with Wrexham and gained valuable experience before he returned to Anfield. He was forced to wait almost three years before he enjoyed an extensive run in the side. His best campaign was during his final year of his time at Anfield where he played in 24 of the 38 league matches. He crossed Stanley Park in 1912 with Billy Lacey and Tom Gracie coming the other way. He was equally as unimpactful for the Blues, playing in only 24 games in a 15-month stay.

He became a provision merchant in 1946 and he was so successful in this profession that he was the President of the Liverpool Provision Trade Association. Both of his sons were capped by England in rugby union.

## ven den BERG, Harman

*Midfielder*
**Born:** *1918 Cape Town*
**Died:** 2006
**Playing career:** *Peninsular, Liverpool (1935-1939)*

Harman Van den Berg had shown great sporting promise from a young age. Growing up he was an avid sports player and excelled in cricket, football and rugby. In fact, prior to joining Liverpool he was capped for Western Province - the South African rugby union team. As was the norm with many South African players – and Liverpool had a few in their history – he stepped off the Union Castle liner from Cape Town on 18 October 1937 and then Liverpool manager, George Kay, was awaiting his arrival. He signed his professional contract and played on the left wing whilst at Liverpool, making his debut against Everton on 16 February 1938 – Liverpool won the tie 3-1. The South African would only feature in 18 more games for the 'Pool, scoring three times. World War II prevented his time at Anfield from elongating but he did remain with the club for short while during wartime. He died on 6 August 2006, aged 88.

Barry Venison

## VENISON, Barry

*Defender*

**Born:** *1964 Consett, County Durham*
**Playing career:** *Sunderland, Liverpool, Newcastle United, Galatasaray, Southampton (1981-1997)*

When Barry Venison was 20 years old, he led out his Sunderland side as captain in the 1985 League Cup final - the youngest captain in a Wembley finale. Unfortunately, The Black Cats lost the match and they were also relegated the same season. He spent one season with Sunderland in the Second Division before he wrote a letter to a host of top clubs asking them if they'd be interested in his services! Liverpool replied and he was signed for £200,000 in 1986. He slotted straight into the starting XI as left-back before moving to right-back after Jim Beglin broke his leg. Sadly, injuries impeded his true potential, but he did win two League Championships and one FA Cup before moving to Newcastle. Venison represented Liverpool on 158 occasions, scoring three times. He also won two caps for his country and made his full international debut at the age of 30. After retiring he became a pundit firstly with Sky Sports and then with ITV. He also launched a non-profit online sports memorabilia auction site. He made an appearance as himself in the 2001 comedy film, *Mike Bassett: England Manager*. Venison moved to America in 2003 and he worked in property development for a short time before moving back into football. He became the Technical Director of Orange County Blues before moving into management with the club to see out the 2016 season.

## VIGNAL, Gregory

*Defender*

**Born:** *1981 Montpellier, France*
**Playing career:** *Castelnau Le Cres FC, Montpellier, Liverpool, Bastia, Rennes , Espanyol, Rangers, Portsmouth, Lens, Kaiserslautern , Southampton, Birmingham City, Atromitos, Dundee United, AS Beziers (1997-Still Playing)*

Gregory Vignal joined Liverpool in September 2000 but never really got a look in until the 2001/02 season. Just as he began to show promise in a red shirt, he fractured his foot and that kept him out for the remainder of the season. He never recovered from the injury and after several loan periods in different countries, he moved to the south coast of England to join Portsmouth.

Despite playing for numerous clubs, he failed to make more than 30 league appearances for any of them and retired when his contract with French club AS Béziers expired in 2013. He moved into coaching and had a period with Rangers' men's teams before being promoted as the head coach of the club's senior women's team in July 2019.

## VORONIN, Andriy

*Striker/Attacking midfielder*

**Born:** *1979 Odessa, Ukraine*
**Playing career:** *FC Koln, Bayer Leverkusen, Liverpool, Hertha BSC (loan), Dynamo Moscow, Fortuna Dusseldorf (loan) (1995-2013)*

Andriy Voronin arrived at Liverpool on a free transfer in 2007 and played occasionally for the Reds. He scored his first goal for the club during a Champions League qualifier against Toulouse. It was clear that Rafael Benitez was no longer considering the Ukrainian going forward and he was loaned to Hertha Berlin, where he impressed. However, they could not afford to bring him on a permanent basis and he signed for Dynamo Moscow. He was capped 75 times by his country. Whilst he was at Liverpool he criticised the city and the 'high rate of crime' that he believed was problematic. He also stated that he could not understand what Liverpool-born players such as Steven Gerrard or Jamie Carragher had to say.

## WADDLE, Alan

*Striker*

**Born:** *1954 Wallsend*
**Playing career:** *Halifax Town, Liverpool, Leicester City, Swansea City, Newport County, Mansfield Town, Peterborough United. (1971-1993)*

Alan Waddle was John Toshack's deputy at Liverpool and spent a large majority of his four years with the club watching the team play just like the fans. He managed to find the net on only one occasion but what a goal to score. Waddle got the winner in the Merseyside derby at Goodison on 8 December 1973. He would have been excused for expecting big things following the goal but quite simply, Liverpool's squad was just too strong at the time and the Englishman was rather unfortunate to be playing in the same team as John Toshack and Kevin Keegan.

Throughout his 22-year career in football he played for 21 clubs! He moved to Australia after his career ended so he could be closer to his daughter and was appointed the technical advisor of amateur Australian side Demon Knights before taking over as the club's head coach during the 2012 season.

## WADSWORTH, Walter
*Defender*
**Born:** *1890 Bootle, Merseyside*  **Died:** 1951
**Playing career:** *Bristol City, Liverpool, Flint Town, New Brighton, Oswerty Town (1926-1931)*
Walter Wadsworth was the first legend of the club who played in defence. He was strong and built like a brick, striking fear into any opposition attacker. He was a local boy who signed for Liverpool in April 1912. Despite his strong build and lack of supposed agility, he was a fantastic footballer who possessed skill and the footballing brain to operate at the highest level. Liverpool had a mean defence during the early 1920s, which helped the club not only win the League Championship but to retain it the following season. When the 'Pool were visiting Brammall Lane, a certain Untied fan had a bit too much to say and Wadsworth turned around and punched the spectator! He spent 14 years at Anfield – although he did have to wait three years for his debut – and played 242 times for the club, scoring eight goals. He left in 1926 for Bristol City and he was appointed club captain, remaining in the west country for two years. When he finished his career in 1931 he went into the haulage business and returned to Bristol to settle. He died one day before his birthday on 6 October 1951, aged 60.

## WALKER, John
*Inside-forward*
**Born:** *1873 Shotts, Scotland* **Died:** 1940
**Playing career:** *Armadale, Hearts, Liverpool, Rangers, Morton (1893-1906)*
John Walker joined Liverpool after signing from Hearts at the climax of the 1897/98 season. He was a fantastic player and helped the club win the Scottish League twice and the Scottish Cup once. He also made his international debut for Scotland prior to joining the 'Pool. He was an ever-present member of the team during his debut season with the club and only missed two matches in all competitions.

In true Scottish fashion, Walker was a little tipsy and got himself in trouble with the police when he was at Liverpool. Himself and a few teammates were being a little rowdy in the street when a policeman arrived to settle things down. Unwisely, the players provoked the copper who then arrested one of them! Despite his off-field antics, he was a fantastic goal scorer for the club and finished with 30 goals from 120 games – not a bad return from someone in a supporting role. When he retired he moved to Canada and became an engineer with Manitoba Telephones. He also enlisted for the Canadian Military Engineers. He died in 1937 after an accident while cutting wood.

## WALKER, William
*Inside-forward*
**Born:** *1871 Uphall, Scotland*  **Died:** 1907
**Playing career:** *Broxburn, Leith Athletic, Liverpool*
William Walker's stay at Anfield was brief but transfer fees were introduced to the game when he requested to leave. A sum of £100 was put on his head but due to an admin error by Liverpool, he was allowed to leave for free! He was tragically killed following an incident in a game. A boot to the stomach caused distress but he continued to play. After the game he went to the hospital and was initially discharged but he returned to the hospital and passed away shortly afterwards, on 23 January 1907.

## WALL, Peter
*Full-back*
**Born:** *1944 Shrewsbury*
**Playing career:** *Shrewsbury Town, Wrexham, Liverpool, Crystal Palace, Leyton Orient (loan), St. Louis Stars, California Surf (1963-1980)*
Peter Wall signed for Liverpool in October 1966 when he was only 21. He had built up a good reputation and he was widely respected as a fantastic full-back. Bill Shankly departed with £35,000 to secure the Englishman but he failed to really settle at the club. In all honesty, Liverpool had a fairly established side at the time and Shankly needed his reinforcements to force their way in – something that Wall could not do. After only 42 games for the 'Pool he was on his way to Crystal Palace where he spent seven years and played in over 200 games for the Eagles.

Paul Walsh

Wall finished his career in America with California Surf and during the final year of his contract as a player, he took over as player-manager. When he retired from playing he managed the side for another year before moving to Los Angeles Lazers to manage for five years.

## WALSH, Jimmy

*Striker*
**Born:** *1901 Stockport*
**Died:** 1971
**Playing career:** *Stockport County, Liverpool, Hull City, Crewe Alexandra, Colwyn Bay (1919-1933)*
Jimmy Walsh signed for Liverpool from Stockport in May 1922 and spent his debut season with the club stuck in the reserves. However, after Dick Johnson had injured his knee, he was given an opportunity to play for the first team. He managed to find the net twice on his debut in the league as Liverpool comfortably beat Birmingham 6-2 on 29 August 1923. He would continue to be an ever-present figure in the side that season and even finished the campaign as the club's top-scorer with 19 from 42 matches. After this season his luck would spiral downwards in a Liverpool shirt and he would only feature 35 more times throughout the next four years. He left for Hull City in 1928 before finishing his career in Wales with Colwyn Bay. He died on 19 June 1971, aged 70.

## WALSH, Paul

*Forward*
**Born:** *1962 Plumstead*
**Playing career:** *Charlton Athletic, Luton Town, Liverpool, Tottenham Hotspur, QPR, Portsmouth, Manchester City, Portsmouth. (1979-1996)*
Paul Walsh made his name with Charlton before impressing again at Luton Town. Liverpool signed the forward for £700,000 in 1984 and he would remain with the club for three years, winning the 1985/86 League Championship. A bidding war between Manchester United and Liverpool took place but the Englishman opted for the latter. Ian Rush was out of the side when Walsh joined the club so he slotted straight into the first team, making ten appearances consecutively. He sustained an injury – in addition to Rush becoming match fit – which kept him on the fringes of the team for the remainder of the season.

His second season with the club was far more entertaining, scoring 18 goals in only 25 matches before rupturing his ligaments. A cruel injury to suffer, just as he was starting to hit the heights at Anfield. The arrival of John Aldridge and Peter Beardsley spelt the end for Walsh's time with Liverpool and he moved to Tottenham. He finished his career with Portsmouth in 1996 and he played in 521 league matches, scoring 128 throughout his entire footballing journey. He was capped five times by England, netting once. When he retired he became a football agent for a short period of time and represented Lee Bradbury during his move to Manchester City. He also invested in property but fell victim to Australian fraudster Peter Foster, where he lost a significant amount of money. He started his punditry career in 2001 with Sky Sports and since that he has appeared regularly on Soccer Saturday and Football First. He continues to work as an after dinner speaker.

## WALTERS, Mark

*Midfielder/Winger*
**Born:** *1964 Birmingham*
**Playing career:** *Aston Villa, Rangers, Liverpool, Stoke City, Wolverhampton Wanderers, Southampton, Swindon Town, Bristol Rovers (1981-2002)*
Mark Walters was a Birmingham-born winger and nearly scored 50 goals in just under 250 games for Aston Villa, where he had started as an apprentice. He moved on to Rangers, where he netted 51 times in 143 matches – impressive stats for someone playing on the wing. He then joined Liverpool and played in a further century of games, although a large majority of these were from the bench. After a couple of loan periods away from Anfield, he moved to Southampton in January 1996. By now, he was past his best and he failed to improve a struggling side which influenced a move to Swindon at the end of the season having made just nine appearances in all competitions for the Saints. Walters retired after competing in another 200 games with Swindon and Bristol Rovers. After retiring he went on to coach in Coventry and then returned to Villa as a trainer in the club's academy. He has since picked up teaching qualifications and became Head of Languages at the academy. He is still playing Masters football for Rangers.

## WARK, John
*Midfielder*
**Born:** *1957 Glasgow, Scotland*
**Playing career:** *Ipswich Town, Liverpool, Ipswich Town, Middlesbrough, Ipswich Town (1974-1996)*

John Wark rose to fame in Ipswich's academies team, where he won the Youth Cup and managed to force his way into their first team. He was voted the PFA Player of the Year during the 1980/81 season thanks to his 14 Goals in Town's victorious UEFA Cup campaign. He finished the season with 36 goals but narrowly missed out on the League Championship as Aston Villa had pipped his team to the title. Wark spent nine years with Ipswich before he moved to Liverpool. He was brought to Anfield as an ideal replacement to the recently departed Graeme Souness in March 1984, for a fee of £475,000. Upon his arrival, he stayed in a hotel with two new additions to the club and spent the first night hitting the nightclubs in Liverpool! When the football started, however, he managed to bring his scoring boots to Anfield with him as he netted on his debut against Watford and made nine appearances as Liverpool had won yet another league title. There were concerns that it was a mistake to buy the Scotsman but he was determined to prove them wrong - and that's exactly what he did. He was the club's top-scorer with 27 in his first full season, which included three hat-tricks.

John Wark

Frustratingly, injuries impeded his next two seasons after he had torn his Achilles before breaking his ankle upon his return to the first team – missing out again on more medals as Liverpool won the double in the 1985/86 campaign. When Jan Molby arrived at the club, Wark was pushed to the side and he eventually returned to Ipswich in January 1988. Town had been relegated by this point but he did not mind dropping down a division. He transferred to Middlesbrough after a dispute about his contract but he returned a year later to finish his career with a third spell for Ipswich before retiring in 1997. Wark played 108 times for Liverpool and scored 42 goals. He returned to Portman Road as a community officer after his playing career.

## WARNER, Tony
*Goalkeeper*
**Born:** *1974 Liverpool*
**Playing career:** *Liverpool, Swindon Town (loan), Celtic (loan), Aberdeen (loan), Millwall, Cardiff City, Fulham (loan), Fulham, Leeds United (loan), Norwich City (loan), Barnsley (loan), Hull City, Leicester City (loan), Charlton Athletic, Scunthorpe United, Tranmere Rovers, Liverpool, Wellington Phoenix, Floriana, Blackpool (1994-2015)*

Injuries are a common feature of football. They happen in nearly every game, which is why it's important to keep a strong squad. When Tony Warner arrived at Liverpool he became the reserve goalkeeper after an injury to Michael Steensgard. He was named on the bench 120 times, waiting for his first opportunity to shine and demonstrate what he could do between the Liverpool sticks. Sadly, his debut never came as David James never picked up an injury whilst Warner was contracted with the club! He was released in 1999 and signed for Millwall, where he was more successful and featured 225 times for the Lions. He eventually returned to the topflight with Fulham but after only seven league appearances in two years, he was on the move again. This would become a common theme in Warner's career as he played for 13 clubs – excluding loan periods to seven other teams. He failed to settle at any club other than Millwall and finished his career with Accrington Stanley. In 2016 he became the goalkeeping coach at Bolton and a pundit for Wirral Radio.

Stephen Warnock

2006/07 campaign and he was shipped to Blackburn midway through the season. He spent two years with the club before moving to Aston Villa for a further four years. He eventually dropped down the divisions and finished his career while contracted to Burton Albion in 2018. He has since moved into punditry and has worked for BBC, BT Sport, DAZN and Quest TV.

## WATSON, Alex

*Central defender*
**Born:** *1968 Liverpool*
**Playing career:** *Liverpool, Derby County (loan), A.F.C. Bournemouth, Gillingham (loan), Torquay United, Exeter City, Taunton Town, Clevedon Town, Liverpool (1985-2005)*

Alex Watson could regard his time with Liverpool as unlucky. He had signed professionally with the club in 1985 but the team was full of superstars who were enjoying great success both domestically and in Europe. He started in the 1988 Charity Shield but that was his highlight for the club. He left Anfield as he knew the task was too mighty for him to break into the first team on a regular occasion. He did, however, carve out a successful football career away with the 'Pool – featuring heavily for both Bournemouth and Torquay. He is the younger brother of Everton player, Dave Watson. In total, he played in over 500 matches and he is now a qualified FA coach.

## WATSON, Dave

*Centre-back*
**Born:** *1961 Liverpool*
**Playing career:** *Liverpool, Norwich City, Everton (1978-2001)*

Dave Watson joined Liverpool's academy in 1978. He spent two years there before being released. What was Liverpool's loss was certainly Everton's gain as he became a club legend with the blue side of Merseyside. Prior to joining the Blues, he had six very good years with Norwich. He won the First Division and the FA Cup with Everton and although Liverpool's team were strong during this period, the club surely would have regretted allowing such as a good player to leave. He played in 528 matches for Everton, ranking third for the most appearances for the club in their history. He had his first taste of management five years prior to his retirement.

## WARNOCK, Stephen

*Full-back*
**Born:** *1981 Ormskirk*
**Playing career:** *Liverpool, Bradford City (loan), Coventry City (loan), Blackburn Rovers, Aston Villa, Bolton Wanderers (loan), Leeds United, Derby County, Wigan Athletic (loan), Wigan Athletic, Burton Albion, Bradford City (loan) (1994-2018)*

Stephen Warnock had to go through hell and back to make his Liverpool debut. He had broken his leg three times during his youth but managed to overcome the setbacks to finally make his debut for the the first team! Prior to making his first appearance for the club, he had impressed on loan with Coventry and was even voted Fans' Player of the Season. He played on 30 occasions during Rafael Benitez's first season at the helm of the club but he had sadly missed out on medals in both the League Cup and Champions League as there were not enough to go around – he played in every round bar the final in the former but Liverpool lost the finale to Chelsea. He dropped down the pecking-order during the

He was appointed manager of the Toffees after Joe Royle had resigned. He reverted back to playing duties but he did move into full-time management with Tranmere for a sole season following his retirement as a player.

## WELFARE, Harry
*Striker*
**Born:** *1888 Liverpool* **Died:** 1966
**Playing career:** *Northern Nomads, Liverpool, Tranmere Rovers, Fluminense (1906-1924)*

Harry Welfare made his debut for Liverpool against Sheffield Wednesday on 15 February 1913. He was brought into the side as Bill Lacey was injured, where he impressed significantly. He scored his sole goal for the club two weeks later when Derby visited Anfield before playing in the next match against Tottenham. When Lacey returned from injury, himself and Arthur Goddard built a formidable partnership on the wing for the 'Pool, keeping Welfare out of the team. He moved to Rio de Janeiro in 1913 to work as a geography and mathematics teacher. The school's PE teacher also ran Fluminense Football Club and utilised Welfare in the team frequently. Professional leagues were not established in the country until 20 years later, so he played on an amateur basis. He later became Vasco de Gama's coach in 1927 and spent ten years with the club. He led the team to victory in the first professional season and remained in Brazil for the rest of his life. He died in Angra dos Reis, Brazil, on 1 September 1966.

## WELSH, John
*Midfielder*
**Born:** *1984 Wavertree*
**Playing career:** *Liverpool, Hull City (loan), Hull City, Chester-City (loan), Carlisle United (loan), Bury (loan), Tranmere Rovers, Preston North End (2001-2012)*

John Welsh joined Liverpool at ten years old and captained both the academy team and England's youth team. He was a dominating central-midfielder who had all-round fantastic qualities. Unfortunately for the local lad, he only made ten appearances for Liverpool's first team before it became apparent that he would have to look elsewhere for regular football. He did, however, feature briefly during the 2005 Champions League last-16 tie, coming on as a last minute substitution. After a successful loan period with Hull, he moved on a permanent basis. He spent the majority of his career in the lower leagues of English football but he did have six years with Preston from 2012-2018. He is currently contracted with Atherton Collieries.

## WEST, Alf
*Full-back*
**Born:** *1881 Radford, Nottingham* **Died:** 1944
**Playing career:** *Liverpool, Reading, Notts County, Mansfield Town, Shirebrook (1900-1920)*

Alf West was a fantastic full-back who may have been one of the best in England during the earlier years of his career. He signed for Liverpool in 1903, having made his name with Barnsley for two years prior. He was so impressive for the Tykes that the club had granted him a testimonial match after only a short period of service! He was not short of contract offers either, with Small Heath – now Birmingham – having a bid rejected. He slotted nicely into Liverpool's side and played in the remaining games of the campaign. Despite his fine performances in red, he could not prevent the club from being relegated after such a poor start to the season before he arrived. A peculiar event took place which kept West side-lined until Christmas 1904. He had been training for the 120 yards handicap when the trainer had accidently shot the full-back in the shoulder with the starting pistol! Nevertheless, he returned to make 16 appearances as Liverpool regained their First Division status. He suffered another minor injury the following season but missed a large majority of the year through a severe family tragedy, restricting him to just four appearances. He returned to the side and played frequently the following campaign but sporadically during his final two years. He moved to Reading in 1909 before returning to Liverpool a year later. He only added four more appearances before he left the club indefinitely in 1911, moving to Notts County where he only missed two matches in two seasons with the club before the advent of World War I. During the conflict, he was shot in the leg and was forced to return home for a year to rehabilitate. He returned to France and survived the remainder of the war. He died on 27 June 1944, aged 62.

## WEST, David
*Striker*
**Born:** *1964 Dorchester*
**Playing career:** *Dorchester Town, Liverpool, Torquay United, Cheltenham Town (1983-1986)*

Bob Paisley signed the striker for £15,000 but he never featured for the club. The closest he came was being named on the bench twice for two European encounters. He did, however, have a career with Torquay United and several other lower-league teams. In December 1986, he was involved in a car crash with a milk tanker and suffered a number of injuries. He retired at 27 to focus on becoming an estate agent with a Dorset-based chain.

## WESTERVELD, Sander
*Goalkeeper*
**Born:** *1974 Enschede, Netherlands*
**Playing career:** *De Tubanters, Twente, Vitesse, Liverpool, Real Sociedad, Mallorca, Portsmouth, Everton, Almeria, Sparta Rotterdam , Monza, Ajax Cape Town (1980-2013)*

When the Dutch international signed for Liverpool, he became the most expensive goalkeeper in English history after a £4 million fee. Within the space of his two-year stay at Anfield he had won three competitions – FA Cup, League Cup and the UEFA Cup, which all came in the same year! He gained a brilliant reputation whilst playing for FC Twente for his approachability, something he took with Liverpool with him as he was often seen interacting with the crowd. When Gerard Houllier informed him that he was third-choice goalkeeper he immediately set out to join another club and found just that when he moved to Spain to join Real Sociedad. He briefly returned to England with Portsmouth and then Everton but failed to impress. He finished his career with Ajax Cape Town and won six caps in total for the Netherlands. When his contract expired in South Africa he became a goalkeeping coach with the club. Whilst Westerveld was at Liverpool, he claimed that he hated scouse humour. People would constantly joke with him about dropping things and he stated that he despised these comments, which resulted in a lack of confidence. He now works as a Licensed Intermediary at World Soccer Consult.

## WHEELER, Johnny
*Wing-half*
**Born:** *1928 Crosby, Lancashire*
**Playing career:** *Tranmere Rovers, Bolton Wanderers, Liverpool, New Brighton (1946-1963)*

Johnny Wheeler was a fantastic midfield player who refused to shy away from a hard-hitting tackle. He had great stamina and always posed a threat when Liverpool were moving the ball forward. He was 28 years old when he arrived at Anfield, having played in 101 league games for neighbours, Tranmere. He was also a member of the Bolton team that had lost the FA Cup final 4-3 after leading 3-1. He was appointed club captain during the 1958/59 season as Liverpool set off on their quest to regain First Division status. Although primarily a wing-half, he demonstrated his versatility by frequently playing as an inside-forward for the club. It was in this position that he scored one of the fastest hat-tricks ever recorded – his goals coming after 81, 82, and 85 minutes! Wheeler was completely left out of the team from the start of the 1961/62 season and only made one more appearance for the club from then. He became assistant-trainer at Bury for six years after he had retired from playing. He died on 16 November 2019, aged 91. Prior to his death, he was the oldest person alive to have captained Liverpool.

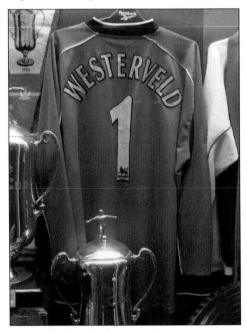

Ronnie Whelan

## WHELAN, Ronnie

*Midfielder*

**Born:** *1961 Dublin, Ireland*

**Playing career:** *Liverpool, Southend (1979-1996)*

It was little surprise that Ronnie Wheelan had managed to forge a successful career in professional sport. His father had represented Ireland and his brother played in the League of Ireland. He started his journey with Home Farm and several English clubs were interested in capturing his signature. He had trained with Manchester United for a little while but he opted to go to Anfield for a fee of only £35,000 – an absolute bargain. Wheelan made his debut on 3 April 1981, only two days after Liverpool had won the League Cup. He scored during the game against Stoke and demonstrated what the next decade would look like with the Irishman anchoring the midfield. Despite his impressive start, he did not feature again for Liverpool that season but when Ray Kennedy was transferred to Swansea the following January, Wheelan made the position his own. He made a fantastic start to his career and many tipped him to become the greatest player in the world. Although he may not have hit that height, he was certainly a brilliant player whenever he put the Liverpool jersey on. He played 493 times for the 'Pool and scored 73 goals. The midfielder won six League Championships, two FA Cups, three League Cups and the 1984 European Cup. He left the club in 1994 and joined Southend for two seasons before he called time on his playing career in 1996. During his final year with United he was appointed player-manager and would eventually move into full-time management in Greece and Cyprus. The Irishman now works as an after-dinner guest and previously as a pundit for RTÉ.

## WHITBREAD, Zak

*Centre-back*

**Born:** *1984 Houston, Texas, United States*

**Playing career:** *Liverpool, Millwall (loan), Millwall, Norwich City, Leicester City, Derby County (loan), Derby County, Shrewsbury Town (1992-2015)*

Zak Whitbread spent 11 years in Liverpool's academy and he even captained the U-19s. His fine performances saw him selected for the reserves and he made his debut on 17 September 2001. After three years with the second-string side, he was finally giving an opportunity to prove himself in the first team when he was selected to go to the 2004 pre-season tour to north America. Unfortunately, the formidable partnership of Sami Hyppia and Jamie Carragher proved too much of an obstacle and after 14 years associated with Liverpool, he left without making a single competitive appearance for the club. He played for several English teams but failed to permanently settle at any of them. He finished his career in 2016 with Shrewsbury Town. In 2018, he set up a player management agency called Perform Sports Management.

## WHITE, Bill

*Inside-left*

**Born:** *1877 Edinburgh*

**Died:** 1960

**Playing career:** *Heart of Midlothian, Woolwich Arsenal, New Brompton, Queen's Park Rangers, Liverpool. Dundee, Middlesborough, Motherwell, Broxburn (1894-1904)*

Bill White scored two minutes into his debut for Liverpool. To make the event even sweeter, it was against Everton in the first home game of the season on 14 September 1901. Despite this, he would only feature in five more games for the club as Liverpool finished in eleventh place the year after they had won their inaugural League Championship. He returned to the country of his birth to join Dundee before crossing the border one final time to turn out for Middleborough. When he retired from football, he became a miner. He died in 1960.

### "DID YOU KNOW?"

*"Liverpool v West Ham (1969) was the first match to be shown in colour on Match of the Day."*

## WHITE, Dick
*Centre-half*
**Born:** *1931 Scunthorpe* **Died:** 2002
**Playing career:** *Scunthorpe United, Liverpool, Doncaster Rovers, Kettering Town (1950-1966)*

Dick White started his career representing his boyhood club, Scunthorpe. He was granted a move to Anfield in November 1955 after playing in 133 league games for United. Don Welsh had travelled to meet up with then Iron manager, Bill Corkhill to offer £8,000 for the player on the spot – they had to take him away from a snooker match that he was currently involved in! It was a club record and hard to decline, resulting with White on his way to Liverpool. He was forced to wait 18 months before he was a regular in the team but he eventually settled and was even appointed captain. The arrival of Ron Yeats stripped the captaincy away from him, but he did finish his time at Anfield as the club won the Second Division title. He played 217 times for the 'Pool, scoring just once. He joined Doncaster Rovers before retiring in 1966 with Kettering Town. White became a garage proprietor in Nottingham after his retirement and he was a keen golfer, serving as both captain and president of Scunthorpe Golf Club. He died on 15 June 2002, aged 71.

## WHITEHURST, Albert
*Centre-forward*
**Born:** *1898 Fenton* **Died:** 1976
**Playing career:** *Bradford City, Liverpool, Rochdale, Stoke, Tranmere Rovers (1920-1933)*

Albert Whitehurst played briefly for Liverpool and scored a goal in his final game to salvage a point against Leeds. He would only feature in eight games for the club before he moved to Bradford City. Prior to joining Liverpool, he had been very impressive for Rochdale, scoring 116 goals in only 168 games. Whilst with City, he had scored seven of a possible eight when his side trounced Tranmere in 1929. Ironically, he would later move to Tranmere and play centre-half for them! He died in 1976.

### "DID YOU KNOW?"

*"The first Liverpool Football Club played rugby and have no connection to the current set-up. "*

## WHITHAM, Jack
*Forward*
**Born:** *1946 Burnley*
**Playing career:** *Sheffield Wednesday, Liverpool, Cardiff City, Reading (1964-1976)*

Jack Whitham had previously spent six years with Sheffield Wednesday. When they were relegated during the climax of the 1969/70 season he moved to Liverpool. He was a good performer for the Reds but injuries once again took over his time with the club. He scored 7 goals in the 18 games that he played in. Bill Shankly was so frustrated with the striker that he once told him to train next to the pigsty as he did not want the rest of the team to be contaminated by his habit of picking up injuries! When he retired from football he ran a public house for ten years in Sheffield before becoming the manager of the South Yorkshire Police Social Club.

## WHITWORTH, George
*defender*
**Born:** *1927 Eckington, Derbyshire*
**Died:** 2006 **Playing career:** *Liverpool (1950-1952)*

George Whitworth had to wait two years to make his debut in red. The day finally came when Liverpool visited Craven Cottage on 1 March 1952. He made a good impression and played in nine of the final 11 games of that campaign. He suffered a nasty injury to his knee in a reserve game the following October and he was forced to retire. He returned to Derbyshire to run pubs in Ilkeston, Beeston and Kirby-in-Ashfield. He died on 16 March 2006, aged 78.

## WIGNALL, Steve
*Central defender*
**Born:** *1954 Liverpool*
**Playing career:** *Liverpool, Doncaster Rovers, Colchester United, Brentford, Aldershot (1970-1991)*

Steve Wignall spent two years in the academy before being released in 1972. He refused to let the rejection define his career, however, and he carved a successful footballing life with Doncaster before becoming a prominent figure for Colchester. He finished his career in 1991 with Aldershot. He managed the Shots following his retirement as a player and spent three years with the club. He also had stints managing Colchester, Stevenage, Doncaster and Southend. He released his autobiography *You Can Have Chips* in 2009.

## WILKIE, Tom
*defender*
**Born:** *1876 Edinburgh, Scotland* **Died:** 1932
**Playing career:** *Liverpool, Portsmouth (1893-1904)*
Tom Wilkie made his debut for Liverpool on the opening day of the 1895/96 season against Notts County. He helped Liverpool win the Second Division before he was established as the club's first-choice left-back. He played 64 times in total and managed one goal for the club. He later signed for Portsmouth and became a firm fan favourite on the south coast. Wilkie later emigrated to Australia and became a fire station officer in Perth. He died in 1932.

## WILLIAMS, Danny
*midfielder*
**Born:** *1979 Wrexham, Wales*
**Playing career:** *Liverpool, Wrexham, Doncaster Rovers (loan), Kidderminster Harriers, Chester-City (loan), Bristol Rovers (1997-2012)*
Danny Williams was another product of Liverpool's youth academy that the team did not benefit from. In all fairness, he spent the majority of his career in the lower leagues of English football, which would suggest he was lacking the quality to make it at a top club like Liverpool. He was named on the bench once for the Reds in a Premiership game against Derby on 10 May 1998. Throughout his career, he had two elongated spells with Wrexham and Kidderminster. In the summer of 2013 he joined Rhos Aelwyd, who are a non-league team in Wales, but there is no record of him being involved with the game any longer.

## WILSON, Charlie
*Wing-half*
**Born:** *1877 Sutton, Shropshire* **Died:** unknown
**Playing career:** *Stockport Co, Liverpool (1895-1905)*
Charlie Wilson joined from Stockport County in 1897 but failed to make an impression with Liverpool during his first two years with the club but did become a regular face in the side. He was in fine form for the 'Pool when he had a strange dream. He dreamt that he would break his leg in the next day's game against Middlesbrough – and that's exactly what happened! He returned to the team later but he never truly recovered from the awful injury. He retired as a player in 1905 but he remained with the club working as a scout up until 1939.

## WORGAN, Arthur
*Striker*
**Born:** *1871 Aigburth Vale, Liverpool* **Died:** 1920
**Playing career:** *Liverpool (1893-1895)*
Arthur Worgan was a member of Liverpool's first-ever squad. As he was an amateur player, he was entitled to play for whoever he wished for – as long as he remained an amateur. He did eventually play in two games for Liverpool's first team, bagging two goals in the process. He netted a brace on his debut against Burton Swifts on March 3 1894, before featuring in his second and last game for the club against Sheffield United on October 6, 1894. His brother, Albert, played in goal for Liverpool casuals during the turn of the century. When Arthur retired as a player he served as director of the club until his death in 1920.

## WRIGHT, Dave

*Forward*

**Born:** *1905 Kirkcaldy, Fife* **Died:** 1955
**Playing career:** *Cowdenbeath, Sunderland, Liverpool*

Dave Wright had to wait ten months until he was given his debut for Liverpool. He broke into the team during the 1930/31 season but eventually lost his place and transferred to Derby. He left Liverpool after exactly 100 appearances and 35 goals. He finished his career with Bradford Park Avenue in 1936 and died 19 years later.

## WRIGHT, Mark

*Defender*

**Born:** *1963 Dorchester on Thames*
**Playing career:** *Oxford United, Southampton Derby County, Liverpool (1980-1998)*

After only ten appearances for Oxford, Southampton snapped Mark Wright up and he spent five years on the south coast. However, it was Derby who Liverpool needed to do business with to bring the experienced defender to Anfield in 1991. County were in desperate need of the Cash and Wright needed to remain in the topflight if he wanted to continue his international career, which suited Liverpool nicely. He suffered a knee injury on his debut that kept him out for three months. However, he did captain Liverpool to FA Cup victory as they beat Sunderland 2-0 in the final. Wright captained the side again the following campaign and scored his first goal for the club in a 1-1 draw with former club Southampton, but another disappointing season meant Liverpool would not be participating in Europe's most prestigious event. He remained with Liverpool until he was forced to retire at the age of 35 due to an ongoing back problem. He was capped 45 times by England and scored one goal. He moved into management after he retired and has had spells with Southport, Oxford, Peterborough and Chester. His most recent role was a return to Southport but he and his entire coaching team left only four months into the tenure - as they lost five straight games and conceded 19 goals in the process. He and his wife have also become foster care advocates and he regularly organises charity football matches to help with the cause. Currently, he contributes to LFC TV as a pundit and appears as an after dinner speaker.

## WRIGHT, Stephen

*Defender*

**Born:** *1980 Bootle, Liverpool*
**Playing career:** *Liverpool, Crewe Alexandra (loan), Sunderland, Stoke City (loan), Coventry City, Brentford, Hartlepool United, Wrexham (1996-2014)*

Both Everton and the 'Pool wanted Stephen Wright's services and he chose the latter – despite growing up an Everton fan! He would have to wait two more years before finally making his debut. He was loaned to Crewe during the following season but once he returned, he was selected for Liverpool for the first time against Stoke in the League Cup – Liverpool ran out as 8-0 winners. The highlight of his career would have been scoring in front of the Kop against Borussia Dortmund in the Champions League group stage. Sunderland submitted a £3 million offer for Wright and he was on his way, after only featuring in 21 games for the club. He spent six years with Sunderland and played over 100 times for the Black Cats before he then began to drop down the divisions. He retired as a player in 2017 and is now working at the youth academy with Wrexham. His father, John, was a kitman at Liverpool.

Mark Wright

## WYLLIE, Tom
*Striker*
**Born:** *1872 Maybole, South Ayrshire* **Died:** 1943
**Playing career:** *Maybole, Rangers, Everton, Liverpool, Bury, Bristol City (1892-1898)*
Tom Wyllie was a fantastic goal-scorer and he was the first person to score in a Merseyside derby – he previously represented Everton, too. He averaged a goal every other game whilst with Liverpool. When the 'Pool went into the Second Division, Wyllie moved to Bury. He played against Liverpool after Bury were admitted into the second tier and Liverpool had finished bottom of the First Division. He remained with the Shakers for two seasons before joining Bristol City. When he retired he remained in Bristol and became a newsagent in Bedminster, south Bristol. He died on 28 July 1943, aged 73.

## XAVIER, Abel
*Full-back*
**Born:** *1972 Nampula, Mozambique*
**Playing career:** *Benfica, Bari, Real Oviedo, PSV, Everton, Liverpool, Galatasaray (loan), Hannover, Roma, Middlesbrough, LA Galaxy (1990-2008)*
When Abel Xavier was playing he was not too difficult to spot – you just needed to look for the player with the brightest hair! Throughout his career he had played in eight different countries: Portugal, Spain, Germany, Italy, Turkey, America, Holland and England. He was part of the Portugal team that lost in the semi-finals of Euro 2000 when he gave a penalty away by handling the ball in the area. He went absolutely ballistic at the referee which saw him brandished with a six-month ban from international football. Xavier joined Liverpool from Everton, becoming only the second player in recent history to cross Stanley Park. Everton fans would have been absolutely furious with his Liverpool debut, too. He failed to find the net with the Blues but scored only 16 minutes into his debut with the 'Pool! He would only add one more goal to his brief Anfield career before departing for Hannover 96 in 2003. He retired with LA Galaxy in 2008 and moved into coaching, having spells with Olhanense, Farense, Aves and his most recent role, Mozambique. He had spent three years with the latter but was dismissed after a poor African Cup of Nations.

## YEATS, Ron
*Centre-half*
**Born:** *1937 Aberdeen, Scotland*
**Playing career:** *Dundee United, Liverpool, Tranmere Rovers, Stalybridge Celtic (1957-1978)*
Ron Yeats was a fine player for Liverpool and he was their leader during the 1960s. His father was a butcher and he worked alongside him before making it as a professional footballer. He was captain of Dundee United and undertook his national service whilst he was playing for the Scottish team. Bill Shankly had previously shown interest in the defender when he was managing Huddersfield but he proved too costly for the team. However, when he arrived at Anfield – where additional funds were available – he finally got his man. He arrived only two months before Ian St. John and Shankly was now comfortable with the squad that he had built. Liverpool were still in the Second Division at the time but they were immediately promoted the season that the two signings joined. He was handed the captaincy midway through that campaign and wore it with distinction. His finest moment in a Liverpool shirt came when he had the honour of lifting the 1965 FA Cup – the first in the club's history.

Ron Yeats

Liverpool continued their fine form and this was the team that laid the foundations for the next two decades, when the club experienced unprecedented levels of success. In total, the Scotsman played 454 times for Liverpool and scored 16 goals. He won two League Championships, the Second Division title and the aforementioned FA Cup. He left Liverpool in 1971 and joined Tranmere for a couple of seasons before dropping into the lower leagues of English football – with the exception of two seasons in America. He retired in 1978 and went into the haulage business before entering the catering trade. He still lives in Liverpool and worked as the club's chief scout until his retirement in May 2006.

## YOUNG, Alexander

*Inside Right*
**Born:** *1880 Slamannan, Scotland*
**Died:** 1959
**Playing career:** *Slamannan Juniors, St Mirren, Falkirk, Everton, Tottenham Hotspur, Manchester City, South Liverpool, (1898-1912)*
Alexander Young was a fantastic servant to Everton Football Club but he certainly had his demons. He is the fourth all-time highest goal-scorer for the club and his goal helped the club win the 1906 FA Cup.

He remained with the Blues for 10 years before he left for Tottenham. He then moved to Manchester City before he finished his career with South Liverpool. His life took a drastic turn when he was convicted of the manslaughter of his brother in Australia in June 1916. He was given a three-year prison sentence and later returned to Britain. Throughout his life, he was considered to have been mentally unstable but Everton continued to help their former player with financial assistance long after he had played for the club. He died on 17 September 1959, aged 79.

## YOUNGER, Tommy

*Goalkeeper*
**Born:** *1930 Edinburgh, Scotland*
**Died:** 1984
**Playing career:** *Hibernian, Liverpool, Falkirk, Stoke City, Rhyl, Toronto City, Leeds United (1948-1963)*
Having started his career with Hibernian, Tommy Younger achieved enormous success with the club, winning two league titles in the 1950/51 campaign and the following season. Phil Taylor signed the Scotsman for £9,000 in June 1959 and he remained with the club for three years. He went straight into the team upon his arrival, finally bringing an end to Liverpool's few years where they had no designated number one 'keeper. Whilst with the 'Pool, he also captained Scotland in the 1958 World Cup. He lost his place to Bert Slater shortly before the 1959/60 season had begun and moved to Falkirk as player-manager, where he momentarily retired due to a back injury. However, the injury was not as severe as once thought and he returned to England to play for Stoke. When Younger retired indefinitely he was voted president of the Scottish Football Association in May 1983 until his death the following year on 13 January 1984, aged 53.

## ZENDEN, Bolo

*Left-back*
**Born:** *1976 Maastricht, Netherlands*
**Playing career:** *PSV, Barcelona, Chelsea, Middlesbrough, Liverpool, Marseilles, Sunderland*
Bolo Zenden had been voted the best player in Holland during his final season with PSV Eindhoven. He had plenty of admirers across Europe and he chose perhaps the biggest of them all – Barcelona.

The Dutch international played frequently for the Spanish giants during a three-year stay before he was shipped to Chelsea in the summer of 2001. He failed to make a significant impact with the Blues and he was loaned out to Middlesbrough before he made the move permanent. Liverpool then signed the full-back and he spent two years at Anfield. He had been impressive for his former team and was even voted supporters' Player of the Year the season. He failed to match that success whilst wearing a red shirt, however, and had to settle for a role as a squad player. He did win the European Super Cup with the Reds but that was about as good as it got for the Dutch defender. He moved to France to play for Marseille before returning for one last spell in his playing career with Sunderland. He retired in 2011 and had his first coaching role when he was appointed assistant to Rafael Benitez when he was made Chelsea interim manager. He returned to Holland when the Spaniard left the Blues and he began coaching Jong PSV, the club's reserve team. Zenden has since made his way up to the first team and focuses on training the attacking players. He also works as a pundit on Dutch television.

## ZIEGE, Christian
*Left Wing-back*
**Born:** *1972 West Berlin, West Germany*
**Playing career:** *FC Sudstern 08 Berlin, TSV Rudow Berlin, FC Hertha 03 Zehlendorf, Bayern Munich, Milan, Middlesbrough, Liverpool, Tottenham Hotspur, Borussia Monchengladbach (1978-2005)*

Christian Ziege won the Bundesliga twice with Bayern Munich before he arrived at Anfield. He had played for AC Milan too for a couple of seasons. He signed from Middlesbrough for £5.5 million in August 2000 but he failed to live up to expectation. Liverpool had a successful season whilst the German was there, winning the treble. Perhaps what best demonstrates Ziege's lack of impact was the fact that he was left out of the squad for four of the final five games of the season. He only featured in the League Cup final, thus that was the only medal that he won with the club. He left Liverpool after one season and moved to Tottenham. Whilst with Spurs, he suffered a horror injury that needed emergency surgery to save his right leg from amputation. He has since moved into management and has had stints with Germany's youth teams. He is currently manager of FC Pinzgau

Christian Ziege

# Photo Credits

We are extremely grateful to the following for the use of their photographs. We have made every effort to ensure that every image used complies with their own individual copyright requirements. A list of the full details including links to the relevant photographers/sites can be found at www.where-are-they-now.co.uk/liverpool-credits

**Ablett House** John Bradley
**Derek Acorah** Ian French
**Daniel Agger** Anthony Booker
**Aldridge, John** Jarle Vines.
**Alonso, Xabi** Rufus46
**Anelka** Rahal18
**Aqualini** cady from my bed, nowhereland
**Arbeloa** Club Deportivo Altorricón
**Babbel** Frank Schwichtenberg
**Baker, Ben** Unknown (Popperfoto)
**Barmby** Mattythewhite
**Baros** Tadeas Bednarz
**Barton** Harold 1923
**Barton-Joey** Johnvedwards
**Bellamy** Jon Candy from Cardiff, Wales
**Benayoun** David Lee
**Berger** Chensiyuan
**Bolder** Jonesy 702
**Bradshaw** commons.wikimedia.org
**Burrows** https://www.thegoodlifefrance.com
**Byrne** Christophe95
**Callaghan** Rebecca Boardman
**Camara, Titi** https://alchetron.com/Titi-Camara
**Carragher, Jamie** md.faisalzaman
**Cisse** Ivan Yakushkin
**Clemence, Ray** Di sconosciuto
**Clough, Nigel** Chris Barnes
**Cole, Joe** md.faisalzaman
**Harry Enield Scousers** Dunk.
**Lee, Sammy** Philip Gabrielsen
**Liddel, Billy** Rodhullandemu
**Litmanen, Jari** Petteri Lehtonen
**Livermore, Doug** Oyvind Vik
**Marsh, Mike** Egghead06
**Mascherano, Javier** Casa Rosada
**McAllister, Gary** helly-b
**McAteer, Jason** Sony Xperia
**McDermott, Terry** Loveless85
**McMahon, Steve** petetambo
**McManaman, Steve** Chensiyuan
**Meireles, Raul** Danny Molyneux
**Molby, Jan** Matt Eagles
**Morientes, Fernando** El Hormiguero
**Photowall** Ben Sutherland
**Meireles, Raul** SAW
**Litmanen, Jari** Petteri
**Molby, Durnin** - Liverpool Legends  Matt Eagles
**Sturridge, Daniel** ShakeFrog
**Reina, Pepe** Rerekirip Benediktov

**Jones, Brad** md.faisalzaman from Worcester,
**Keane, Robbie** Michael Kranewitter
**Torres, Fernando** Mattythewhite
**Kuyt, Dirk** Saw
**Arbeloa, Alvaro** Willtron
**Can, Emre** commons.wikimedia.org
**Fowler, Robbie** Jonesy702
**Wark, John** Bertil Holen
**Busby, Matt** Bernt Rostad
**Paisley, Bob** Rodhullandemu
**Hunt, Roger** Christophe95
**Moran, Dalglish, Evans** wekkuzipp
**Crest** Rodhullandemu Bus
**Shirts** Ben Sutherland
**Cups** Sanjiva Persad
**The Liverpool Football Club Stadium**, Humphrey Bolton
**UEFA Super Cup 2019** Mehdi Bolourian
**Alonso, Xabi** Rufus 46
**Hillsborough Memorial**, Terry Robinson
**Shankly Gates** G Laird
**1936 flag** EL Loko
**1892** https://commons.wikimedia.org
**Agger, Daniel** Saw
**Gayle, Howard** Jarvin
**Gerrard, Steve** Pannathorn Sukman
**Liddell, Billy** Rodhullandemu
**Shankly wall** Ben Sutherland
**Sturridge, Daniel** Ruraidh Gillies
**Crowd** Eric Kilby
**Moreno, Albert** https://commons.wikimedia.org
**Can, Emre** https://commons.wikimedia.org/
**Barnes, John** Sjur Bjokly
**Bradley, James** Memorino
**Callaghan, Ian** Rebecca Boardman
**Suarez, Luis** https://it.wikipedia.org
**Poulsen, Christian** Mattythewhite
**Liverpool University** Vita Student
**Anfield** Robert Cutts
**Spirit of Shankly** James Mughal
**Liverpool 4 Barcelona 0** cchana

# Our Website

We hope that you enjoyed this book. If you like this topic, why not visit our website? Not only will you be able to keep up to date with changes, you can leave your own comments, memories, or stories.

www.where-are-they-now.co.uk/club/Liverpool

Printed in Great Britain
by Amazon